THE BRAIN
ADVANTAGE

THE BRAIN
ADVANTAGE

BECOME A MORE EFFECTIVE LEADER
USING THE LATEST BRAIN RESEARCH

MADELEINE L. VAN HECKE,
LISA P. CALLAHAN, BRAD KOLAR,
AND KEN A. PALLER

Prometheus Books

59 John Glenn Drive
Amherst, New York 14228-2119

Published 2010 by Prometheus Books

Inquiries should be addressed to
Prometheus Books
59 John Glenn Drive
Amherst, New York 14228–2119
VOICE: 716–691–0133, ext. 210
FAX: 716–691–0137
WWW.PROMETHEUSBOOKS.COM

14 13 12 11 10   5 4 3 2 1

Library of Congress Cataloging-in-Publication Data

The brain advantage : become a more effective business leader using the latest brain research / by Madeleine L. Van Hecke . . . [et al.].
    p. cm.
Includes bibliographical references and index.
ISBN 978–1–59102–764–5 (pbk. : alk. paper)
    1. Leadership. 2. Leadership—Psychological aspects. 3. Brain—Research. 4. Executive ability. I. Van Hecke, Madeleine L.

HD57.7.B726 2009
658.4'092019—dc22

2009025001

Printed in the United States

DEDICATION

Madeleine Van Hecke dedicates this book to her husband, Greg Risberg, with thanks for all the love and laughter he brings to her life.

Lisa Callahan dedicates this book to her husband, Ron, who always sees the moon, and to her children, Charlie, Audrey, and Jack, whose wildly different outlooks on life never fail to interest and inspire her.

Brad Kolar dedicates this book to Peg, Zak, and Rebecca, who always remind him that a sound mind is nothing without a strong heart.

Ken Paller dedicates this book to his family and all his teachers.

CONTENTS

SECTION IV: DECISION MAKING

SECTION V: PERSONAL EFFECTIVENESS

CONCLUSION: HOW WILL TODAY'S BRAIN RESEARCH SHAPE THE FUTURE?

AFTERWORD: THE ADVANTAGES OF BRAIN RESEARCH
by Ken Paller

BIBLIOGRAPHY

INDEX

ACKNOWLEDGMENTS

Authors Madeleine, Lisa, and Brad would especially like to thank their coauthor, neuroscientist Ken Paller. Ken contributed his expertise as a researcher and a neuroscientist to this book to ensure that we portrayed the brain research accurately. In the process, he strengthened the book but he also did much more than that. He was a true teacher. He educated us about many issues related to brain research and he deepened our appreciation of the challenges that neuroscientists face.

We also want to thank our gifted illustrator, Tom Kerr, for his engaging "Kerrtoons." Tom is the creator of all the illustrations in this book. He was a pro at translating ideas into images that were both fun and effective. Plus he was great fun to work with! Tom's Web site is http://www.tom-kerr.com.

Many thanks to Steven L. Mitchell, editor-in-chief at Prometheus Books, for his support. We know that a host of other people behind the scenes at Prometheus also made this book possible. Our thanks to everyone from editing to accounting, sales, and marketing.

Finally, we want to thank our families. Madeleine would like to thank her husband, who spent many a lonely hour watching reruns of *Scrubs* while she shut her office door and worked on this manuscript. Lisa would like to thank her husband for holding down the fort during all of those Monday-night working sessions and she would like to thank her kids for having missed out on editing their English homework while she was editing the manuscript instead. Brad would like to thank his family for their patience on Monday nights.

THE BRAIN ADVANTAGE

"LEADING WITH THE BRAIN IN MIND"

L eaders are in charge. They are in charge of people, of budgets, of production lines. Most leaders also believe that they are in charge of their greatest resource—their own brain.

But how true is that?

The more we understand about how the brain works, the clearer it becomes that our brain often makes decisions before we get a chance to consciously decide anything for ourselves. Here are just a few examples:

1. THE MORE EXPERT WE BECOME, THE LESS WE "THINK."

As chapter 2 discusses, the brain automates much of what we do repeatedly. As people increase their expertise in driving a car, writing a computer program, or painting a portrait, their brain can shift routine aspects of that skill over to "autopilot." Sometimes people say, "I could do this in my sleep." That's a sign that what they are doing requires no conscious thinking. In his book *Everyday Survival*, Laurence Gonzales describes what happened to international rock climber Lynn Hill.[1] Hill threaded her rope through her harness but then, instead of tying the required knot, she stopped to put on her shoes. Distracted by a conversation, she never returned to tying her harness rope. As Gonzales says, the similarity between tying her shoes and tying the rope "tricked" Hill's brain into thinking she had done what she needed to do. Fortunately, Hill survived the seventy-two-foot fall that resulted.

2. OUR BRAIN CAN TRICK US INTO BEING SURE THAT WE ARE RIGHT— EVEN WHEN WE'RE WRONG.

Neurologist Robert Burton argues that our brains often manufacture a sense of certainty that we are right. Sometimes, of course, we *are* right. The problem, discussed in chapter 14, is that the brain can create this feeling even when we are drastically wrong.[2] In a dramatic example, neurological patients with *Cotard's disease* ignore logic and insist that they are dead. When we make decisions based solely on the feeling that "I am sure I'm right," we are often in trouble. As Burton points out, the brilliant mathematician Srinivasa Ramanujan had a notebook of theorems that he was sure were correct—he just needed more time to prove them. After his death, other mathematicians were able to demonstrate that some of Ramanujan's concepts were right on target. But others turned out to be "dead wrong."[3] We should not always believe it when our brain broadcasts an internal message that says "You are absolutely right about that!"

3. WITHOUT CONSULTING US, OUR BRAIN DECIDES WHOM TO TRUST.

When editors at the *New Republic* trusted journalist Stephen Glass, they were probably influenced by his likability. Glass endeared himself to his colleagues, regularly inquired about their families, and brought bagels to the office. Glass created a sense of connection between himself and others. As chapter 5 notes, the brain reacts to this feeling of connection by producing *oxytocin*, a hormone that, in turn, increases our tendency to trust. Maybe oxytocin led the editors at the *New Republic* to trust Glass— until *Forbes* revealed his reporting to be full of fabrications.

So who really is in charge? Our conscious, thinking selves—or other brain processes that work outside of our awareness? Clearly, we are not in control of as much as we thought we were. As neurologist Richard Restak says, "*The brain has a mind of its own.*"[4]

That is the unsettling news.

The good news is that leaders can use insights from the latest brain research to manage their own brains more effectively. That is the first Brain Advantage. Just as important, leaders can use that knowledge to manage other people more effectively. That is the second Brain Advantage. Here are some brief examples of how neuroscience can help business leaders be more effective:

1. With neurons firing at breakneck speeds, the brain spurs us to act fast—sometimes too fast.

The brain works at high speed. It processes incoming information in milliseconds. It formulates responses in a heartbeat. As a result, people sometimes have regrets simply because they acted so quickly. In 2008, radio broadcaster Don Imus used a racial slur to refer to members of the Rutgers women's basketball team. CBS ultimately fired Imus because of the comment. Later, Imus acknowledged that what he had done was "really stupid."[5] In discussions, people often whip out responses before they have considered what they are about to say. No wonder we sometimes regret the words that come out of our mouths! As discussed in chapter 9, leaders who understand how the brain reacts can intentionally slow down the pace during important situations.

2. You are not as objective as you think.

Leaders pride themselves on their objective thinking and decision-making skills, but both neurological and psychological research show that people are rarely as objective as they think they are. For example, research in chapter 15 shows that when we react to another person's mistake, it is the emotional brain circuits that determine whether we condemn or forgive them. We may *try* to judge others reasonably, using only relevant information, but often our emotional circuits make up our minds for us.

This is not the only way the brain makes up our minds. Neuroscientist Chris Frith argues that the brain determines our experience at the most basic level—it determines what we perceive.[6] Our eyes are involved in *seeing*, of course. But what we *perceive* depends on how other brain regions interpret the neural impulses from the retina. That is why optical illusions can fool us, even when we *know* that we are viewing an illusion. For instance, in the classic illusion shown in chapter 17, two equal lines seem unequal because of the way our brains perceive perspective. Leaders who appreciate how much the brain interprets—in fact, *creates*—what we experience are at an advantage. For example, the brain is a genius at coming up with theories of causality. It generates reasons to explain everything that happens. But sometimes it is wrong. Sometimes the causal patterns the brain sees are as illusory as an actual optical illusion. Leaders who know this can compensate for it and make better decisions.

3. Don't let your attention wander around on its own!

Most of us believe that our conscious intentions dictate what we pay attention to and what we ignore. As discussed in chapter 16, neuroscience research tells a different story. Often our brain, below the level of consciousness, determines what we notice. Most of the time, the brain does a good job of alerting us when we need to pay attention—but not always. Leaders try to ensure that employees pay attention to what is most important. Traditionally, leaders do this by having employees develop goals, often by using systems designed to improve goal setting, such as the SMART system. Unfortunately, SMART goals are not always the best goals. They do not always direct employees' attention—and efforts—to activities that benefit the organization. They may even do the opposite of what is desired. In chapter 16, we discuss alternative ways to set goals.

These examples give you a small taste of the brain research reviewed in this book. But the book goes beyond presenting captivating studies and facts. *The Brain Advantage* shows you how the brain research relates to your own leadership practices.

WHAT THIS BOOK DOES FOR YOU

The Brain Advantage gives you an executive summary of the latest brain research and its implications for your leadership style and practices. Each chapter has the following structure:

"What's the Story?"

The opening section of each chapter gives you an intriguing glimpse into how people think and the brain science behind the process.

"Interesting, but so what?
How can I use this information as a business leader?"

This section shows how the research ties to leadership.

"What if .. ?"

The final section of each chapter answers the question "What might leaders do differently if they took this brain research into account?"

The human brain is a three-pound miracle. But of all its miraculous features, there is one that is too precious to neglect. We have the power to "step outside of ourselves" and be aware of what our brain is doing. Consider a rat that has mastered a tricky maze to find food. Move the food closer to the starting point, and the rat will run right past it.[7] The rat is trapped in its routine. As humans, we too get trapped in mindless behaviors. But unlike the rat, we can take a step back and realize what we are doing. A chimp can experience an insight; it can see a new way to use a tool to solve a problem. But lacking the ability to use language in the ways that people do, the chimp will not ask herself, "How did I come up with that idea?" She will not plan research to test hypotheses about other ways to solve the problem. She won't say to herself, "Hmmm. I wonder if I should get a team together to brainstorm better ways of doing this?"

The Brain Advantage does what few business leaders have the time to do for themselves. It consolidates research from a wide range of studies, articles, and books. This research delves into the *neurocognitive* underpinnings of how people think and act, leading to provocative insights into the human condition. Then it draws on key research findings and insights to help make you a better leader. You can use *The Brain Advantage* to become an even more effective decision maker, communicator, and change agent.

As a business professional, you can "lead with the brain in mind." You can take a step back to admire all that brain activity, think about what it means, and change your behavior to become more effective. That is *The Brain Advantage*. It's in your hands now.

Visit www.thebrainadvantage.com for additional resources.

NOTES

1. Laurence Gonzales, *Everyday Survival: Why Smart People Do Stupid Things* (New York: Norton, 2008).

2. Robert Burton, *On Being Certain: Believing You Are Right Even When You're Not* (New York: St. Martin's, 2008), p. 160.

3. Ibid., p. 151.

4. Richard Restak, *The Brain Has a Mind of Its Own* (New York: Crown Trade Paperbacks, 1991).

5. Judy Faber, "CBS Fires Don Imus over Racial Slur," CBS News, April 12, 2007, http://www.cbsnews.com/stories/2007/04/12/national/main2675273_page2.shtml (accessed February 1, 2009).

6. Chris Frith, *Making Up the Mind: How the Brain Creates Our Mental World* (Malden, MA: Blackwell, 2007).

7. Gonzales, *Everyday Survival*, p. 27.

INNOVATION

Chapter 1

USING CONSTRAINTS TO FREE UP THE MIND

WHAT'S THE STORY?

What is going on in the brain of a jazz pianist? This is a tough question for neuroscientists to answer. How do you tuck a piano—or even a keyboard—into the tight enclosure of an MRI machine, where the top is only inches from the reclining person's nose? How can the jazz artist hear the music he is creating over the din of the MRI contraption itself? And if you are doing this research in order to study creativity, how can you tell that what you are seeing in the brain scan reflects actual improvisation and not simply the playing of a prearranged jazz piece?

These were the challenges faced by researchers Charles Limb and Allen Braun as they planned their study of jazz improvisation.[1] They met the first challenge by leaning a specially designed nonmagnetic keyboard against the slightly raised knees of the reclined musicians. The researchers suspended a mirror above the area so that the jazz artists could see the keys reflected there. The musicians wore earphones. These allowed them to hear the music they were creating. The earphones also allowed the musicians to hear a prerecorded jazz quartet accompaniment. This accompaniment made the situation more similar to the conditions in which the musicians ordinarily played. The researchers wanted to see if there were parts of the brain specifically involved in improvisation rather than in simply playing jazz. To do this, they had the musicians play two pieces—a jazz piece they had previously memorized and a piece that they improvised on the spot.

What did the researchers find? As expected, some areas of the brain were active no matter what the musicians played. These were the areas involved in looking at the keyboard, touching the keys, and listening to the music. In the improvisational piece, there was also activity that possibly reflected the brain encoding new combinations of sounds. But there were three other areas that were noticeably different when the musicians improvised compared to when they played the memorized piece.

Limb and Braun found that the *medial prefrontal cortex*—an area of the brain that is a few inches behind the center of the forehead—was much more active during improvisation. Some investigators have associated this part of the brain with self-expression, and with an intentional focus on inner thoughts and sensations rather than external stimuli. In some ways, this is similar to what Mikhail Csíkszentmihályi called "flow."[2] When creative artists are in a state of flow, they are not consciously thinking ahead about the next note to play or the next brush stroke to make on a painting. This doesn't mean that their actions are random; they don't play just any old note. Instead, it is as if they are being guided by a set of internalized rules or strategies. These rules influence the result, but the artist doesn't need to consciously "will" each intention into an action.

It also turns out that what is *not* happening in the brain may be just as important as what *is* happening. While the medial prefrontal cortex was *more* active, there were two parts of the brain that were significantly *less* active when the musicians improvised, compared to when they played the memorized piece. One of these areas, the *orbital frontal cortex*, is involved with monitoring our behavior to keep it socially appropriate. This is the area that prompts us to worry about what others think of us. It tells us to behave—to stifle a giggle at a funeral and not to swear in front of Grandma. During these tests, this part of the prefrontal cortex was *less* active while the musicians improvised, perhaps because being concerned about judgment from others inhibits creativity.

There was a second area that was quiet during improvisation, the *dorsolateral prefrontal cortex*. This part of the brain is involved in what are sometimes called the brain's "executive functions." When we are consciously pursuing a goal, planning to achieve it, and monitoring our progress, this part of the brain is at work. In children, the prefrontal cortex is not fully developed. It continually develops through the teenage years, probably up until age twenty-five. That's why many ninth graders struggle to write a long research paper. Teachers have to point out the steps the students need to take that would seem obvious to us; steps including narrowing a topic to a manageable size, figuring out how to find basic information, and planning their work so that they can turn the assignment in on time. The point is that this kind of thinking and planning that can be so essential to accomplishing many goals is *not* what drives improvisation. In fact, it may interfere with the state of flow.

In the flow state, thoughts and sensations can come through without being controlled, judged, or censored. In contrast, when executive functions are activated, the flow state is interrupted. For example, when an artist steps back from her painting to consciously consider her progress, she is activating the executive parts of the brain. When this happens, the self-expressive parts become idle. Bringing in the "director" who consciously analyzes and evaluates temporarily shuts down the "playful wanderer" who discovers new connections.

A similar pattern of conscious analysis interfering with creativity has been found in research that focuses on what happens when people attempt to solve problems. Psychologist Jonathan Schooler, now at the University of California at Santa Barbara, showed that if you made people explain their thinking while they were trying to solve a puzzle, they were less likely to experience a spontaneous insight that revealed the answer.[3] This shows that it is not only artistic expression that is interrupted by thinking analytically about what we are doing. In some circumstances, conscious analysis can also interfere with creative problem solving and innovation.

INTERESTING. BUT SO WHAT?

HOW CAN I USE THIS INFORMATION AS A BUSINESS LEADER?

Companies need innovation to thrive; leaders are expected to encourage innovative thinking. This creates a challenge for many leaders since it requires a neural orientation that they typically avoid. A successful leader, for example, relies heavily on the area of her brain that controls executive functions. Whether the goal is increasing revenues or changing the corporate culture, she needs to plan a strategy, monitor progress, and make adjustments when things go off track. Goal-oriented business leaders are consciously, intentionally, and deliberately thinking about what they are doing.

None of these adjectives describe what jazz musicians do when they improvise. While the business leader consciously creates plans and monitors them "on purpose," the only thing the virtuoso jazz musician does on purpose is decide to improvise in the first place. After that, conscious control fades, and he enters into that state of flow where unconscious processes take over.[4] The jazz musician does not continually shift to that controlling mode, engaging the prefrontal cortex to monitor the piece that is emerging. He does not consciously ask: "Well, what should I do next with this theme?" Instead, he improvises in a "twilight zone" where expert decisions about what to do are made unconsciously.

This means that the process of improvisation is at odds with the thought processes that business leaders usually foster. Indeed, the kind of thinking most likely to result in innovative ideas is at odds with many typical business goals. For example, efficiency is valued in business, and standardization is the way to achieve it. Leaders systematize business procedures so that employees don't have to reinvent the wheel but can instead use proven methods. The leader's job in this scenario is to reduce variability, not to introduce it.

In contrast, creating variations on a theme is exactly what jazz artists do. Leaders don't want employees to reinvent the same old wheel, but they do want new wheels that improve what already exists. They want better products and services and original ways to solve problems. At

upper levels of management, companies want leaders who are imagina-
tive enough to see the entire industry from different perspectives. But
the values that are typically embraced in business, such as careful planning and efficiency, make it hard for some leaders to endorse the kind of
thinking that leads to innovation.

This tension between efficiency and the apparently inefficient mean-
derings of the innovative mind are what led Mark Fishman, MD, president of the Novartis Institute for BioMedical Research, to criticize Six
Sigma. At a Creativity Colloquium sponsored by the Harvard Business
School, Fishman commented, "If there is one device that has destroyed
more innovation than any other, it is Six Sigma." The problem is that
"models like Six Sigma attempt to reduce variability, establish norms,
and then increase adherence to those norms."[5] This is great for efficiency
but disastrous for innovation. Such standardization is especially problematic during the formative stages of creative ideas. As creativity guru
Teresa Amabile notes, "The early discovery phase of the creative process
is inherently confusing and inefficient. So don't impose efficiency-
minded controls during that phase."[6] The point is not to say that Six
Sigma isn't valuable—just that there are times and places to apply it.

Another way in which innovation is at odds with typical business goals
is that, by its very nature, improvisation entails risk taking. In contrast,
reducing risks is often a crucial part of a leader's job. This means that
leaders may need to manage their own risk aversion in order to encourage
innovative thinking in their employees. Ed Catmull, president of the innovative animation film studio Pixar remarked, "We as executives have to
resist our natural tendency to avoid or minimize risks, which, of course, is
much easier said than done. In the movie business and plenty of others, this
instinct leads executives to choose to copy successes rather than try to
create something brand-new. That's why you see so many movies that are
so much alike. It also explains why a lot of films aren't very good."[7]

Does this mean that leaders should proclaim free zones where innovators have no constraints? For example, should they be encouraged to
ignore the practical realities of cost production or even the company's
strategic plan as they dream up new products and services? Well, no. The
fact is that jazz artists do have constraints. The genre of "jazz" has its own
rules. There are many moves that an accomplished artist would not make
during the improvisation of a particular piece. The jazz artist who excels

doesn't have to think consciously about those rules. Rather than restricting innovation, these constraints free creativity because jazz musicians know that within those rules, they can try any innovation they like. If not overly suffocating, constraints won't destroy creativity—just the opposite—they create a safe space within which the jazz artist can wander at will.

Business leaders can similarly impose constraints that encourage rather than stifle creativity, but these must be the right sorts of "nonsuffocating" constraints. What are the right sorts of constraints? First, they are broad. The conventions that constrain the jazz artist are general. They don't dictate, for example, specific moves like "rest for two beats here" or "use a B-flat here." In her article on "How to Kill Creativity," Teresa Amabile advises leaders to "give people freedom within the company's goals. Tell them which mountain to climb, but let them decide how to climb it."[8] The mountain—the company's goals, vision, and mission—constitutes the broad parameters within which the innovative employee must function.

Stephan Haeckel, director of strategic studies at IBM's Advanced Business Institute, advises companies to go further than merely using the company's vision, goals, or mission as a guide for employees. He writes that companies should also develop governing principles that clearly define "how far managers can go without seeking approval." For example, one governing principle might be "Always get and respond to customer feedback on new products under development." Another might be "Always assess the market need for a new product before implementing it." This principle could be written to include a statement of just how large a projected market must exist in order to move ahead. It is impossible to prescribe a specific set of governing principles that all organizations should embrace. The principles need to grow out of the company's primary purpose and goals. In *Adaptive Enterprise*, Haeckel shows leaders how to create governing principles that are clear without being suffocating. He also shows how these governing principles, combined with a clear definition of an organization's purpose and identification of any absolute constraints, can free up creativity. As Haeckel writes, leaders who provide this kind of clear context provide "an unambiguous framework for individual activity, aligning and bounding organizational actions without dictating what those actions should be."[9]

Many organizations create guiding or governing principles. That is not necessarily new. One of the key differences in Haeckel's approach is the way that these principles drive decision making and management. Often in organizations, guiding principles serve as high-level reminders of how people should behave. However, Haeckel uses them in a more structured, pragmatic way. Governing principles are not *reminders*—they are *boundaries* for both employees and managers. He advocates giving people considerable latitude in their jobs as long as they stay within those principles. The principles "define the boundaries of empowerment to ensure that creative, unprecedented responses remain consistent with organizational purpose and policy. They help the system find the balance between freedom and clear direction."[10]

Done well, boundaries that create safety for the employee also alleviate the problem of micromanagement. Micromanagement comes from the leader's fear that costly mistakes might occur—mistakes for which they will be held responsible. So managers adopt "no surprises" as their mantra. This in turn gets translated as a requirement to notify the leader about every change in direction or every decision that is made. One employee, for example, complained that even though the project was well within budget, the supervisor insisted on approving every expenditure, no matter how small. As Pixar's Ed Catmull comments, "Managers need to learn that they don't always have to be the first to know about something going on in their realm, and it's OK to walk into a meeting and be surprised."[11] Leaders who have set boundaries may find it easier to relinquish tight control. The boundaries create a sense of safety for the leader as well as for the employees.

WHAT IF . . . ?

1. WHAT IF LEADERS SEE THEMSELVES AS FACILITATORS OF INNOVATIVE PEOPLE?

Sometimes "powerful people hold forth in meetings even though others in the room [have] much better ideas for solving problems."[12] Robert Sutton, a professor at Stanford University's School of Engineering, made this comment during the Harvard Creativity Colloquium. The group was discussing the idea that leaders need to stop viewing themselves as the major source of innovative ideas. Instead, they should take on the role of facilitating innovation in others. Theresa Lant of New York University suspected that many leaders would not be attracted to this role. Lant asked, "Where is the glory in being a 'facilitator' as a manager? How do you get a management layer made up of real humans who aspire to that role and will do it?"[13]

As Lant's comment indicates, it is easy to be more impressed with a leader whose own inspirations make headlines than with the leader who stimulates innovation from behind the scenes. But what if leaders adopted the attitude of Pixar's Ed Catmull? Catmull commented, "For 20 years, I pursued a dream of making the first computer-animated film. To be honest, after that goal was realized—when we finished *Toy Story*—I was a bit lost. But then I realized the most exciting thing I had ever done was to help create the unique environment that allowed that film to be made."[14]

When leaders view themselves as facilitators, they no longer have the burden of coming up with all the ideas that the organization needs. Instead, their role becomes threefold. First, create and then actively manage the kind of constraints that will fuel innovation. Second, find ways for people to get useful feedback while protecting them from debilitating criticism. Third, put together teams and assignments that will build on the innate passion of creative people. Each of these steps is discussed below.

2. WHAT IF LEADERS FOCUS MORE ON "WHY" AND LESS ON "HOW"?

Actively managing constraints doesn't just mean that the leader sends an e-mail with a brief reminder of the organization's vision. Instead, leaders should ensure that employees not only genuinely share that vision but also understand how their specific tasks or projects help achieve it. Once they have carefully established boundaries, leaders should resist the temptation to dictate what happens within them. Instead, leaders should push their teams to the limits of those boundaries, encouraging (even demanding) new ideas and ways of working within them.

Plans that are too prescriptive activate the parts of employees' brains associated with self-regulation and executive function. Those are specifically the areas that were *not* used during improvisation. Instead, leaders should focus on keeping the "big picture" in front of their employees— the desired outcome and its associated requirements. Leaders should then back off and empower employees to improvise within the constraints of the outcome and requirements.

3. What if Leaders Use Feedback to Move People Forward Instead of Stopping Them in Their Tracks?

New ideas are fragile. It is a given in the field of creativity that having one's ideas ridiculed or rejected out-of-hand kills creativity. As Teresa Amabile noted, "Virtually everyone in the [Harvard Creativity Colloquium] agreed that managers must decrease fear of failure and that the goal should be to experiment constantly, fail early and often, and learn as much as possible in the process."[15]

To learn from mistakes, people need feedback that energizes the creative process instead of stopping it in its tracks. For example, innovative employees are likely to resent feedback from a bureaucratic leader who has little understanding of what it takes to nurture an idea from an initial inspiration to a viable product. A better approach is for innovative people to receive feedback from respected peers in their own field. At Pixar, innovators regularly present their emerging ideas to their peers. Another possibility is to test prototypes of the idea in the target market. Prototypes provide data that is more likely to be viewed as an objective and valuable source of information. Feedback from the target market doesn't have the personal sting of a supervisor's dismissal of an idea.

4. What if Leaders Include Employee Passion and Interests as Criteria for Staffing Decisions?

To build on the innate passion of creative people, leaders can match innovative individuals with the teams and tasks that fuel their natural creativity. Simply by determining assignments, leaders can have a huge impact on the intrinsic motivation of their employees. All too often, staffing decisions are made carelessly. As Amabile notes, "Something of a shotgun wedding occurs. The most eligible employee is wed to the most eligible—that is, the most urgent and open—assignment."[16] Leaders also influence the creative process when they construct project teams. Jazz musicians describe the incredible high that comes from cocreating with spirits who are both kindred and different. By bringing together people who are diverse enough to stimulate different possibilities and yet able to work in harmony, leaders can have a profound impact on what emerges.

Overall, leaders have a huge impact on innovation because their decisions shape the space within which creative employees can improvise. They can protect emerging ideas and ignite the passions of their creative people. Working with the least predictable, most volatile medium possible—people—the skilled leader sculpts the environment in which creativity can flourish.

NOTES

1. Charles J. Limb and Allen R. Braun, "Neural Substrates of Spontaneous Musical Performance: An fMRI Study of Jazz Improvisation," *PLoS ONE* 3, no. 2 (February 2008), http://www.plosone.org/article/info%3Adoi%2F10.1371%2Fjournal.pone.0001679 (accessed March 14, 2008).

2. Mikhail Csikszentmihalyi, *Flow: The Psychology of Optimal Experience* (New York: HarperPerennial Modern Classics, 2008).

3. J. W. Schooler, S. Ohlsson, and K. Brooks, "Thoughts beyond Words: When Language Overshadows Insight." *Journal of Experimental Psychology: General* 122 (1993): 166–83.

4. Teresa Amabile and Mukti Khaire, "Creativity and the Role of the Leader," *Harvard Business Review* (October 2008): 7.

5. Ibid., p. 3.

6. Ibid.

7. Ed Catmull, "How Pixar Fosters Collective Creativity," *Harvard Business Review* (September 2008): 3.

8. Teresa Amabile, "How to Kill Creativity," *Harvard Business Review* (May 2007): 5.

9. Stephan Haeckel, *Adaptive Enterprise: Creating and Leading Sense-And-Respond Organizations* (Boston: Harvard Business School Press), p. 17.

10. Ibid., p. 123.

11. Catmull, "How Pixar Fosters Collective Creativity," p. 8.

12. Amabile, "Creativity and the Role of the Leader," p. 8.

13. Ibid., p. 11.

14. Catmull, "How Pixar Fosters Collective Creativity," p. 10.

15. Amabile, "Creativity and the Role of the Leader," p. 10.

16. Amabile, "How to Kill Creativity," p. 5.

Chapter 2

DO EXPERT BRAINS THINK LESS?

WHAT'S THE STORY?

Brain imaging techniques allow researchers to witness the brain's activity reflected in a rainbow of colors on a computer screen. When brain cells are highly active—working harder—the result shows up as brighter colors on the screen. Brilliant reds and yellows indicate brain areas that are most active. In contrast, the blues and greens on a scan show a quieter, less active brain area.

What would we expect to find if we compared the brain scans of people with high IQ scores versus their average IQ counterparts? We might picture the active brain of an Einstein as a hotbed of smoldering colors—but we'd be wrong. Neurologist Richard Restak summarized a UCLA study that compared individuals with high IQs to those with average IQs. Restak wrote, "The researchers started off with the seemingly reasonable idea that 'smarter' brains work harder, generate more energy, and consume more glucose. Like light bulbs, the brains of 'bright' people were expected to illuminate more intensely than those of 'dimwits' with a reduced wattage."[1] What they discovered instead was exactly the opposite. Higher IQ people had cooler, more subdued brain scans "while their less intellectually gifted counterparts lit up like miniature Christmas trees."[2] Other research has amplified these findings. When individuals undergo training and gain expertise, their brain activation may be reduced following learning. As efficiency develops, fewer neurons may be required. Restak concluded that "smarter brains" don't have to work as hard.

Now, of course, the brain itself isn't *really* lighting up like a Christmas tree. If we were able to peek directly into the gray matter of the brain, we wouldn't see blobs of yellow or blue like the ones we see in brain scans. Neuroimaging includes an assortment of different ways to gauge brain activity and metabolism, from measuring glucose levels in a PET scan to measuring features like blood flow in an MRI. Indicators like these are translated into the colors seen in a brain scan.

Why would "smarter" brains work less hard? One strong bet is that when we are inexperienced—when we still have a lot to learn—we have to make a conscious effort to think about what we're doing. But later, after we've become more adept, much of what initially took effort becomes automatic. This is why it's possible for us to ride a bike or drive a car while barely thinking about what we're doing. Pianists can play *Für Elise* without ever thinking "what note comes next?" Office personnel can type effortlessly. The brain automates well-learned responses. It may feel to us as if our *fingers* are playing the music or typing the letters. But the only way our fingers can do this is because repetition has enabled brain cells to efficiently take charge of the movement of our fingers.

Many repeated actions will become automatic over time. The good news is that functioning on autopilot allows us to expend less of our brain's energy on routine aspects of the work. Our expertise allows us to direct our energy elsewhere. For example, novices use different parts of their brains than experts do. This happens in areas as different as playing chess[3] and swinging a golf club.[4] These studies show that less-experienced people think more about carrying out the mechanics of the task and encoding information.[5] Experts, on the other hand, function on autopilot in these areas. In fact, experts sometimes falter—flubbing a basketball free throw or a golf putt—when their focus shifts back to the mechanics.[6]

So functioning on autopilot can be a great advantage—but it can also work against us. As mentioned in the introduction to this book, international rock climber Lynn Hill was preparing to climb a wall in Buoux, France, in 1989. She threaded her rope through her harness, but then, instead of tying the knot, she stopped to put on her shoes. While tying her shoes, she talked to another woman. "The thought occurred to me that there was something I needed to do before climbing," she later recalled.[7] But Hill "dismissed the thought" and climbed the wall. When she leaned back to rappel to the ground, she fell seventy-two feet. Fortunately, tree branches broke her fall and she survived.

Laurence Gonzales, who tells this story in his book *Everyday Survival*, points out that more training would not have helped Lynn Hill. "In fact," as Gonzales writes, "experience contributed to her accident." She could tie her rope to her harness on autopilot, but the similarity between tying her shoes and tying the rope "tricked" her brain into thinking she had done what she needed to do.

So there are two sides to our ability to function on autopilot. Doing so can lead to major mistakes, as Lynn Hill's story illustrates. On the other hand, there are distinct benefits to this behavior as well. When we are trying to become more expert, in many cases our goal is to get good enough so that we *can* be on autopilot!

INTERESTING, BUT SO WHAT?

HOW CAN I USE THIS INFORMATION AS A BUSINESS LEADER?

Among their many challenges, leaders have two key responsibilities: developing their people and increasing efficiency. Increasing efficiency often involves standardizing, automating, or simplifying processes. However, carrying out routines more automatically also has one major drawback. It increases the risk that, like Lynn Hill failing to knot her rope, people will at times implement these procedures "mindlessly."

In an ideal world, for efficiency's sake, employees would conduct much of their work on autopilot. Then they would shift off autopilot when the situation required more conscious thought. The key question for business leaders is how to ensure that people stick to autopilot when it's working well, yet make the shift to more conscious deliberation when it's needed.

Think of autopilot as a well-practiced script, one that employees have mastered so well that they can follow it with little conscious thought. As people develop expertise, they acquire many such scripts. The sales professional may be explicitly trained in a verbal script of what to say when the potential buyer poses a particular objection. But there are many *types* of scripts to consider. They are not necessarily verbal. When a software designer automatically chooses a particular design as her starting point, or an executive instinctively poses a series of questions about a possible acquisition in order to evaluate its feasibility, both may be drawing on well-learned scripts. On autopilot, they follow steps that have proven to be effective in the past.

But scripts don't always improve performance. First, problems can occur when employees fail to notice that an actual situation differs in important ways from the situation that their "script" was based on. Second, difficulties may arise when employees focus on the script so much that they miss other important information. Finally, employees who are used to a script that works well often won't consider more effective ways of doing the job. Leaders need a way to preserve the benefits of autopilot while avoiding the drawbacks. The following section explores each of the drawbacks in more detail.

1. EMPLOYEES FAIL TO NOTICE THAT THE REAL-LIFE SITUATION IS DIFFERENT FROM THE TRAINING SITUATION.

Example:

Dave Grossman, a former lieutenant colonel in the army and retired professor of military science at Arkansas State University, describes a law enforcement officer who was determined to become an expert at snatching a gun from the hand of an assailant.[8] Putting in hours of practice, the officer would repeatedly grab a pistol from whomever he was practicing with: his wife, his training partner, or his friend. Then he would return it and try again and again until he felt proficient. The first chance he had to use this maneuver occurred when he answered a call about a potentially dangerous man in a convenience store. He and his partner went down separate aisles. As he reached the end of his aisle, he was startled when the suspect stepped around the corner, pointing a gun at him. The officer automatically snatched the man's gun right out of his hand. His assailant was surprised! But he was even more astonished when the officer then promptly returned the gun to him—just as he had practiced so many times before. Luckily, the officer's partner stepped in at that moment.

What would have happened if the officer, during the training exercises, had built in one additional step? He could have built a "stop" into the training so that returning the gun stood apart from the script. He might simply take the gun and then pause. If he waited a few seconds, he could "reset" before handing the gun back for more practice. In training, leaders sometimes take shortcuts to make the training more efficient. They might not realize that those shortcuts are being built into the scripts.

Another way to minimize this kind of mistake is to ensure that the practice training resembles the actual situation as closely as possible. Dave Grossman points out that if you practice shooting at blank, male-shaped silhouettes, you are learning to shoot at anything threatening that jumps in front of you. Training with photorealistic targets is a far better approach. Some of these targets clutch innocent items like cell phones or wallets instead of guns. The trainee learns to shoot at genuine threats and to hold fire in other situations.

2. Employees stay overly focused on the demands of the immediate situation.

Example:

In *Everyday Survival*, Laurence Gonzales describes a fire captain who sets his watch alarm so that it will sound once an hour when he's in an extended battle against an inferno.[9] The captain does two things when his alarm goes off. First, he steps back from what he's been doing on autopilot and stops to think. He looks around, asks himself what he might have missed, and considers the big picture. Second, he takes a moment to pay attention to what his gut may be telling him. As a simple example, the captain might stop and then notice that he's thirsty. This is a reminder to have his men also stop and take a drink of water so that they don't become dehydrated. In this way, the captain takes advantage of his ability to function quickly and efficiently on autopilot. But he increases the odds that he'll catch problems that the autopilot approach sometimes misses.

In high-intensity situations, it's useful to have an external reminder like the watch alarm given in the example to remind us to periodically step out of the autopilot mode. An extension of this is the idea of building quality reviews or audits throughout your processes. Quality reviews can provide the necessary pauses to ensure that people are thinking through all of the alternatives.

3. WHEN AUTOPILOT IS WORKING ADEQUATELY, EMPLOYEES FAIL TO CONSIDER THAT THERE MAY BE EVEN BETTER WAYS OF DOING THE JOB.

Example:

There is a classic 1940s water jar puzzle that psychologists use to demonstrate how autopilot can lead to inefficiency.[10] In this puzzle, you

Figure 2.1

Figure 2.2

Problem	Jar A	Jar B	Jar C	Desired Quantity
1	21	127	3	100
2	14	163	25	99
3	18	43	10	5
4	9	42	6	21
5	20	59	4	31
6	23	49	3	20
7	15	39	3	18
8	28	59	3	25

The Water Jar Problem:
How could you pour water in and out of these jars so that you end up with 100 units?
Answer:
Fill Jar B. Pour water from Jar B into Jar A so that Jar B now holds 106 units.
Pour water from Jar B into Jar C twice.
You'll have 100 units left in Jar B.
How would you solve the similar problems in figure 2.2 so that you ended up with
    the desired quantities?

see three containers that will hold different amounts of water, like the ones shown in figure 2.1. Your job is to use the jars as measuring cups, pouring water into the different containers so that you end up with the designated amount of water. Figure 2.1 shows a strategy of pouring water into various cups that works to solve problem 1. This same strategy works for the first five problems shown in figure 2.2. But in problems 6, 7, and 8, a different strategy would be more efficient. You could simply add (or subtract) water from one or two of the jars. Yet many people doing this little exercise fail to notice the simplest solution because they have already gotten into a mind-set of following a script on autopilot. Since that script is working, they never step back and notice a better way.

Imagine that individuals solving this set of problems had trained themselves to periodically step back and ask, "Am I doing this in the most efficient possible way?" "Is there a different way to approach this?" To keep from mindlessly carrying out routines that work well enough but are not optimal, employees can periodically step out of autopilot and critique the scripts that they have acquired.

WHAT IF . . . ?

1. WHAT IF BUSINESS LEADERS USE AUTOMATED SYSTEMS TO REMIND THEM TO PERIODICALLY GO OFF AUTOPILOT?

Professionals often step back from recently completed projects and debrief. They assess how things went and consider what they might do differently next time. Why not extend this practice to well-established routines? Team members could, for example, look at the plans they are creating for carrying out a project. Then they could take some time to discuss questions like "Is this the most efficient possible way to do this?" and "Is there someone else whose perspective we should get on this before we start?" Similarly, individuals can take a few minutes before they jump into their own work to ask "Is there a better way to do this?" "Would it be better to have someone else do this?" One business leader experimented with sending herself questions like these as instant messages that appeared throughout the day. When one of these "prompts" appeared, it didn't usually change her behavior immediately because it didn't apply directly to what she was doing. But over time, she internalized the questions and they started popping into her head at times when they did apply.

Leaders can incorporate questions like the ones above into their own routines. In many organizations, quality or continuous improvement reviews are intended to serve a similar purpose. But all too often, the reviews themselves become scripts that are executed with little thought or consideration. Leaders should shift their mind-set from thinking of quality or other reviews as administrative tasks and instead approach them as opportunities to turn off autopilot for a moment.

Most leaders come to know their weak spots in carrying out projects. They may realize, for instance, that all too often they get lost in the details and lose sight of the overall vision. Or they get sidetracked pursuing research that is tangential to the decision they are trying to make. Or they fiddle around for hours with presentation graphics when the payoff for the additional time investment is miniscule.

Once leaders are aware of their own foibles, they can develop a system to remind themselves to avoid these quirks. For example, a leader might send a reminder to himself saying, "Am I getting lost in the details?" to appear at random times throughout the week. He might set up a prompt saying, "Is the time I'm devoting to this worth the payoff?" to pop up on his calendar each morning. A leader who often immerses herself in projects before adequately considering the input of others could post a reminder in her office that says, "Whose input do you need before you make that decision?" Over time, these prompts will become automated so that leaders may no longer need external reminders.

2. WHAT IF LEADERS NOT ONLY INCORPORATE SUCH QUESTIONS ROUTINELY INTO THEIR OWN HABITUAL WAYS OF WORKING BUT ALSO TRAIN THEIR EMPLOYEES TO ASK SIMILAR QUESTIONS?

One manager described how her boss would sometimes pause by her desk as she created a complicated spreadsheet. Then he would ask a question like "Why are you copying the same information over and over?" He'd work with her for ten minutes, showing her a better approach that ultimately saved her hours of labor. Given this payoff, she paid attention. Over time, she learned to spot signs of inefficiency on her own. Ultimately, she got into the habit of asking herself "What is the most efficient way to create this spreadsheet?" Stepping back and thinking consciously about what she was doing and how she was doing it became part of her "automatic" routine. She also began to ask "big picture" questions, such as "How am I going to be using the information that I'll get from the survey I'm designing?" and "Will it be easy to analyze this data with this method?"

Einstein once said that if you gave him an hour to solve a problem and his life depended on getting the right answer, he would spend fifty-five minutes figuring out what questions to ask. In order to shift out of autopilot, it's crucial that the questions people pose to themselves be genuinely thought provoking. In one exploratory study of the use of prompts, for example, when some professionals were asked "Have you considered a sufficient number of alternatives?" they simply answered "yes," and then they went on with their work. But when they were instead asked "What are two other alternatives you could use in this situation?" they discovered new possibilities.

3. WHAT IF LEADERS CONSCIOUSLY SEEK OUT THE "BEGINNER'S MIND"?

Often leaders turn to the "experts" when things get tough. However, the experts might not be the ones in the best position to solve a problem. They may be trapped in well-learned scripts that reflect traditional ways of thinking. Instead, what if leaders involved people who weren't mired in the status quo? What if they purposely sought the opinions of people who didn't know how things were "supposed" to work? Leaders need to understand that sometimes a fresh perspective is as valuable as a well-seasoned one. They should build teams and organizations that are not only cross-functional in nature but are also *cross-experiential* in nature.

NOTES

1. Richard Restak, *The Brain Has a Mind of Its Own* (New York: Crown Trade Paperbacks, 1991), pp. 138–39.

2. Ibid., p. 139.

3. William M. Bart and Michael Atherton, "The Neuroscientific Basis of Chess Playing: Applications to the Development of Talent and Education," paper presented at the American Educational Research Association Meeting, Chicago, Illinois, April 2003.

4. S. L. Beilock and S. Gonso, "Putting in the Mind versus Putting on the Green: Expertise, Performance Time, and the Linking of Imagery and Action," *Quarterly Journal of Experimental Psychology* 61 (2008): 920–32.

5. J. G. Milton et al., "Expert Motor Performance: Limbic Activation Is Inversely Related to Skill Level," *Neurology* 60 (2003): A345.

6. S. L. Beilock, S. L. Carr, and T. H. Carr, "On the Fragility of Skilled Performance: What Governs Choking under Pressure?" *Journal of Experimental Psychology: General* 130 (2001): 701–25.

7. Laurence Gonzales, *Everyday Survival: Why Smart People Do Stupid Things* (New York: Norton, 2008), p. 24.

8. Dave Grossman and Loren W. Christensen, *On Combat: The Psychology and Physiology of Deadly Conflict in War and Peace* (Milstadt, IL: Warrior Science Publications, 2008).

9. Gonzales, *Everyday Survival*, pp. 69–70.

10. Bruce Goldstein, *Cognitive Psychology: Mind, Research, and Everyday Experience* (Belmont, CA: Wadsworth, 2008).

Chapter 3

EUREKA! HOW TO MAKE NEW CONNECTIONS

WHAT'S THE STORY?

Barbara McClintock, who later earned a Nobel Prize for her work in genetics, was puzzled over the results of her latest study. She and her research colleagues were baffled. Then the solution hit her like a bolt. Her colleagues were skeptical as they tried to follow the rough outline of her solution, but McClintock herself had no doubts. As she wrote, "The answer came fast . . . [but later] I worked it out step by step—it was an intricate series of steps—and—it worked out exactly as I'd diagrammed it."[1]

In their book *Sparks of Genius*, Robert and Michele Root-Bernstein tell us that McClintock literally shouted "Eureka! I have the answer!" at her moment of insight. "Eureka," roughly meaning "I have found it," is the exclamation commonly attributed to the ancient Greek scholar Archimedes.

Archimedes needed to determine the purity of the king's gold crown. His idea was to weigh the crown and then use its weight-to-volume ratio to calculate its density, a measure of its purity. But how could he determine the volume of the crown without melting it down? Supposedly, the answer came to Archimedes as he stepped into the baths and saw the water rise. He realized that he could immerse the crown and use the displacement of the water to gauge its volume.

As Northwestern University neuroscientist Mark Jung-Beeman observes, "In the two millennia since Archimedes shouted 'Eureka!,' it has seemed common knowledge that people sometimes solve problems—whether great scientific questions or trivial puzzles—by a seemingly distinct mechanism called insight. This mechanism involves suddenly seeing a problem in a new light, often without awareness of how that new light was switched on."[2]

Jung-Beeman was intent on discovering what happens in the brain at that moment of insight. But he couldn't just tuck people into MRI machines and wait, hoping that they'd have an insight. He needed some kind of puzzle that would at least sometimes require insight to solve. To provide an experimental comparison, he also needed puzzles that could be solved more methodically.

Jung-Beeman found an exercise from earlier research that he thought might fit the bill. In this exercise, the researcher presented participants with sets of three words, such as pine, crab, and sauce. The participant's job was to come up with a single word that could be joined with each of these to form a commonly used word or phrase. For example, "cone" works with "pine cone" but doesn't make sense with "crab" or "sauce." "Meat" works with both crab and sauce—as in crab meat and meat sauce—but doesn't work with "pine." Proceeding in this way, searching for possible words and trying them out to see if they are correct, is a methodical, analytic way to search for solutions. Alternatively, after viewing the words pine, crab, and sauce, a participant might suddenly think "apple" and just know that it is correct. This is a flash of insight.

In one study, Jung-Beeman and his associates presented people with 124 sets of words and scanned their brains as they tried to find a word that tied all three together. The participants in this study solved more than half of the problems. They solved these problems with insight 56 percent of the time and used a methodical approach 41 percent of the time. This gave Jung-Beeman hundreds of instances where he could compare their insightful brains to their methodical brains. What did he learn?

Several areas of the brain were especially active when participants solved the problems with insights. One of these areas stood out. This was a part of the cortex with the rather daunting name *anterior superior temporal gyrus*. It's called the aSTG for short, and it clearly plays a crucial role in our "aha!" moments. When Jung-Beeman's research participants solved one of the problems with insight, the flash of insight was preceded by a flare of intense activity in the right hemisphere aSTG.

What do aSTG neurons do? It turns out that other research impli-
cates the right hemisphere aSTG in making novel connections between
ideas. The right aSTG is active, for example, when we interpret a
metaphor or "get" a joke. Here's what is especially intriguing. Both the
right and the left hemispheres have temporal lobes, and each has an
aSTG area. But only the aSTG in the right hemisphere lights up when
we have an insight. Jung-Beeman notes, when describing his results,
"There is no insight effect anywhere within the temporal cortex of the
LH [left hemisphere]."[3] This reinforces the idea that the right hemisphere is more involved with creativity, especially with the ability to see
unusual perspectives and come up with new ideas.

The neurons in the right hemisphere seem to be ideally suited to
help us discover distant associations. Compared to brain cells in the left
hemisphere, the ones on the right have longer branches, called *dendrites*,
that reach further across the cortex. The branches also have more nubs,
called *dendritic spines*, that connect with other cells. These neural and
cognitive attributes help people "to see connections that previously
eluded them."[4]

In a follow-up study, Jung-Beeman and his colleagues made another
interesting discovery. Participants who were in a good mood solved more
of the word problems overall—and solved more of them with insight.
People in a more positive mood at the beginning of the study showed an
interesting pattern of neural activity. Right before they saw the next set
of words, they showed activity in a part of the brain associated with cognitive control. This area is called the *anterior cingulate cortex*. It helps us
to be more mentally flexible—to recognize when a response is correct
but also to move on when a response is wrong. It tells us, "Cone works
with pine but not with sauce. . . . OK, let's try something else."

Creativity experts have long recognized that creative people tend to
be more flexible in their thinking. They also remind us that a playful
atmosphere will stimulate more unusual ideas when we brainstorm. Playfulness may do this by helping us to be in a good mood and a more
relaxed frame of mind. Jung-Beeman suggests that we get so many good
ideas while showering or half dozing because a relaxed frame of mind is
conducive to insight. Like playfulness and a positive mood, the "drowsy"
brain induces a relaxed state and encourages insights.

Figure 3.1. Sometimes your best ideas come through relaxation instead of perspiration.

INTERESTING, BUT SO WHAT?

HOW CAN I USE THIS INFORMATION AS A BUSINESS LEADER?

What lessons does Jung-Beeman's research have for leaders who want to encourage insightful thinking? We can't "force" insights or methodically march toward them using preprogrammed steps. In fact, just the opposite seems to be true. Sometimes we need to shift away from our methodical left-brain orientation and let the right brain take over. Our right brains let the insights "happen" and help us notice them when they occur. What can we do to spend more time in this right-brain state?

Insights involve making new connections among ideas that we

already have. As Jung-Beeman notes, Archimedes already knew how to compute density from volume and weight. He just couldn't figure out how to calculate volume without damaging the crown. "His observation of water displacement allowed him to connect known concepts in new ways," Jung-Beeman writes. "This is the nature of many insights, the recognition of new connections across existing knowledge."[5]

We can get better at finding unusual ways to "connect the dots" by increasing our existing knowledge. Creativity expert Teresa Amabile points out that one way to help people be more creative is to encourage them to expand their expertise in their own fields. Our expertise, she says, "constitutes what Nobel Laureate, economist, and psychologist Herb Simon calls [our] 'network of possible wanderings,' the intellectual space [within which we] explore and solve problems. The larger the space, the better."[6]

Another way to look at this is that if we want our brains to "connect the dots" to form insights, we need plenty of "dots" to connect. To borrow a phrase from innovation expert Stephen Shapiro, we need to "collect and connect." Shapiro writes, "I contend that creativity is about collecting and connecting dots . . . dots being ideas, disciplines, ways of looking at problems, and experiences."[7]

To get better at this, we can practice bringing different "dots" together. This is the basis of many creativity exercises. In one simple example, individuals randomly choose five words from a dictionary. Then they think about a given problem in terms of those words. Such "forced associations" prod our brains to connect the dots in a new way, fostering insights. Are exercises like this the same thing as trying to "methodically march" toward insights? No—they are exercises designed to free our minds from analytical thinking.

We can also foster insights by bringing different fields of expertise together. A chance encounter between people from different fields caused a major breakthrough with the deadly disease kuru. A veterinarian who was an expert in scrapie, a sheep disease, visited an exhibit that a friend had recommended. The exhibit featured the work of D. Carleton Gajdusek, a physician who had been trying to discover the cause of kuru. The veterinarian was stunned by the photographs that showed the damaged brain tissue of kuru victims; the tissue was almost identical to sheep who had scrapie. He convinced Gajdusek that, like scrapie, a slow-acting infectious agent might cause kuru. Gajdusek's successful efforts to demonstrate this ultimately earned him a Nobel Prize in Medicine.[8] Leaders who bring people together from adjacent fields increase the odds that insights will occur.

In addition to helping people "collect and connect the dots," leaders can help influence their people's moods. We have seen that people who are in a good mood are more likely to think creatively. Providing recognition, challenging assignments, and fun workspaces can foster positive moods. Conversely, some leaders seem to create bad moods. One employee commented that within minutes of the district manager entering the building, word spread and the tension in the building became palpable. His teams would certainly have trouble achieving the relaxed state of mind needed for creativity! Leaders influence the mood of employees in many ways, often setting the tone for a team or even an entire organization.

WHAT IF . . . ?

1. WHAT IF LEADERS ENCOURAGE THEIR PEOPLE TO EXPLORE FIELDS OUTSIDE THEIR AREA OF EXPERTISE?

Many organizations pay for people to attend training and conferences and may even provide tuition reimbursement. But typically, there are restrictions on the experiences that are funded. Usually experiences must directly relate to the individual's job. If employees have more breakthrough insights when they associate disparate elements, then this policy may be too narrow. Purposeful support of learning in other fields could pay off with innovation.

2. WHAT IF LEADERS ARE MORE INTENTIONAL ABOUT BRINGING VARIOUS FIELDS TOGETHER?

Leaders often foster connections by creating diverse teams. Another way to do this is through the arrangement of physical space. Pixar's animation studio intentionally designed its building "to maximize inadvertent encounters." Pixar located the cafeteria, meeting rooms, and mailboxes in a large atrium at the center of the building. People meander through this area several times a day. As Pixar's president says, "It's hard to describe just how valuable the resulting chance encounters are."[9]

3. WHAT IF LEADERS PURPOSEFULLY WORK TO CREATE A MORE POSITIVE MOOD IN THEIR ORGANIZATIONS?

Insightful solutions are more likely to occur when people are in a positive state of mind. As author Jonah Lehrer concluded in his *New Yorker* article on insight, "A clenched state of mind may inhibit the sort of creative connections that lead to sudden breakthroughs."[10]

Maybe the antidote to a "clenched" state of mind is an unclenched jaw. In *The Levity Effect*, authors Adrian Gostick and Christopher Scott note that introducing levity at work can be "as simple as unfurrowing a brow or relaxing clenched jaws."[11] They discuss studies showing that lightheartedness increases creative ideas. In one of these studies, watching a comedy increased creativity in brainstorming groups.[12] In another, humor in divisive work groups "cultivated a climate in which creative, playful, unconventional problem-solving could mature."[13]

Southwest Airlines is the poster child for organizations where lightheartedness prevails.[14] Henry Ford would be astounded at Southwest's success. In the 1930s and 1940s, laughter at the Ford Motor Company was prohibited. British management scholar David Collinson tells the tale of a Ford worker who was fired after being "caught in the act of smiling" and "slowing down the line maybe half a minute."[15] Ford would be surprised to learn that levity can actually improve the bottom line by decreasing employee absenteeism and turnover.[16] Apparently "managing to have fun" is not just fluff but is a valuable tool for leaders.[17]

"Laughter and good humor are the canaries in the mine of commerce—when the laughter dies, it's an early warning that life is ebbing from the enterprise." —Paul Hawken

NOTES

1. Robert Root-Bernstein and Michele Root-Bernstein, *Sparks of Genius* (New York: Houghton Mifflin, 1999), p. 2.

2. Mark Jung-Beeman et al., "Neural Activity When People Solve Problems with Insight," *Public Library of Science Biology*, April 2004, http://biology.plosjournals.org/perlserv/?request=get-document&doi=10.1371/journal.pbio.0020097&ct=1 (accessed July 5, 2008).

3. Ibid., p. 7.

4. Ibid., p. 1.

5. Ibid., p. 15.

6. Teresa Amabile, "How to Kill Creativity," *Harvard Business Review* (May 2007): 3.

7. Stephen Shapiro, "Unleash Your Inner Motivator," *Stephen Shapiro's 24/7 Innovation*, http://www.steveshapiro.com/unleash-your-inner-innovator (accessed March 3, 2009).

8. June Goodfield, *Quest for the Killers* (Boston: Birkhauser, 1985).

9. Ed Catmull, "How Pixar Fosters Collective Creativity," *Harvard Business Review* (September 2008): 9.

10. Jonah Lehrer, "The Eureka Hunt," *New Yorker*, July 28, 2008, p. 44.

11. Adrian Gostick and Scott Christopher, *The Levity Effect: Why It Pays to Lighten Up* (Hoboken, NJ: Wiley, 2008), p. 18.

12. A. M. Isen, K. A. Daubman, and G. P. Nowicki, "Positive Affect Facilitates Creative Problem Solving," *Journal of Personality and Social Psychology* 52 (1987): 1122–31.

13. C. M. Consalvo, "Humor in Management, No Laughing Matter," *Humor: International Journal of Humor Research* 2 (1989): 285–97.

14. Kevin Freiberg and Jackie Freiberg, *Nuts! Southwest Airlines' Crazy Recipe for Business and Personal Success* (New York: Random House Broadway Books, 1998).

15. David Collinson, "Managing Humour," *Journal of Management Studies* 39 (2002): 269–88.

16. Gostick and Christopher, *The Levity Effect*, p. 133.

17. Matt Weinstein, *Managing to Have Fun: How Fun at Work Can Motivate Your Employees, Inspire Your Coworkers, and Boost Your Bottom Line* (New York: Fireside, 1997).

Chapter 4

CAN YOU REWIRE YOUR OWN BRAIN?

WHAT'S THE STORY?

T he first chapter in Norman Doidge's best seller, *The Brain That Changes Itself*, is called "A Woman Perpetually Falling." Doidge tells the story of Cheryl, who at the age of thirty-five was given the antibiotic *gentimicin* to treat a postoperative infection. Gentimicin is typically prescribed for only short periods of time because of a potentially disastrous side effect—it can damage the structures of the inner ear that we rely on to maintain a sense of balance. Apparently given too much of the drug, Cheryl "became one of a small tribe of gentimicin's casualties, known among themselves as Wobblers."[1] Cheryl wobbles because her lack of inner ear balance makes her feel as if she is perpetually falling. She cannot know whether she is stable and upright, or tilted and collapsing, except by using what she sees. She must constantly look for visual cues such as the line that the edge of a dresser creates in a room. Being in the dark is totally debilitating to Cheryl. One night when the lights went out, she immediately collapsed to the floor.

Cheryl was no longer able to make all the automatic adjustments that the rest of us make unconsciously to keep our balance. Unable to drive or keep her job, she lived on a $1,000 monthly disability check and was constantly exhausted by the effort of keeping her body stable in space. Then Cheryl became a patient of the inventive neurologist Paul

Bach-y-Rita. He constructed a special helmet for Cheryl to wear in hopes that it could provide her with cues to replace the natural feedback system that she had lost. The helmet is an odd contraption. It works in conjunction with a computer and plastic strip about the size of a stick of gum that has small electrodes on it. Cheryl places the strip on her tongue. A device in the helmet sends signals to the strip. These signals are extremely mild electrical impulses that feel like the fizzing of a drink on her tongue. When Cheryl's head moves backward, she feels the fizzing sensation toward the back of her tongue. When her head is listing to the left or to the front, she feels the fizz in a corresponding area toward the side or front of her tongue. Cheryl is able to use these signals to keep her balance. Putting on the helmet, Cheryl was able to walk across the room without wobbling for the first time in five years.

Dr. Bach-y-Rita only had Cheryl wear the helmet for one minute that first day. But something odd happened after she took it off. She was able to feel balanced for twenty seconds before the sense of falling returned—a small residual effect that initially seemed pretty inconsequential. Except that the next time, when Cheryl donned the helmet for two minutes, the residual effect lasted twice as long—forty seconds. Cheryl then wore the helmet for about twenty minutes, and Bach-y-Rita expected a residual effect of just under seven minutes. But instead, it lasted a full hour. Cheryl kept the helmet on for longer and longer periods of time. The residual effect increased from hours to days and finally to months.

Today, Cheryl no longer needs the device and no longer feels as though she is perpetually falling. Her brain has somehow learned to send her "balance signals" on its own. Bach-y-Rita believes that the signals from the helmet were able to strengthen secondary pathways in Cheryl's brain—pathways that were previously masked by neural "noise" from the damaged tissue.

What happened to Cheryl is an example of one of the most dramatic insights to emerge from neuroscience—the realization that the brain is much more malleable than we suspected. Many remarkable studies show this *neural plasticity*, as neuroscientists call any functional change in neurons or networks of neurons. Science author Sharon Begley describes several of these studies in her book *Train Your Mind, Change Your Brain*. Begley describes a study of string musicians by neuroscientist Edward

Taub and his colleagues.[2] Violinists and cellists develop great sensitivity in the pads of their fingers—at least on the hand that touches the strings. Taub was able to show how the string musicians' long hours of practice affect the brain. There is a strip of cortex called the *somatosensory cortex*. It runs below the place where the band from a set of headphones might fit on your head. Taub compared how much cortical space on this strip was devoted to registering sense impressions from the musicians' bow hands versus the hand that plays the strings. He found that the string-playing fingers commanded a significantly larger area of the brain.[3] While this may seem only logical, it ran counter to the accepted wisdom. Most neuroscientists at the time knew that our neurons form stronger connections as a result of learning experiences. But prior results in humans had not shown that such specific aspects of a person's experience could directly change how much "neural real estate" is devoted to different functions.

The brain can even take over neural real estate that is usually dedicated to a totally different purpose. One of the most striking examples of this can be seen in research by Alvaro Pascual-Leone. Pascual-Leone and his lab group showed that when blind individuals learn to read Braille, the brain uses cells in the *visual cortex* to process the signals from the blind person's fingertips.[4] It is as if the brain is saying, "Well, here is a lot of unused space in the visual cortex. I need more room to process some very subtle signals from the fingertips. Why don't I just register Braille touch in this empty space?" We used to think that visual cortex neurons could only detect visual input. Now we realize that brain cells can sometimes assume different functions, if they receive relevant information. In this case, some visual neurons normally organized to process spatial information from the retina apparently assumed the spatial processing role required for reading Braille.

The brain's plasticity has phenomenal implications for people whose brains have been damaged by stroke or other disease. At one time, many healthcare professionals gave up on stroke patients after the first year of physical therapy, assuming that little further change was likely. We now realize that patients can regain functioning even years later and that intensive training may help. That training stimulates other parts of the brain to take over the functions of the damaged areas. Edward Taub's *constraint-based therapy* is designed to do just that.

Taub showed that one of the reasons stroke patients do not regain more use of affected limbs is because they naturally use their "good" arm. Why struggle to pick up a cup with your weak arm if you can effortlessly lift it with your good one? But if a stroke patient who has little use of an arm receives intensive therapy *and* puts her good arm into a sling to prevent her from using it, her weak arm can often regain function. Taub is a pioneer of this constraint-based therapy approach in which patients are constrained from using their "good" arms while performing various repetitive activities for hours and hours a day. For example, the patient might painstakingly place a peg in a board over and over while the physical therapist supports the patient's hand. Ultimately, the signals the brain is receiving from those movements can establish new neural pathways and even take over different neural real estate. Some stroke victims who had lost hope of ever moving a limb again have been able to train their brains to process input from the weak limb, even though their strokes occurred as long as seventeen years earlier.[5]

INTERESTING, BUT SO WHAT?

HOW CAN I USE THIS INFORMATION AS A BUSINESS LEADER?

For business leaders, the neuroscience lesson that the brain is more plastic than we realized is a lesson about change. It is both a hopeful and a cautionary tale. The hopeful part of the lesson is the incredible power of the brain to change as a result of learning and practice. The cautionary part is that it often takes a lot of time and intensive practice to create those changes. How can leaders get employees to make the needed effort? People are unlikely to change if the changes require a great deal more effort than the old way. Instead of adopting new approaches, employees will be like the stroke victim who is tempted to use only the stronger arm. They will be tempted to continue the old way of doing things.

All new learning involves changes in the brain. In most cases, these changes do not require the complex rerouting that happens in the brain of a stroke patient. Often, existing neural circuits are progressively modified in the process of learning. During learning, connections among cells may be strengthened or new connections may be formed. Neural processing in the network can then take place more quickly and efficiently. Some neuroscientists use the analogy of ruts in a road to describe this process. When you are learning something new, you have to carve out a new rut—a new groove in the brain. That takes effort and concentration. As you practice, the rut becomes deeper and smoother.

In some cases, new learning may involve even more than the creation of a few new connections among cells. Intensive practice can sometimes cause the very structure of the brain to change. For example, there is a structure called the *hippocampus* on each side of the brain, deep inside, that is heavily involved in learning and memory. The back portion of the hippocampus is especially involved with helping us remember certain types of spatial relations, such as spatial maps of the world. Neuroscientists at University College London wondered what would happen to that area if a person memorized a large number of detailed maps. Then they realized that they could answer their question by studying London cab drivers.

London cabbies have to pass a stringent navigational exam. They have to know, not only the location of streets, but details like the fastest routes from one place to another. It takes most cabbies two years of study to pass the test. Using MRI brain scans, Eleanor Maguire and her associates at University College compared the cabbies with other men about the same age. They found that the rear portion of the hippocampus was larger in cabbies. In fact, the more years of experience a cabbie had had, the larger this area was. The taxi driver study was momentous. As neurologist Jeffrey Schwartz writes, "Published in 2000, this was the first demonstration that the basic anatomy of the adult brain, not just the details of its wiring, can be altered by the demands its owner places on it."[6]

When leaders initiate change, they are placing demands on people's brains. Not only do employees have to master new routines, but they have to overcome the natural tendency to rely on the "easier," well-learned, old routines. In particular, when the change requires that we do the *same* task but in a *different* manner, those neural circuits will find it hard to adapt to the new reality. Simple changes help us realize this. We shift a set of files from one file drawer to another or move a clock to a different wall. We realize just how hardwired our habits are as we repeatedly open the wrong file drawer or search the wall where the clock previously hung. It takes effort and practice to change this habit because we are literally trying to rewire our brains.

Organizational change often requires shifts that are much more fundamental than remembering the new location of the file drawer. Executive coach David Rock and neurologist Jeffrey Schwartz point out that many of the more complex duties of workplace managers become hardwired because "how [leaders] sell ideas, run meetings, manage others, and communicate are . . . [so] well routinized."[7] The fact that so much has become habitual means that implementing change is likely to be more difficult than most leaders anticipate. A certain amount of fumbling is a given.

WHAT IF . . . ?

The conventional wisdom about change is that if leaders can motivate their employees and communicate effectively, they will be successful. This neuroscience lesson teaches leaders that people are likely to have trouble implementing change even when they receive excellent training and *want* to cooperate.

1. WHAT IF BUSINESS LEADERS FACTOR THE NEUROLOGICAL "LEARNING CURVE" INTO THEIR EXPECTATIONS OF THE SPEED OF CHANGE?

When changes require people to adopt new patterns, it is going to take practice and repetition to rewire the brain. Business leaders can see just how difficult change is when they witness employees struggling with new computer software or hardware. For example, the new computers adopted by one organization had the "delete" key in exactly the same position where the "page up" key had been in their previous computers. People lost work as they inadvertently pressed "delete." In this case, people changed quickly, most adapting to the different key placement within a few days. Why? Well, the consequences of making this mistake were costly. The feedback telling people that they had made a mistake was both immediate and relentless. They could always tell when they had erred.

Contrast this with an example of a different hardwired habit. Imagine that a new CEO joins a company called Business Solutions. One of the first actions the CEO takes is to change the organization's name to Business Systems Solutions. This phrase captures the vision he has for the company more closely than the old one. It is easy for him to make the change—he is new. He has not spent the past five or ten years using the name Business Solutions with his clients. But other employees have, and it will not be easy for them to change the name that has become hardwired in their brains.

It is more difficult to make this change than to avoid the "delete" key in the computer example because a person could revert to saying Business Solutions without anyone even noticing, much less pointing out the error. Like the stroke patient unthinkingly using her good arm because it is natural and easy to do so, employees will automatically revert to "the old way." In this case, the CEO has two choices. He can accuse people of being stuck in the past or he can understand that, despite their best intentions, employees' brains will need a bit more time to strengthen the new neural circuit.

2. What if Leaders Use "Constraints Plus Encouragement" to Implement Change?

Constraint-based therapy demonstrates that new neural connections are more likely to be formed if we prevent the usual or dominant way of doing things. Leaders usually understand the need for constraining "the old way" of doing things if change initiatives are to succeed. But constraint-based therapy also shows how slow and arduous the brain's learning curve can be. The therapy succeeds when motivated stroke patients work intensively with physical therapists who do two crucial things. They push patients to their limits and they give them the support they need. For example, the stroke victim tries to pick up a cup and raise it to her lips to drink. In the beginning, she may only be able to touch the cup handle with her index finger. The physical therapist has to literally move her thumb and finger to grasp the handle, then complete the job by supporting her arm and lifting the cup to her mouth. But the two continue to work at this task, repeating the same movements over and over. With each repetition, the brain receives signals establishing this circuit. Slowly, the patient will regain movement until ultimately she can take a sip of coffee unaided.

The physical therapists succeed because they tailor what they are doing to the needs of the patient. They give the minimum support needed for the patient to succeed, and the maximum encouragement. Successful change agents can use this idea in a business setting. Leaders need to make sure that the challenges that change presents are balanced by the degree of support offered. In an attempt to make today's world "greener," for example, many offices are going paperless. For example, some medical offices now use electronic health records systems where information such as changes in medications can be instantly updated or a prescription can be sent to the patient's pharmacy with a keystroke.

In this particular example, medical professionals often have trouble adopting new electronic systems, even though they can clearly see the potential benefits. They are using unfamiliar equipment and software, and are often nervous about making a mistake. It would help if they had an assistant by their side to help them when they got stuck or confused. If only they could call on an expert like the physical therapist in the previous example who could provide exactly the type and degree of support that they needed! While this isn't practical in business settings, what about using innovative training and support approaches to provide the necessary coaching? Support does not have to be expensive either. For example, a list of easily accessible troubleshooting FAQ's ("frequently asked questions") might be enough to help employees get through all but the most difficult situations. Simply rearranging desks to place new learners next to experienced people can also help. The more leaders can calibrate the support their people need with the new learning that is required, the more successful they will be as change agents.

3. What if Leaders Recognize that Learning Takes Time?

In the fast-paced, frenetic world of business, leaders are constantly looking for ways to do things faster. Unfortunately, learning and understanding can't be rushed. Leaders need to make time for their people to learn. Too often, leaders view learning and training experiences as impediments to time spent on the job. They try to minimize the time spent in such activities. Instead, what if leaders identified a few key areas in which they wanted their people to become fully engaged? Leaders could then give their people greater amounts of time to spend on those few things rather than trying to put them through a large number of short, disparate experiences that probably won't "stick" anyway.

NOTES

1. Norman Doidge, *The Brain That Changes Itself* (New York: Penguin, 2007), p. 4.
2. T. Elbert et al., "Increased Cortical Representation of the Fingers of the Left Hand in String Players," *Science* 270 (1995): 305–307.
3. Sharon Begley, *Train Your Mind, Change Your Brain* (New York: Ballantine, 2008), p. 126.
4. Ibid.
5. Jeffrey Schwartz and Sharon Begley, *The Mind and the Brain: Neuroplasticity and the Power of Mental Force* (New York: Perennial Press, 2002), p. 193.
6. Ibid., p. 252.
7. David Rock and Jeffrey Schwartz, "The Neuroscience of Leadership," *Strategy+Business*, February 6, 2007, http://www.strategy-business.com/press/freearticle/06207 (accessed March 22, 2000).

RELATIONSHIPS

Chapter 5

CAN I TRUST YOU?

WHAT'S THE STORY?

W hat makes us trust another person? Trusting the wrong person, as the Bernard Madoff scandal all too painfully illustrated, can be catastrophic. FBI agents arrested financier Bernard Madoff on December 11, 2008.[1] He was charged with duping investors out of an estimated $50 billion. Madoff's alleged securities fraud hit investors hard. Numerous charities—as well as individual investors and pension funds—lost millions. Beyond the financial losses, Madoff's alleged crimes damaged the Jewish community. As Rabbi Burton L. Visotzky, professor at the Jewish Theological Seminary, said, "The fact that he stole from Jewish charities puts him in a special circle of hell. . . . He really undermined the fabric of the Jewish community, because it's built on trust."[2]

Trust is risky. Yet without trust, we would never rely on a friend to pick us up at the airport, or depend on a colleague to steer us in the right direction as we worked on a project. So how do we decide whom to trust? Economists look at trust as a calculation. Based on how someone has treated us in the past, we calculate the odds that we can trust that person in the current situation. Bernard Madoff was trusted partly because over the years his investors enjoyed consistent financial gains.

One of the ways that economists test this calculation theory is by having people play "the trust game." In this game, you are given some money—say, $20—and told that you can hand over whatever amount you want to a "trustee" in the next room. You are also told that whatever you give the trustee will automatically triple, so that if you send $10 into the next room, the trustee will be given $30. The trustee then decides how much money to return to you. If the trustee keeps everything, you won't be likely to send any more money to that person. But if, for example, the trustee sends back half ($15), then your investment will have paid off and in the next round you might send even more. Over several rounds, your gains could increase. But you also might lose a lot if, in the last round, the trustee keeps every penny.

It turns out that what we do in the trust game depends mainly on how fairly we feel we've been treated previously. It is as if our brains are calculating the odds that the other person will treat us fairly, based on our past interactions with him or her. For example, if the money I send you triples each time it gets to you and you split those proceeds evenly with me every time, then my brain ups the odds that you will continue to play fair so that we are both winners. This inclines me to trust you with more and more of my money each round.

Through a recent technological development called fMRI hyperscanning, neuroscientists are now able to scan the brains of two people at the same time. Frank Krueger and his colleagues used fMRI hyperscanning during a variation of the trust game. In this version, the two players switched roles on different rounds. Sometimes one player would hand money over to the other, and the receiving player would decide how much money to return. At other times the roles were reversed.[3] This variation more closely resembles what happens in our everyday lives. Sometimes we decide how much to trust a colleague or acquaintance, while at other times that person decides how much to trust us.

What did the researchers find? About half of the pairs in this study always reciprocated trust, meaning that at no time during the thirty-six rounds of play did either partner keep all the money and leave the other penniless. For these players, two areas of the brain were involved. One of these areas, the *paracingulate cortex*, helps us imagine the mental states of other people. This area was active in the early rounds of the game in the people who never betrayed one another. The researchers speculated that these players' ability to imagine what the other person was thinking made it easier for trust to develop. Their past interactions helped them build up a positive history of trustworthy behavior. Later in the experiment, this more calculating part of the brain was less active in these players. They no longer needed to think hard about what the other person might be planning because they had established a sense of trust.

The second finding was that people who never betrayed each other showed greater brain activity in the *septal area* of the brain, which is a part of the *limbic system*, the region of the brain known to be involved in social learning. Researchers also speculate that this area may control the release of *oxytocin*, a hormone associated with attachment and bonding. This is important, because other research has shown that oxytocin influences trust. In this research, men who were given whiffs of synthetic oxytocin before playing the trust game were more trusting,[4] even to the point of continuing to trust after being betrayed.[5]

The neuroscience research suggests that fairness is not the only element that influences trust. The brain does try to imagine what the other person might be thinking in an attempt to predict how that person will behave. And the brain does appear to keep track of what has happened in the past to determine the odds that our partner will play fair or betray us. But once trust is established, we take it for granted and our brains no longer need to engage in careful calculations to decide what to do. We simply trust. And, in fact, we have a good "oxytocin" feeling about the person we have trusted. Feelings of trust make us feel more connected to others. The people in Frank Krueger's research who never betrayed one another reported feeling closer to their partners.

INTERESTING, BUT SO WHAT?

HOW CAN I USE THIS INFORMATION AS A BUSINESS LEADER?

Leaders need to make wise decisions about whom to trust, to what degree, and with what tasks. Every time a leader assigns a task or project—indeed, in every act of "empowerment"—leaders are also deciding how much to trust the person who takes on the task. How does a leader decide who is trustworthy? The brain performs a calculation. It recounts past experience to predict how others will act. But that calculation is more complex for leaders in the workplace than it is for people playing the trust game in the laboratory. To make the right decision, leaders need to accurately evaluate not only integrity and goodwill but competency as well. Leaders can't trust an employee to deliver on a promise if that person lacks the necessary skills to do the job.

Trust is crucial to organizations. Leaders can react in harmful ways when they don't trust their employees to perform competently. Some leaders simply refuse to delegate responsibility and instead do the work themselves. Others assign the task, but later spend hours rechecking the figures or rewriting the PowerPoint deck. In this way, these leaders avoid a poor outcome. But they also overburden themselves and fail in their responsibility to develop their people.

Some leaders delegate the work but then micromanage the process. These leaders breathe down the employee's neck to make sure that the employee carries out the assignment in exactly the same way that they would. Other leaders micromanage in a more roundabout way by demanding a step-by-step description of what the employee did to finish the job. Some leaders even give the same assignment to multiple people and choose the "best" output as the final product. This not only shows a lack of trust in employees, but it significantly reduces both employee engagement and productivity as well. All of these actions increase stress and fuel employee frustration. They also make it impossible for employees to demonstrate that they can be trusted to carry out assignments on their own, since they never have the opportunity to do so.

So should a leader simply accept reports, recommendations, and analyses with a smile—never questioning or doubting the results? Well, no. It is part of the leader's job to evaluate outcomes. But leaders can make a distinction between monitoring the *outcome* of people's work and micromanaging the *process* that people follow to create that work. Sometimes leaders act as if being more hands-off in managing people means they must also be more hands-off in holding them accountable. But that's not necessarily true.

For example, leaders can use their knowledge of the business to ask questions about the results that come in. Knowledgeable leaders have hypotheses about what factors are at play in their businesses. If a leader looks at an analysis of sales data that contradicts her own experience and insights, then she has a clue that something might be amiss. Either the leader has something to learn or the employee has erred somewhere. The two can discuss the case more fully to resolve their differences.

Trusting others doesn't mean abdicating responsibility or completely eliminating oversight. It does mean making more conscious decisions about whom you can trust, to what extent, and with what assignments. It means considering the degree to which an employee's skills match the requirements of the task. It also means working out ways to provide additional support if needed. Once all this is in place, it means backing off and trusting the employee.

Doesn't trusting others mean that leaders take on some additional risk? Sure. As psychologist Roger Mayer and his associates point out, it is not possible to develop trust in a risk-free environment.[6] If there is nothing at risk, then there is no real need to truly trust others. Sometimes organizations try to reduce risk by instituting tight controls to ensure compliance. Paradoxically this inhibits the development of trust. When employees comply, leaders will likely attribute their compliance to the company's policies and not to the employees' trustworthiness.

WHAT IF . . . ?

Leaders can make better decisions about whom to trust. They can also proactively manage the risks involved in trusting others. Here's how:

1. WHAT IF LEADERS ACKNOWLEDGE THE PERSONAL FACTORS THAT AFFECT THEIR ABILITY TO TRUST?

In a thought provoking article titled "The Decision to Trust," Robert Hurley describes personality characteristics that influence our ability to trust. These include our personal tolerance of risk and our natural inclination to trust or distrust others in general. It will be hard for us to trust if risk makes us anxious. For example, leaders who find it very difficult to accept any imperfections will find it harder to trust that others will do the job to their exacting standards. Leaders who have the self-knowledge to recognize their own quirks in these areas have already made an important first step. By recognizing these kinds of factors, they can intentionally base their decisions about whom to trust on a more objective case-by-case basis.

2. WHAT IF LEADERS MONITOR HOW MUCH "OXYTOCIN TRUST" IS INFLUENCING THEIR DECISIONS?

In reviewing research on organizational trust, F. David Schoorman and his associates note that emotional attachments are so powerful they can cause people to risk even when that risk is "not warranted by the available evidence."[7] One key factor influencing trust is similarity. We tend to trust people who are similar to ourselves and who share our interests. Leaders can monitor how much similarity is influencing their decisions. A leader can ask herself, "Why am I reluctant to trust Miranda with a major overseas project? Is it because of how she has performed in the past, or just because her style is so different from my own?" A leader might feel less trust just because an employee has different priorities. For example, a workaholic manager may find it harder to trust family-oriented employees.

To avoid either excessive trust or mistrust, leaders can ask themselves questions such as, "Whom do I typically trust with high-profile assignments?" "Whom do I trust with our most difficult clients?" Leaders can then create a list of team members who are on the high end of the leader's own "trust continuum" versus those who are lower. Then leaders can ask themselves some hard questions about the list: Do I tend to trust this person at the top of the list because he is similar to me? Because I like him? If someone on the low end were behaving exactly like a high-end person, would I question that person's actions more? How much real evidence do I have that a person on the low end of the list is likely to let me down?

This kind of review can encourage a leader to be more objective when deciding to trust people. It might also raise a red flag about someone that the leader has come to trust implicitly. In her article "Duped," Margaret Talbot tells a story of misplaced trust in Stephen Glass, an up-and-coming reporter for the *New Republic*, who turned out to be "the most egregious liar I ever knew."[8] Glass's rise and fall is documented in the movie *Shattered Glass*. This film shows how Glass's career crumbled when *Forbes* revealed that his story—about a genius teenage hacker who was paid off by CEOs to leave their computer systems alone—was a total fabrication.

How did Glass fool so many editors and colleagues for so long? It seems that he was able to create a sense of connection that stimulated powerful feelings of trust. As Talbot recalls, "I liked Steve; most of us who worked with him did. A baby-faced guy from suburban Chicago, he padded around the office in his socks. Before going on an errand, Steve would ask if I wanted a muffin or a sandwich; he always noticed a new scarf or a clever turn of phrase, and asked after a colleague's baby or spouse."[9] The Stephen Glass story is a vivid demonstration that unconditional "oxytocin trust" can lead to betrayal.

3. WHAT IF LEADERS ACTIVELY MANAGE THEIR PART OF THE "TRUST" EQUATION?

For trust to develop between leaders and employees, both parties need to demonstrate their trustworthiness. Leaders need to earn a reputation for competency, honesty, and dependability. Both leaders and followers need to make sure that they keep their promises. In a business setting, this often involves a promise about meeting a deadline or providing necessary resources. In "The Decision to Trust," Robert Hurley urges leaders to "underpromise and overdeliver."

Hurley also points out that sometimes employees will promise more than they should for reasons that have nothing to do with integrity. Maybe they aren't good at predicting what is possible in a given time period, or maybe they get carried away by their own enthusiasm. The result is still a breach of trust. As Hurley writes, "When a person fails to deliver, he's not just missing a deadline; he's undermining his own trustworthiness."[10]

Such small breaches can often snowball because of the reciprocal nature of trust. In Frank Krueger's brain research based on the trust game, when one participant betrayed the other early in the rounds, both became overly guarded and set off a downward spiral. Trust can deteriorate quickly when one party feels that he or she has been let down by the other. The good news is that leaders can also trigger an upward spiral. Candid conversations about what went wrong can disrupt the descent and turn things around. As Hurley observed, "To some degree, one person's openness induces openness in others, and the decision to put faith in others makes it more likely that they will reciprocate."[11]

NOTES

1. Allistair Barr and Ronald D. Orol, "Madoff Arrested in Alleged Ponzi Scheme," *MarketWatch*, December 11, 2008, http://www.marketwatch.com/news/story/madoff-arrested-charged-may-facing/story.aspx?guid=%7BB7353 DBD-688D-47D4-B7F8-D257A018405F%7D&dist=msr_14 (accessed January 12, 2009).

2. Robin Pogrebin, "In Madoff Scandal, Jews Feel an Acute Betrayal," *New York Times*, December 23, 2008, http://www.nytimes.com/2008/12/24/us/24jews.html (accessed January 12, 2009).

3. Frank Krueger et al., "Neural Correlates of Trust," *Proceedings of the National Academy of Sciences* 104, no. 50 (2007): 20084–89.

4. M. Kosfeld et al., "Oxytocin Increases Trust in Humans," *Nature* 435 (2005): 673–76.

5. T. Baumgartner et al., "Oxytocin Shapes the Neural Circuitry of Trust and Trust Adaptation in Humans," *Neuron* 58 (2008): 639–50.

6. Roger C. Mayer, James H. Davis, and F. David Schoorman, "An Integrative Model of Organizational Trust," *Academy of Management Review* 20, no. 3 (1995): 709–34.

7. F. David Shoorman, Roger C. Mayer, and James H. Davis, "An Integrative Model of Organizational Trust: Past, Present, and Future," *Academy of Management Review* 32, no. 2 (2007): 344–54, quote from page 349.

8. Margaret Talbot, "Duped," *New Yorker*, July 2, 2007, http://www.newyorker.com/reporting/2007/07/02/070702fa_fact_talbot (accessed December 7, 2008).

9. Ibid., p. 1.

10. Robert Hurley, "The Decision to Trust," *Harvard Business Review* (September 2006): 7.

11. Ibid., p. 7.

Chapter 6

OUCH! YOU LEFT ME OUT

WHAT'S THE STORY?

I was at a park with my dog and suddenly a frisbee rolled up and hit me in the back. I looked around and there were two guys playing, so I threw it back to them thinking that I'd go back to my dog—but then they threw it back to me. So I threw it to them and they threw it to me, so I sort of joined their group and we were throwing it around for a couple of minutes and then all of a sudden they stopped throwing it to me and they just threw it to each other . . . I was amazed at how bad I felt . . . and finally I just sort of slithered back to my dog.

The speaker, social psychologist Kip Williams, made these remarks in a 2004 interview for ABC News.[1] Williams studies the pain of being ignored and ostracized, and his experience suggested a solution to a research puzzle he had been trying to solve—namely, how to temporarily induce feelings of being excluded in research participants.

As a result of his experience in the park, Williams developed *Cyberball*,[2] a computer game in which you see two figures, like the ones shown in figure 6.1, tossing a ball back and forth. *You* are represented at the bottom of the screen, and when given the ball, you can throw it back to whomever you choose. When participants in research play Cyberball, the computer figures initially include them in the game. But later, the computer figures exclude the human participants. These participants experience what Williams himself experienced in the park with the Frisbee.

Figure 6.1. Research shows that feeling left out is more painful than we realized.

Neuroscientists Naomi Eisenberger and Matt Lieberman, who are husband and wife, teamed up with Williams. They adopted Cyberball as a way to test out a hunch Eisenberger had about social pain. Eisenberger suspected that phrases like "he broke my heart," "I was cut to the core," and "it was like a slap in the face" might be more than just metaphors. Previous research with animals had suggested that our brains may actually register social pain in exactly the same structures that register physical pain. To test this possibility, Eisenberger and her colleagues scanned people's brains as they played Cyberball. First, however, she led the research participants to believe that the two figures representing the other players were being controlled by real people instead of the computer. This made it seem that the two other "real" players, after initially including the participants in the game, would suddenly stop throwing the ball to them.

What was going on in the research participants' brains when they were left out of the game? Eisenberger reported that the upper portion of the *anterior cingulate cortex* reacted when the participants experienced the social pain of feeling excluded.[3] Other experiments show that this brain area is also active when people experience physical pain. There may be something in common between physical pain and emotional pain, though exactly what is unclear. The researchers could also tell that this part of the brain reacted specifically to the social exclusion. How did they know this? The researchers told some participants that the reason they were excluded was because of a glitch with the equipment. These participants' brains did not react in the same way.

How did the research participants who experienced this social pain react? In interviews after they had played Cyberball, these participants reported strong feelings of being rejected. They searched, sometimes tearfully, for explanations: "What happened? Maybe I threw the ball too hard at them?" A few of the participants were so upset by the experience that the researchers had to spend considerable time helping them calm down—even after these participants had been told that there were no "real people" other than themselves involved in the game.

As this research highlights, it doesn't take much to make us feel excluded. This kind of exclusion seems to affect us in ways that are out of proportion to the harm done to us. We are in conversation with someone at a party and then notice that person's gaze drifting across the room . . . to whom? Someone more interesting or more attractive? We walk toward a table in the cafeteria and the three people sitting there shift their positions ever so slightly, seemingly forming a closed circle that implicitly shuts us out. We make a joke in the midst of a lively conversation but no one notices and the group goes on talking as if we hadn't spoken. Psychologists used to think of social pain mainly in terms of what we feel when we are humiliated or insulted. But as social exclusion research clearly indicates, we also feel pain simply from being left out.[4]

Eisenberger's husband and research collaborator, Matt Lieberman, speculates that social pain has an evolutionary advantage. Physical pain alerts us to a danger that we need to address. Similarly, social pain makes us aware that something is going wrong in our social relationships. To survive as a species, humans need to be connected to other humans. Any signal that we are at risk of being excluded from a group could theoretically help us. Social pain spurs us to mend the damage and stay connected to others. It also makes evolutionary sense that the brain could most easily evolve if it did not have to create an entirely new signal system to alert us to exclusion. Instead, it could simply connect the pain of rejection with a system that was already in place. Why not use the neural system that already alerts us to the presence of physical pain?

While we are highly sensitive to the pain that *physical* abuse causes others, we seem to be less sensitive to the effects of *social* pain. As Eisenberger commented in the ABC interview, "We need to be more careful. While kids are taught not to physically hurt each other or hit each other, they're not taught the importance of not rejecting each other—that the pain they can cause each other is real and can last for a long time." One blogger, commenting on Eisenberger's research, wrote, "This study gives us some hard scientific evidence backing what we have always known in our inner hearts to be true; that being left out matters and that it hurts—the pain of exclusion is as real as that of any other kind of injury."[5]

INTERESTING. BUT SO WHAT?

HOW CAN I USE THIS INFORMATION AS A BUSINESS LEADER?

Every effective leader will, at times, use strategies that include some people while excluding others. For example, most leaders rely on an inner circle of trusted advisers. During succession planning, leaders often invest more time and resources in people who have the highest potential for growth. The neuroscience research explained above alerts leaders to how much real pain these strategies can cause for those who feel excluded.

Leaders cannot dole out their time and attention in precise or equal measures—nor should they try to do so. But they can shoot for a balance to ensure that whole segments of their organization do not feel left out and that individuals do not feel routinely overlooked. Leaders can ask themselves how publicly their partiality manifests itself. How obvious is it to individuals that they are being overlooked? In an effort to develop its potential leaders, one company hosted a monthly dinner at a fancy restaurant for line managers—but only included those managers who had college degrees. This fact was widely known, and it is not hard to imagine the effect this exclusion had on the managers who often had more experience but were not "college grads." While this is a clear-cut example, an exclusion can often be much more subtle.

When a leader responds to some team members by rephrasing their points or jotting down their ideas but then appears to barely listen to the comments of others, those who are seemingly overlooked will feel excluded. The signals that make people feel invisible are often slight, such as letting one's gaze wander to the next item on the agenda while someone is talking. Such a trivial action will not devastate team members if it happens occasionally. But when leaders are consistently less responsive to certain employees, it matters. People notice when no one throws the ball to them.

Sometimes leaders inadvertently cause an entire department or team to feel excluded. One leader habitually failed to acknowledge a team that performed work that was important, albeit behind the scenes. For a variety of understandable reasons, he rarely met with the team face-to-face and was not familiar with the details of their work. As a result, he never recognized their efforts publicly—though he was conscientious about expressing his appreciation of other teams. This overlooked team became demotivated and cynical. When the situation was pointed out to the leader and he began recognizing the team, the situation improved. But it took years to completely eliminate the cynicism.

What effect does feeling ignored have on people? While some people may step up their efforts to be noticed when they feel invisible, many others simply withdraw. Team members whose ideas are rarely given any attention think, "Why say anything? No one listens to me anyway." So they are mute during the next team meeting, making it easy for both the leader and other team members to forget that they are there. Feeling more and more invisible, these team members withdraw even more. Some of the major barriers to engagement are the very same experiences that trigger the social pain of feeling ignored and left out. Feeling like you are contributing to the organization in a meaningful way, feeling connected to your team or coworkers, and valuing your relationship with your manager are three of the key drivers of engagement.[6] All three of these motivators are harmed when people feel excluded.

Sometimes people are ignored because their own behavior causes others to avoid them. For example, everyone can predict that Jose will pontificate, or that Sally will meander from one irrelevant remark to another, or that Ravi will churn out reams of data while his listeners' eyes glaze over. People like Sally, Jose, and Ravi are typically unaware of the impact they have on others. They suffer from the common blind spot of not seeing themselves. Leaders may want to consider mentoring or coaching to help such people recognize and change their behavior so that they will be better accepted by the team. This will not only increase engagement; it will also increase the odds that everyone's valuable ideas are noticed and not lost.

Some people feel estranged because the culture of the organization is not a close match to their style, philosophy, or values. They may consider leaving the organization, feeling that they don't fit in. When an alienated person adds significant value, leaders sometimes try to address this problem by adding incentives, such as bonuses, so that the person will stay. However, if the employee is experiencing real pain, these quick fixes are unlikely to succeed. One member of a leadership team, for example, was repeatedly told that her ideas were delightfully innovative but could not be implemented because they were too far afield from the organization's standard practices. A leader's best bet in such situations may be to support that employee in finding a different home for her talents, an organization where she can truly belong.

WHAT IF . . . ?

What if leaders found ways to balance their investment in high performers with the creation of an inclusive environment? Most people—leaders and colleagues alike—are well aware of the behaviors that make people feel excluded or devalued. We are often conscious of our actions when we roll our eyes at a particular person's comments, or when we barely acknowledge that someone has joined the group, or when we ignore that person's timid attempts to join in the discussion. What we fail to realize is how much real pain our actions cause. As former Electrolux CEO John Case commented, "No leader would slap an employee in the face."[7] Yet the sting of social pain hurts so much that, as Cyberball inventor Kip Williams observed, many people would prefer to be hit than ostracized.[8] What if leaders reframed actions that create social pain by asking themselves, "Would I be willing to hit this person in this situation?"

1. WHAT IF LEADERS VIEW EMPLOYEE ENGAGEMENT SURVEYS AS A KIND OF PAIN INDEX?

Most leaders have at least a few strategies that they can use to create a culture in which inclusiveness is valued. They know ways to encourage people to be more sensitive to signs of social ostracism. But what if leaders also applied this brain research to their employee engagement or satisfaction survey data? Leaders often use such data to "prove" that under their leadership, employee engagement and satisfaction have increased.

Used in this way, these survey results can distance leaders from the real people who take the surveys. It is easy to focus on the scores and fail to remember that some of these questions are not merely indicators of engagement or satisfaction—but indicators of real human pain. In hospitals, patients are sometimes asked to quantify the level of pain they experience by picking a number on a scale from one to five. In a very real sense, survey questions like "To what extent do you feel listened to?" are a measure of how much social pain an employee is experiencing. Instead of focusing on numbers, leaders can focus on impact. If 80 percent of employees feel that they are listened to, that might seem like a pretty good result. But the one in five people who doesn't feel listened to might be experiencing social pain. Would it be acceptable to slap every fifth person in the face? Leaders would not physically hit their employees, but when they see these ratings, they should remember that some employees are in real pain.

2. WHAT IF LEADERS INCREASE THEIR AWARENESS OF HOW THEIR MESSAGES AND COMMUNICATION MIGHT INADVERTENTLY EXCLUDE OTHERS?

If we have underestimated the pain people experience when they feel left out, then we have probably also greatly misjudged the pain caused by noninclusive speech and practices. What about the gay person in the midst of people who persist in speaking as if the whole world were heterosexual? Or a person of color viewing a training film that is exclusively filled with white faces? In cases like these, the invisibility that people feel can be a source of social pain. This neuroscience lesson reminds us that diversity can sound like a soft issue, but the hard reality is that excluding others causes real pain. People who are rarely included in a meeting or asked to share their views because of their gender, race, ethnicity, age, sexual orientation, or physical appearance suffer social pain, however unintentional their exclusion may be.

3. WHAT IF LEADERS THINK ABOUT THE IMPACT THAT TECHNOLOGY MIGHT HAVE ON IGNORING OTHERS?

Virtual meetings and conference calls can induce feelings of not belonging when half the participants are in the room and the other half are connected only through a computer or phone line. The virtual participants are at high risk for feeling invisible. In addition, they miss most of the nonverbal cues that help people understand what is going on. One leader decided to have *all* the team members participate in team calls from their own desks even though some of them could have met in person. This created a more level playing field and made it less likely that those in remote locations would "check out" because they felt ignored.

The latest telepresence technology enables people to see "virtual" attendees on large screens as if they were sitting right across the table. But there is a caution. One of the unintended consequences of telepresence is that virtual attendees sometimes forget that others can see them. They may even get caught reading a newspaper or having a side conversation on mute while in the middle of the discussion. Having become accustomed to multitasking during conference calls, these virtual attendees can forget that they are now visible to others. When leaders are virtually present at meetings, they need to take special care not to convey the same subtle signs of excluding others that hurt so much in real life. A look of boredom can be much more noticeable on a large screen!

While there have been great strides in communication technology, many organizations don't have the latest equipment. Or they might have the right equipment, but they don't implement it properly. For example, the room may be too big or there aren't enough ancillary microphones or cameras. Some teams have a lot of meetings in which a large contingent meets in person while the rest are virtually present. Leaders of these teams should make a regular practice of participating as virtual team members. This will help them understand firsthand how well the technology is working to bring people together.

NOTES

1. "Pain of Rejection," ABC News Story Archive, September 9, 2004, http://www.abc.net.au/catalyst/stories/s1195656.htm (accessed October 4, 2008).
2. Kipling D. Williams and B. Jarvis, "Cyberball: A Program for Use in Research on Ostracism and Interpersonal Acceptance," *Behavior Research Methods, Instruments, and Computers* 38 (2006): 174–80.
3. Naomi I. Eisenberger, Matthew D. Lieberman, and Kipling D. Williams, "Does Rejection Hurt? An fMRI Study of Social Exclusion," *Science* 302 (2003): 290–92.
4. Geoff MacDonald and Mark R. Leary, "Why Does Social Exclusion Hurt? The Relationship between Social and Physical Pain," *Psychological Bulletin* 131, no. 2 (2005): 202–23, quote from page 202.
5. Allen J. Comeau, "Why Rejection Really Hurts," http://www.drcomeau.com/Why-rejection-really-hurts.htm (accessed January 15, 2009).
6. Patricia Soldati, "Employee Engagement: What Exactly Is It?" *Management-Issues* (March 8, 2007): http://www.management-issues.com/2007/3/8/opinion/employee-engagement-what-exactly-is-it.asp (accessed March 11, 2009).
7. John Case, comment made as part of "Panel on the Neuroscience of Leadership," October 30, 2008, Neuroleadership Summit, New York, http://www.neuroleadership.org (accessed November 1, 2008).
8. K. D. Williams, "Social Ostracism," in *Aversive Interpersonal Behaviors*, ed. R. Kowalski (New York: Plenum, 1997), pp. 133–70.

Chapter 7

WILL THE "REAL" YOU PLEASE STAND UP?

WHAT'S THE STORY?

How do you think you might react if you were placidly watching a movie when the scene abruptly broke and the camera zoomed onto a surgeon's gloved hands—streaming with blood—lifting intestines out of a patient's gaping torso? Stanford University neuroscientist James Gross compiled a series of such film clips that consistently repelled people who viewed them, including scenes of surgery, vomiting, and animal slaughter. Why? Gross wanted to learn what was happening in our brains when we feel intense aversion and disgust, and these fifteen-second clips were ideal for triggering those reactions.

Two areas of the brain that react strongly when we witness these kinds of scenes are the *amygdala* and the *insula*. The amygdala is a core part of an area of the brain called the *limbic system*. This system includes a number of interconnected clusters of neurons with various functions. One of the functions that ties many parts of this system together is the need for involuntary emotional responses. When you instinctively spit out rancid food or freeze at the sight of a bear at your campsite, it is these brain areas that direct your actions. You can see the evolutionary advantage of having a part of the brain that causes you to spit out rotten food *before* you have a chance to swallow it, just as you can see the advantage of instantly freezing at the sight of a bear.

In the modern world, however, we rarely taste strange plants or bump into bears. Instead, the dangers we face often require us to hide our feelings of disgust, fear, or anger rather than to act on them. As Gross writes, we may wish to "hide the anger we feel toward a boss, the anxiety we feel during an interview, or the amusement we feel at a coworker's decidedly politically incorrect joke."[1]

It was this phenomenon of hiding what we really feel that most intrigued Gross and his collaborator, Philippe Goldin. They arranged to scan the brains of people viewing the disgusting film clips. While the participants in this research watched the clips and described their emotional reactions, a camera photographed their faces. In addition to viewing the film clips of revolting sights, the participants also watched other scenes like mountain ranges and sunsets for comparison purposes.

Because Goldin and Gross were particularly interested in what happens when we intentionally attempt to hide our emotions, at times the participants were instructed to try to suppress their facial expressions. At other times they were told to just react naturally. In addition, the researchers sometimes asked people to try to rethink the meaning of what they were seeing in a more positive way. For example, they asked some people to focus on the ultimate benefit of the surgery to the patient rather than on the bloody intestines. The researchers discovered that when people were viewing upsetting film clips and then reconsidered the meaning of what they were seeing, the intense emotional reactivity of the amygdala and the insula areas of the brain decreased. But when people tried to maintain poker faces during these disgusting scenes, those same areas of the brain became *more* active.[2]

The significance of findings like these is that they demonstrate that there are costs associated with trying to hide our emotions. We may suppress the expression of those feelings, but that does not mean we are no longer actually experiencing them. In the more primitive part of the brain, our reactions grow stronger when we try to hide them. Other research reveals that it takes a lot of cognitive effort to keep that stiff upper lip.[3] This is so pronounced that when we try to hide our reactions, it is harder for us to later remember the whole experience. For example, it is harder for us to recall what we actually saw in that upsetting film.[4]

There is another cognitive cost that comes when we hide our feelings—we monitor ourselves. For example, in today's business world it is socially unacceptable to express racial prejudice. People try to stop themselves from saying or doing anything that might reflect racial bias. This kind of monitoring takes effort. That effort uses brain resources to such an extent that it temporarily impairs our ability to do other cognitive tasks.

Research shows that after interacting with black individuals, white people with racial biases do more poorly on cognitive tasks involving attention. Northwestern University social neuroscientist Jennifer Richeson and her collaborators found that people who were more racially biased had higher levels of activity in brain regions controlling attention when shown photographs of the faces of black males.[5] The same people also did more poorly on a cognitive task after having a brief interaction with a black male. As Richeson writes, it is as if our ability to control attention "is a limited, renewable resource that can be depleted temporarily"[6] by our efforts to hide our prejudice. The solution is not to become indifferent to political correctness or to stop monitoring ourselves. The solution is to find ways of genuinely shifting the feelings we have. As discussed in chapter 15, experiences such as having more positive contacts with people from different races can help.

Another cost attached to hiding our feelings is that it is physically stressful for us to do so—and for others to witness. In some studies, two women would watch a disturbing video, like one depicting the terrible suffering caused by the atomic bombing of Hiroshima. Afterward, they would discuss the film. But during the discussion one of the women, based on secret instructions from the researcher, would try *not* to show any emotion. The result was that her blood pressure would rise during the conversation as she attempted to maintain a blank expression. What was surprising was that the blood pressure of her partner would also rise. This did not happen because of the troubling nature of the topic, since the partner's blood pressure did not rise when the other person displayed her natural feelings. We apparently find it disturbing to be with someone whose outward demeanor does not match what we assume their inner feelings to be.

But what if one of the women, rather than trying *not* to show what she really felt, used a different strategy to change her reactions? Like the people watching the disgusting film clips, she might try to think of the film from a different perspective. What if, for example, one woman in the Hiroshima discussion said, "That film was terrible," and the other—instructed to reconsider the viewing experience from a more positive perspective—responded, "Well, I don't know. Maybe it is good to watch something like this so that we do not forget the terrible suffering that war involves." Gross notes that when this kind of exchange occurred, the stress indicators from both women *decreased*.[7]

There is a big caveat related to studies like these. You may have noticed that this research referred to the "women" in the studies. That is because so far only women have been selected for this type of research. This is done in part because researchers believe that women are more emotionally reactive. Until more research is done, we won't know if men who try to hide what they feel experience the same amount of stress, or trigger it in others to the same degree. It is possible that research with men might not turn out the same way. Similarly, these studies with North American individuals may not be applicable to other cultures, particularly cultures where the suppression of emotion is valued. For example, research suggests that Japanese people suppress their negative emotions in the presence of others more than Europeans do[8] and that Asian Americans mask their true feelings more than Caucasians do.[9]

Nevertheless, at least for American women, the bottom line is that hiding their emotions does not change what they feel, and the effort of hiding those emotions carries a hefty price tag. Within the brain, this effort and stress increases the intensity of an emotional reaction. The effort to restrain our emotions is so cognitively taxing that it distracts us from what is happening; this exacerbates our physical stress reaction as well. Moreover, it creates stress for others around us. In contrast, *reappraising* a troubling experience early on—before our emotional reactions escalate—helps. Thinking about what is happening from a more positive perspective calms our brain's reactivity and calms us.[10]

INTERESTING, BUT SO WHAT?

HOW CAN I USE THIS INFORMATION AS A BUSINESS LEADER?

In recent years, the idea that leaders should be authentic has become widespread. In their article "Managing Authenticity: The Paradox of

Great Leadership," Rob Goffee and Gareth Jones point out one of the great paradoxes of authenticity—namely, that leaders have to be many things to many people while remaining true to themselves.[11] One solution to this quandary, Goffee and Jones suggest, is to recognize that our authentic selves are complex and multifaceted. They argue that it is possible to express only those aspects of ourselves that are appropriate in a given setting and still remain authentic. To illustrate this point, the authors quote Jean Tomlin, former HR director at Marks and Spencer. She comments, "Before I go into a situation, I try to understand what it is [people] will be thinking, I prepare what I am going to say. . . . I want to be me . . . [but] what you get is a segment of me. It is not a fabrication or a facade—just the bits that are relevant for that situation."

As Tomlin's remark implies, being authentic does not require us to reveal every random thought and feeling we have. Yet one major facet of authenticity, as humanistic psychologist Carl Rogers emphasized decades ago, is to make sure that our inner selves—what we truly think and feel—match our outer behavior.[12] For example, we may feel a nagging sense of unease after a meeting with our team; something feels "off" to us. We may later realize that we pretended to support a policy that we personally questioned, or we tried to boost the team's morale by feigning more confidence than we actually felt in their ability to complete a project. Leaders often choose not to reveal their true feelings for perfectly understandable reasons. This is where the neuroscience research on hiding emotions meets the issue of authenticity.

As the brain research shows, it costs us to consciously hide what we are really feeling—but it does not only cost *us*. When we act in ways that are not congruent with our genuine feelings, other people detect it and react. In response, they may not only feel physiologically stressed, but they may also have negative feelings about us. In one study, when one member of a pair intentionally tried to hide her feelings, the other woman reported experiencing discomfort, diminished rapport, and less desire to continue the relationship. [13]

How are others able to detect the lack of congruence? One big reason is that our body language betrays us. Most of us have had lots of practice in molding a bland facial expression when we actually feel embarrassed or upset. However, because our limbic system can trigger a grimace faster than we can suppress it, we sometimes unconsciously

Figure 7.1. When you try to fake authenticity, your body language might betray you.

reveal what we initially meant to keep secret. Even though we quickly suppress a frown and put on a smile, our disclaimer, "It's no problem, I don't mind staying late to help out," rings false to our boss. Similarly, people detect this kind of falsity when they say "his smile never reached his eyes."

The upshot of all this is that you can't fake authenticity. In fact, it is very hard to fake anything convincingly—being nonchalant when you are really concerned, being untroubled when you are furious, or being cheerful when you are sad. This is why "practicing" authenticity back-fires. Nick Morgan, the author of "How to Become an Authentic Speaker,"[14] point outs that in the natural course of events, nonverbal behaviors like making eye contact occur just *before* conscious thought. There is a sequence in which the gesture always comes first. This happens because the gesture is involuntarily fueled by that speedy limbic system. It is then *followed* by our words. Though these events may be separated by only tenths of a second, others detect that something is inconsistent if the order changes. So what happens when a speaker begins an impassioned statement, and then remembers he was planning to make eye contact at that point in his talk? When he now looks at his audience, the potentially powerful effect is likely to instead feel contrived.

So leaders can't fake being authentic. But showing their true feelings has a downside too. Leaders don't want to be human mood rings, where everything they think and feel is totally transparent to others. How can they resolve the paradox of authenticity?

Leaders can begin by deciding how emotionally self-revealing they want—and need—to be in different situations. Being authentic is not the same thing as relinquishing one's right to privacy or permitting every thought and feeling to pop out completely uncensored. Effective leaders think through the repercussions of their actions. This is as much a part of who they are as authentic people as the feelings that they experience. When leaders decide to suppress their feelings until they have time to figure out how to deal constructively with a situation, that decision can also be authentic.

In some situations, leaders are reluctant to tell their teams how they are really feeling because they do not want to spread their anxiety to others. They may think they need to pretend an optimism that they do not feel, which makes them feel inauthentic. But there is a third possibility. Leaders don't necessarily have to choose between being reassuring but phony versus overwrought but authentic. Leaders may be able to genuinely shift their feelings by reappraising the circumstances. As discussed in more detail in chapter 20, a leader who initially reacts to an economic downturn with dismay might discover some positive aspects to the changes that are occurring if she rethinks the situation.

No one is encouraging leaders to paint on a false Pollyanna face. But leaders who step back from disasters to reflect on the positive aspects of the situation may find that their own emotions genuinely shift for the better.

WHAT IF . . . ?

1. WHAT IF LEADERS REALIZE THAT THEY ARE ALWAYS EVOLVING IN THEIR ABILITY TO BE AUTHENTIC?

In one organization, nearly everyone loved to work with a particular team leader, Joe. One of Joe's peers asked someone to tell him what Joe did that made him so popular, "so I can do it, too." The response? "Don't bother. . . . it won't be the same." This reply reflects our intuitive sense that Joe's leadership style is successful partly because it expresses *him*. Merely copying his style is doomed to fail. We cannot successfully become a carbon copy of someone else.

On the other hand, we have all learned to get better at what we are doing by using others as models. It is not uncommon for young artists to sit in museums with their sketch pads, copying the masters. Novice musicians often realize that they tend to play in the style of whatever professional musician is their current favorite. Most of us need to imitate others as a step toward developing our own artistic style or our own identities. So how can we reconcile this "pretending" with developing our own authentic style?

What if we recognize, as Carl Rogers put it, that we are always "becoming" a person? We are always evolving. Perhaps the most authentic identity we have is the one that simply acknowledges the stage of development that we are in. This would mean saying, "Well, I am not Joe and I cannot be Joe. But I can try out some of Joe's strategies and adapt them to my own personality and style." Like creative artists who ultimately blend various approaches to create their own inimitable styles, leaders can get a feel for different tactics and adjust them to suit their own strengths and styles.

2. HOW CAN PEOPLE CHANGE IF "THAT'S JUST HOW THEY ARE"?

When team members complained about the brusque style of one leader, he told them, "I know I'm not good at the touchy-feely stuff. This is just how I am. Deal with it." This leader is trying to use being authentic as an excuse for not changing. Employees use the same ploy. When criticized for dominating every conversation, for example, an employee shrugs her shoulders helplessly, "I have always been a talker. That's just me. It's just how I am." She says this as if being true to oneself means acting on every impulse.

There is a kernel of truth in these objections, however. People often feel as if they are playacting when they try to behave differently. Pretending feels just the opposite of being authentic. Leaders are also sometimes concerned that if they try to change, they will appear weird to their employees. "What's with her?" people will wonder as a previously tough leader now inquires solicitously about how people are feeling.

How can leaders try to change without acting in ways that ring false to themselves and their employees? One esteemed physicist always opened his lectures by addressing his class as "fellow students." Viewing ourselves as always learning and evolving offers a solution to this dilemma. Leaders can change without acting phony by being up front with others about what it is that they are trying to do. In a business setting, this might mean telling a team, "Look, part of who I am is that I am a brusque, no-nonsense kind of person who does not like to beat around the bush. But I realize that my style has created some pretty big problems lately, so I am trying to do something about that. This is not going to be easy, so I am asking for your patience and your help." When leaders are genuinely trying to change, words like these ring true. Plus they are likely to elicit understanding and support from others.

3. WHAT IF LEADERS THINK TWICE BEFORE PROMOTING INAUTHENTIC PEOPLE?

Some leaders assume that candidates for promotion can acquire *soft* skills like authenticity. They promote people who have the necessary *hard* skills, and then fall into the trap of thinking that they can coach or train these new leaders to be more authentic. Too often the upshot is that the organization ends up with executive team members who are insensitive and inauthentic. Leaders who are genuinely motivated to become more authentic *can* do so. But attending a training class alone won't do the trick. Authenticity doesn't come from a checklist—it comes from a desire to be more self-reflective and to genuinely connect with others. It is a critical behavior for a leader. So when making promotion decisions, leaders should not assume that people will grow into their authentic selves. Wise leaders should find people who have already demonstrated a commitment to being authentic.

NOTES

1. James J. Gross, "Emotional Regulation," in *Handbook of Emotions*, ed. Michael Lewis, Jeannette Haviland-Jones, and Lisa Feldman Barrett (New York: Guildford), p. 504.

2. Louis Bergeron, "Suppression as Coping Mechanism Increases Stress," *Stanford News Service*, March 24, 2008, http://storybank.stanford.edu/stories/suppression-coping-mechanism-increases-stress (accessed June 7, 2008).

3. Gross, "Emotional Regulation."

4. Jane M. Richards and James J. Gross, "Personality and Emotional Memory: How Regulating Emotion Impairs Memory for Emotional Events," *Journal of Research in Personality* (2005); *Science Direct* (September 2005): http://www.sciencedirect.com/science?_ob=ArticleURL&_udi=B6WM0-4H0YYSW-1&_user=7438643&_rdoc=1&_fmt=&_orig=search&_sort=d&view=c&_acct=C000050221&_version=1&_urlVersion=0&_userid=7438643&md5=765992aa971a92711382b75b2c8b27d2 (accessed November 15, 2008).

5. Jennifer A. Richeson et al., "An fMRI Investigation of the Impact of Interracial Contact on Executive Function," *Nature Neuroscience* 6 (2003): 1323–28.

6. Ibid., p. 1323.

7. Gross, "Emotional Regulation."

8. W. V. Friesen, "Cultural Differences in Facial Expressions in Asocial Situations: An Experimental Test of the Concept of Display Rules," unpublished doctoral dissertation, University of California, San Francisco, 1972.

9. J. J. Gross and O. P. John, "Mapping the Domain of Expressivity: Multimethod Evidence for a Hierarchical Model," *Journal of Personality and Social Psychology* 74 (1998): 170–91.

10. Phillippe R. Goldin et al., "The Neural Basis of Emotion Regulation: Reappraisal and Suppression of Negative Emotion," *Biological Psychiatry* 6 (2008): 577–86.

11. Rob Goffee and Gareth Jones, "Managing Authenticity: The Paradox of Great Leadership," *Harvard Business Review* (December 2008): 86–95.

12. Carl Rogers, *On Becoming a Person* (London: Constable, 1961).

13. E. A. Butler et al., "The Social Consequences of Expressive Suppression," *Emotion* 3 (2003): 48–67.

14. Nick Morgan, "How to Become an Authentic Speaker," *Harvard Business Review* (November 2008): 115–19.

Chapter 8

WALKING A MILE IN SOMEONE ELSE'S MIND

WHAT'S THE STORY?

I magine a couple in love who are participating in research that involves physical pain. While the woman is in an MRI machine, her partner sits nearby. He will sometimes receive a painful shock through electrodes placed on the back of his hand. At those times, she won't be shocked but will instead feel a mild, painless sensation through the electrodes on *her* hand. At other times, the opposite will happen. She'll receive a painful shock but he will experience only a mild sensation. From within the MRI machine, the woman can see both her own hand and her partner's hand. Different colored lights flash to let her know if she or her partner will receive the next electric shock.

Though this eerie scenario is reminiscent of a similar scene in the novel *1984*,[1] unlike "Big Brother" in the novel, the researchers are not trying to induce one partner to betray the other. Instead, the researchers are studying the opposite phenomenon—the empathy that people feel when someone they care about is in pain.[2] What happens in the brain in this situation? The woman receives a shock, and her brain reacts. The brain scan shows high activity in the areas that register our subjective experience of pain.

In the next round, the woman sees a light indicating that her hand will experience the mild sensation, but her partner will receive the painful shock. What happens in this case? In her brain, the same neural circuits that registered her subjective experience of pain when she herself was shocked once again go into high gear. As Tania Singer and Ernst Fehr, the neuroscientists who did this research, commented, "If a loved partner suffers pain, our brains also make us suffer from this pain."[3]

To feel empathy, people have to be able to understand what others are feeling. People have to put themselves in someone else's shoes. This is a fairly high-level intellectual ability—one that seems beyond a young child, for example. In his extensive study of children's thinking, Jean Piaget found that children were often trapped in their own point of view. For example, a four-year-old who sees Mommy crying after he has spilled his milk will think, "I made Mommy cry." He won't think, "Mom just found out that Daddy lost his job, so she's overreacting to a little spilled milk." Piaget called this tendency to see things solely from one's own viewpoint "egocentrism." It was easy to conclude that egocentrism would prevent children from showing empathy.

But that conclusion never quite matched later research. For example, developmental psychologist Martin Hoffman demonstrated that very young toddlers show empathy.[4] They will, for example, try to help another child who is crying. However, these very young children are also egocentric—they see the situation from their own perspective. For example, in one study, a thirteen-month-old baby tried to help another child who was in distress. But to do so, she pulled the distressed boy over to her own mother, ignoring his mom who was sitting nearby. The helpful toddler did not have the cognitive ability to realize that the boy would want his own mom, not hers. But she did understand that her friend was unhappy, and she felt for him. How is this possible if empathy requires the intellectual capacity to take another person's perspective?

Brain research now points to a different explanation for how human beings understand the feelings of others. This explanation doesn't assume that we need highly developed intellectual abilities to feel empathy. Instead, merely witnessing the emotions of others causes us to unconsciously mimic their facial expressions. We probably don't realize it, but when we listen to a tale of woe from a friend, our face assumes an expression of concern. That expression is much like the distressed look on our friend's face. Brain research shows that assuming this expression of sadness activates some of the same brain regions that actually feeling

Figure 8.1. When people "mirror" our own moods and expressions, we feel they understand us.

sad does. So there is a dual process going on. First, we physically mirror the emotions of another person in our own facial muscles. That mirroring in turn triggers the same emotion in us. When this happens, we literally "feel with" that person. In other cases, as in the study of couples in love discussed earlier, just knowing that someone we care about is in pain creates brain activity that triggers pain in us as well.

Some neuroscientists believe that our brains contain cells that specialize in mirroring the feelings, actions, and even intentions of other people. In his book *Mirroring People*, neuroscientist Marco Iacoboni argues that such "mirror neurons" are the key to empathy. [5] The brain cells that have been dubbed mirror neurons were first identified by researchers in Parma, Italy. They were measuring a monkey's neural activity in a region of the brain that registers hand movements related to actions such as gripping.[6] By inserting electrodes into the monkey's brain, they were able to measure the activity in individual brain cells. They discovered that the same neurons that fired when the monkey reached for a slice of apple to eat also fired when the monkey saw a researcher reaching for a slice of apple. Iacoboni theorizes that this kind of activation is what makes it possible for humans to understand one another.

Brain scans cannot be used to discover mirror neurons. Brain scans can show us what regions of the brain are more active, but they cannot pinpoint individual brain cells. To observe human mirror neurons, researchers would have to insert electrodes into the brains of humans. This procedure would not be done just for the sake of research. Until the monkey studies are replicated with people, we can't know whether people also have mirror neurons.

In the meantime, some findings suggest that a process similar to mirroring *is* going on in the human brain. In one MRI study, people saw a film clip in which someone would pick up a cup to drink out of it. The brain scans showed that the same area of the brain was active when people watched someone else pick up a cup to take a drink as when they themselves picked up a cup to drink. Iacoboni uses this research to argue that the brain takes the intentions of others into account. When the participant watched someone pick up the cup to clear the table (not to take a drink), this brain area failed to respond.

Neuroscientists conclude that this area of the brain does not see two similar actions as identical if their goal is clearly different. The brain takes the intention of the person, or the goal of the action, into account. This is an extraordinarily useful ability. Imagine, Iacoboni says, that he is having a disagreement with his wife. If his wife reaches for a glass from the dishwasher while they are arguing, he wants to be able to tell whether she is doing that in order to put the glass in the cupboard or to hurl it at him.

Whatever specific processes are involved, it is clear that the brain uses some sort of mirroring process to help us understand the feelings, actions, and intentions of others. In some way, our brain activity reflects emotions and intentions that are similar to theirs. This, in turn, gives us an intuitive sense of what others think and feel.

INTERESTING, BUT SO WHAT?

HOW CAN I USE THIS INFORMATION AS A BUSINESS LEADER?

The mirroring process that goes on in the human brain helps leaders understand both the feelings and the motives of their employees. These reactions make it possible for leaders to connect with employees on an emotional level, a key to increasing employee engagement. Mirroring processes also enable leaders to be aware of how their own actions affect employees. This awareness is an essential aspect of emotional intelligence. Of course, this same kind of brain activity influences employees as well as leaders. In a business setting, it is particularly important that employees grasp the intentions and goals of the leader. This is crucial to the success of empowerment programs.

1. CONNECTING TO OTHERS

Leaders want to increase employee engagement. One of the key drivers of engagement is feeling connected to others in the workplace. When leaders relate to employees as individuals, they create a sense of genuine connection. In contrast, the opposite happens when leaders interact in ways that don't ring true. An employee may think, for example, "She says she understands how demanding this project is, but she says the same thing to everyone. I don't think she has any idea what she has been asking of me." Leaders who pay attention and take the time to really know what their employees are experiencing have an edge. By paying careful attention, the leader's brain gains the information needed to "read" employees accurately and respond to them with more empathy.

Many leaders understand the importance of empathy on an intellectual level, but often they don't act on their understanding. As Daniel Goleman points out, "When it comes to business, we rarely hear people praised, let alone rewarded, for their empathy. The very word seems unbusinesslike, out of place amid the tough realities of the marketplace."[7] Empathy can sound like a soft emotion that makes leaders cave in every time an employee appears to be distressed. But in a business setting, empathy simply means that leaders understand the feelings of the people around them and take those feelings into account as they decide how to respond.

When our facial expressions mirror the looks on other people's faces, they feel more connected with us. So should leaders go around intentionally mirroring their employees? Hardly. If artificial imitation were enough, a mimic would be a powerful leader. But it is unlikely that sham behaviors affect us in the same way that genuine behaviors do. Remember the studies in which the neurons that fired when a monkey picked up a slice of apple also fired when that monkey merely watched someone else pick up a slice of apple? In one of these studies, the other person didn't actually pick up the object. The researcher only *pantomimed* the action of picking up the object. The monkey's mirror neurons ignored the gesturing researcher. Apparently our brains can often tell the difference between authenticity and parody. They help us tell the difference between someone who is genuinely experiencing empathy for us and someone who is only faking it. And as discussed in chapter 7, authenticity is key to effective leadership.

2. UNDERSTANDING WHAT OTHERS FEEL

To be effective, leaders need to monitor the impact that they have on their employees. Goleman and his colleagues argue that leaders who are "emotionally tone-deaf" can't succeed. All too often, these kinds of leaders will say things that deflate a team's enthusiasm or alienate the very individuals whose support the leader needs most. Moreover, these leaders won't realize what they have done. The emotional reactions of employees are one of the best barometers that leaders have to measure the effects of their actions. Leaders who can't read that barometer are at a distinct disadvantage. As Goleman writes, "When leaders are able to grasp other people's feelings and perspectives, they access a potent emotional guidance system that keeps what they say and do on track."[8]

Leaders' own brains can help them read people. Imagine, for example, that a leader begins telling his team about the great initiative that another department has proposed. He doesn't realize it, but the team members are astounded and upset by his story—they are recalling the time when they proposed a similar idea, and he dismissed it as foolish. The leader might not pick up on the team's reactions directly, but as he unconsciously mimics their facial expressions, he starts to sense that something is "off."

A leader's developed sensitivity to others is an asset when dealing with clients, customers, and vendors, as well as with employees. Leaders who pay attention and really listen can pick up subtle clues about what matters to others. They will be more likely to notice and address a client's apparently minor concern—a concern that could later turn into a major roadblock to a sale. These leaders will be more able to respond to the aspirations of talented employees, making it more likely that they will retain people with high potential. Emotionally intelligent leaders stay tuned-in to nuances of body language, tone of voice, and behavior. This gives them insights into the emotions and intentions of other people.

3. HELPING EMPLOYEES GRASP THE LEADER'S INTENTIONS

Not only do leaders need to understand their employees' intentions, but employees need to understand their leaders' intentions as well. Empowered employees especially need to appreciate the leader's goals. Empowerment entails giving employees more latitude in deciding how to accomplish organizational goals. To make effective judgments without needing a list of specific "dos and don'ts," employees must grasp the overall goal or intent so that they can align their actions with that goal.

How can leaders ensure that people understand their intentions? The mirror neuron research with monkeys suggests that face-to-face communication may be a key component. Employees are more likely to accurately understand the leader's goals when they can see that leader's facial expressions and listen to that person's voice. Obviously, people don't always have to see another person's face to understand that person's intentions, but the brain research shows that we respond powerfully to the physical presence of others. When it is crucial for employees to deeply understand a leader's message, face-to-face communication is vital.

WHAT IF...?

1. WHAT IF LEADERS FOCUS ON BEING "REALLY PRESENT"?

The brain research suggests that being physically present to other people can help us understand them. It also helps *them* understand *us*. But simply being physically present isn't enough. We have to *actively notice* one another. We have to *pay attention*. This is especially important when leaders want to change direction. When leaders are not just issuing marching orders, but need employees to understand their intention, it is critical that these leaders be really present. If the leader is fully present, employees will understand the leader's goals more easily. In addition, the leader will more easily feel genuine empathy for employees who struggle with the proposed changes.

So, what does it mean to be really present? Jon Kabat-Zinn, founder of the Center for Mindfulness at the University of Massachusetts Medical Center, wrote that to be fully present "we have got to pause in our experience long enough to let the present moment sink in; long enough to actually feel the present moment . . . to hold it in awareness."[9] To be fully present means that we are mindful of what is happening *right now*. We pay attention, intentionally, but without judging. We might notice that we are thinking, "Uh-oh, Joe is scowling, I sure hope he doesn't start right in with his objections. It's about time people here just shut up and listened to me." When we are mindful, we will notice these thoughts, but we won't be captured by them. Instead, we will notice these thoughts, let them go, and turn our attention back to what is important.

Sounds simple, doesn't it? As Kabat-Zinn says, mindfulness is "simple, but not easy."[10] It takes practice and discipline to be consistently mindful. It requires that we resist the temptations of the Blackberry and pay attention to the current situation. Mindfulness may sound far afield from the skills that leaders typically try to develop. But the focused attention involved in mindfulness can strengthen some of the same executive functions of the brain that leaders need to be effective. Kabat-Zinn is convinced that mindfulness is not just for Buddhist monks, and he conducts intensive retreats for organizational leaders to help them develop this mindful attitude.[11]

2. WHAT IF LEADERS TAKE ADVANTAGE OF VIRTUAL TOOLS TO BE MORE "PRESENT"?

Today's technology allows a grandmother in India to see her three-year-old grandson in Canada as they talk together through her computer. In business, similar videoconferences enable people across the world to connect at virtual meetings. New technology makes these meetings increasingly realistic. Cisco corporation's product TelePresence can make a dozen people feel they are literally sitting at the same conference table.[12] In reality, those attending the meeting might be located in several different countries. But the image projected of everyone sitting around the same table is so realistic that the impression of actually being in the same room is uncanny.

Leaders have long recognized that how people communicate influences how easy it is to understand—or misunderstand—one another. We misinterpret e-mails more often than phone calls because with e-mail we have fewer cues to interpret meaning. Similarly, we catch other people's reactions more easily in a videoconference than over the phone. It is obvious that we have more cues in some situations than in others. But the brain research shows just how important these additional cues are. They help us get more than just the meaning of what someone says. They give us a glimpse into what other people feel and what their intentions are. Global leaders who don't want to lose the benefits of face-to-face communication but cannot afford frequent costly trips can look into realistic video conferencing services like TelePresence.

3. WHAT IF LEADERS BREAK THE "SCOWLING" CYCLE?

Our brains trigger us to mimic the facial expressions of others. This usually makes us feel empathy for others. For example, if our friend looks sad, we feel her sadness because our own facial expression mimics hers. But what happens when someone gets angry with us? Now we mimic that person's scowl and feel his anger. But we often don't react with empathy, saying, "I am really sorry that I just made you so angry." Instead, we feel angry right back at that person. Our scowls mirror each other and feed into our anger.

Leaders sometimes call for a time-out during contentious discussions. The brain research suggests that it would be best for agitated people to physically separate during that time. Of course, people need to do more than just readjust their facial muscles during time-outs. But stopping the mutual scowling is a reasonable first step to ending the rising exasperation. Leaders who can empathize with people who are upset—without mirroring their anger back—can help those people get back on an even keel.

Leaders need more than empathy in conflict situations. They need good conflict resolution techniques and strong communication skills, like those advised in the classic resource *Getting to Yes*.[13] But the brain research adds an important reminder—leaders who are able to pick up on the mirroring of negative emotions that may threaten the cohesion of a group can intervene and shift the cycle sooner.

NOTES

1. George Orwell, *1984* (New York: Signet Classics, 1950).

2. Tania Singer et al., "Empathy for Pain Involves the Affective but Not Sensory Components of Pain," *Science* 303, no. 5661 (2004): 1157–62.

3. Tania Singer and Ernst Fehr, "Neuroeconomics of Mind Reading and Empathy," *American Economic Review* 95 (2005): 340–45.

4. Martin L. Hoffman, "Developmental Synthesis of Affect and Cognition and Its Implications for Altruistic Motivation," in *Social and Personality Development: Essays on the Growth of the Child*, ed. William Damon (New York: Norton, 1983), pp. 258–77.

5. Marco Iacoboni, *Mirroring People: The New Science of How We Connect with Others* (New York: Farrar, Straus, and Giroux, 2008).

6. G. R. Rizzolatti et al., "Functional Organization of Inferior Area 6 in the Macaque Monkey. II. Area F5 and the Control of Distal Movements," *Experimental Brain Research* 71 (1988): 491–507.

7. Daniel Goleman, Richard Boyatzis, and Annie McKee, *Primal Leadership: Learning to Lead with Emotional Intelligence* (Cambridge, MA: Harvard Business School Press, 2004).

8. Ibid., p. 50.

9. Jon Kabat-Zinn, *Wherever You Go, There You Are* (New York: Hyperion, 1994), pp. xiii–xiv.

10. Ibid., p. 8.

11. Jon Kabat-Zinn retreat information is at http://www.umassmed.edu/cfm/pom/index.aspx?linkidentifier=id&itemid=41276 (accessed February 12, 2009).

12. Cisco product information is at http://www.cisco.com/en/US/prod/collateral/ps7060/ps8329/ps8330/ps7073/prod_video_data_sheet_telepresence_1.html (accessed March 21, 2009).

13. Roger Fisher, William L. Ury, and Bruce Patton, *Getting to Yes: Negotiating Agreement without Giving In* (New York: Penguin, 1991).

Chapter 9

FIRE, READY, AIM?

What Goes Wrong When Our Actions Get Ahead of Our Brain

WHAT'S THE STORY?

You are in the batter's box and the pitcher is winding up. You see the ball leave the pitcher's palm and come flying toward you. Here's the question: At the moment you see a fastball leave the pitcher's hand, how far has it already traveled?

Answer: About nine feet.

Think about that for a second. When you think the ball is just leaving the pitcher's hands, it is no longer there. It has already traveled nine feet.

Neurologist Robert Burton uses this example to explain that we are often on a time delay when we perceive the world around us.[1] Think of what happens when a radio contest winner is at home while talking to the host on the phone. "Turn down your radio," the host says. Otherwise, the winner will hear the host's voice on the radio just after hearing it on the phone—a delayed feedback system that will result in a disjointed conversation. Something like this happens whenever we see, hear, smell, taste, or touch anything. There is a tiny delay between what we experience and our conscious awareness of it.

Why aren't we aware that the ball has left the pitcher's hands at that exact moment? The light that hits our retinas travels much faster than the ball itself can—it travels at the speed of light! So why the delay?

The problem is what happens *after* the light hits the retina. There, as molecular biologist John Medina puts it, the retina converts the light into electrical impulses—"a language the brain can understand."[2] After this step, signals are conveyed through several layers of cells in the retina. Signals are then sent beyond the retina via the optic nerve, but not on a direct path to the cortex. First, there is a stopover deep within the brain, in a place called the *thalamus*. Cells at this level do not generate visual awareness on their own. That is thought to happen much later, after information is transmitted from the thalamus to the cortex. Time is spent on neural processing at each of these levels, as well as for projecting impulses from one place to another. Although neural signals travel very fast, reaching our visual cortex in about a twentieth of a second, the trip still takes long enough that the ball travels nine feet before we see it.

The point is that the batter only has a fraction of a second to make a *conscious* decision about what to do. This is especially true when the pitcher throws a fastball. At the moment the pitch begins, the brain of the batter must process the visual information of the throw and begin to swing the bat as well. This all happens on an unconscious level. It happens before neural signals representing the ball's trajectory have a chance to reach awareness. The ball approaches so quickly that the batter only has a small window of time to decide how to react. In fact, if the batter realizes that he has misjudged the pitch, he does not have enough time to correct his swing. The best he can do in this case is to check swing.

It turns out that external stimuli, like light and sound, aren't the only events that require neural processing time before we become aware of them. The very decisions we make appear to begin with brain activity that is outside of our awareness. Imagine, for example, that I were to say to you, "Whenever you feel like it, lift your index finger." Imagine, too, that you have a way to pinpoint the exact moment that you decide to do this. Researcher Benjamin Libet found that he could tell when participants were going to decide to move their fingers *before they did*.[3] How? Libet detected characteristic brain activity that occurred just before the moment when participants said their decision came to mind.

Libet's research showed that there is a delay between the instant when one's brain makes a decision and when that decision enters the person's consciousness. He carefully constructed his experiments to show that this delay was not due to how these events were measured or reported. The conclusion Libet draws is that the brain signal to take an action begins to occur before we are aware of "deciding" to act. The time difference is miniscule—the brain activity shows up about a half second before we move the finger. Yet, we usually pinpoint the moment of deciding to move the finger three-tenths of a second later.

The implications of Libet's research continue to be hotly debated today, especially in relation to the notion of free will. In psychology, for example, some theorists argue that genetics combined with environmental events determine how we will behave. This belief is called *determinism*. From the perspective of determinism, people feel as though they are free agents in deciding what they do, but in fact they are not. Determinism argues that our genes, combined with the experiences we have had, ultimately cause us to make the choices that we make. To people who believe in determinism, our sense of being a free agent is an illusion.

Consistent with determinism, some neuroscientists see Libet's findings as evidence that free will is an illusion. If the brain "knows" or "decides" when we will lift a finger before we make the conscious decision to do so, they argue, then we are not really free agents in control of our actions. Rather, our decisions are dictated by our brain in ways that escape our awareness. However, Libet takes a different position. We still have what he calls "veto power." During that two-tenths of a second when we are conscious of a decision—"I'm going to lift my finger now"—we can veto that decision. Like the batter who checks his swing, we can decide not to act.

As neuroscientist Jeffrey Schwartz put it, we may not have "free will," but we appear to have "free won't." We have a window of time in which we can decide what we want to do about our decision. So, for example, the decision to grab that extra piece of cake may be made at a neurological level below our level of awareness—but once we consciously decide to head for the fridge, we still have time to veto that decision. How much time we have depends on how fast we have to react. The batter has very little time to react. In other situations, like heading for the fridge or reacting with an angry outburst, we can stretch out the amount of time we have to make a decision. But even when we have very little time—like two-tenths of a second—we at least have time to veto our original intended action.

Naturally, these neuroscience findings do not solve the philosophical debate about free will. Philosophers continue to argue about the nature of volition, even examining the "who" in the question "who has free will?" Does "who" refer to the totality of one's conscious intentions? Does it include unconscious processing? The nature of free will is undoubtedly tied up in various other philosophical conundrums. Clearly, though, the intention to act is more complex than our conscious experience of making a decision.

INTERESTING, BUT SO WHAT?

HOW CAN I USE THIS INFORMATION AS A BUSINESS LEADER?

In his discussion of the baseball player, Robert Burton draws a parallel between the batter's situation and a person engaged in a conversation. In a fast-paced conversation, information speeds toward us and we respond just as quickly. Sometimes, we have a brief exchange in a hallway or swap ideas in a brainstorming session. At other times, we are in a heated discussion where people shoot their ideas in rapid-fire. As Burton asks, how much time do we really think about what someone else has said before we answer?

We only have a small window of time to take in what other people are saying. Imagine, for example, that we respond in a half-second to what someone has just said. Subtract from that half second the time it takes for the auditory signals to lead to comprehension and conscious awareness. We may barely consciously register what has been said before we answer. Sometimes we do *not* register what has been said before we answer. As Burton points out, the faster we respond, the more likely that we won't accurately grasp the incoming information.[4] No wonder the person we are talking with sometimes says, "Would you just *listen* for a minute?" We may be responding to the other person, believing that we have accurately heard what she has said—when we haven't accurately heard anything at all.

Leaders recognize that communication is a challenge. Brain research shows that communication is even more of a challenge than we realized!

First, we misunderstand others because we don't take much time to think about what they have said to us. Second, to make matters worse, we answer before we have taken enough time to think about our response. No wonder we sometimes think "I can't believe I said that!" and wish we could retrieve the words that just flew out of our mouths.

All too often, we answer before we fully take in what someone else is saying, and before we fully consider what we are about to answer. When emotions run high, the conversation is like a flurry of speeding bullets. As one insightful person at a seminar commented: "It's like we each have rifles, and I'm loading my gun with arguments against what he just said while he's shooting his ideas at me. He does the same thing—he's not listening while I'm shooting my arguments back, he's reloading."

We end up saying words we wish we could retract. What we could do instead of "reloading" is to use that two-tenths of a second to exert our veto power—to tell ourselves to keep quiet and think for a moment before we respond. Maybe that's why Bonnie Jacobson, director of the New York Institute for Psychological Change and author of *If Only You Would Listen*, asserts that "keeping your mouth shut" is the main skill people need to be effective leaders.[5] Jacobson points out that the leaders' silence is what gives team members a chance to express their views. But silence also gives leaders time to make sure they understand what others mean and to consider their own response before speaking.

WHAT IF . . . ?

Author David Stauffer opens his article on listening, "The Most Neglected Communication Skill," by quoting the Greek philosopher Zeno.[6] Zeno wrote, "The reason why we have two ears and only one mouth is that we may listen the more and talk the less." In one company, Stauffer notes, the CEO documented that his top sales people "asked more questions and listened more" than less successful sales people. Motivational speaker and Cleveland sales professional Hal Becker argues that "it doesn't matter whether you're selling, negotiating, supervising, or reporting—a manager in any situation is going to be more effective by listening than by talking."[7]

Many leaders pay lip service to the importance of listening. But do they act on what they know?

1. WHAT IF LEADERS FOLLOW ZENO'S ADVICE AND LISTEN MORE THAN THEY SPEAK?

To be better listeners, leaders could exercise their veto power more often. They could shut down the immediate response that springs to their lips and take more time to understand the other person. This is hard for leaders who are uncomfortable with silence. They may need to practice pausing before they react. They may need to deliberately do something to help them slow down. For example, leaders who take notes while someone else is talking are less likely to jump in with a response. These leaders will get more used to building in some thinking time while talking with someone else. Plus the person who an attentive leader speaks to will have the satisfying experience of seeing that leader carefully noting her comments.

Leaders set the pace in many of their conversations. Employees can tell when a leader genuinely wants to hear more and is willing to devote time to the matter. They will take their cues from the leader. If they sense impatience, employees may assure the leader that no further discussion is needed, even if that is not what they truly believe.

2. WHAT IF LEADERS REALLY SEE HOW THEY TALK WITH OTHERS?

"Be a better listener." "Ask questions." "Don't interrupt." These communication rules are very familiar to leaders. Yet we all know people who are poor communicators despite this knowledge. We know the "rules," but we don't know how often we violate them. It is hard to see ourselves.

In his article, Stauffer offers five steps to improve our ability to listen. The first crucial step is for leaders to realize where they need improvement. How many leaders could accurately answer the question "What proportion of the time do you listen versus talk?" How many leaders could say how often they respond instantaneously to what has been said? To discover this information, most leaders will need to get feedback from others or record conversations that they can later analyze.

There is another way in which leaders can get immediate feedback that will improve their listening skills—that is to simply check out how accurately they have understood others in their day-to-day conversations. As Stauffer points out, good listening is an active endeavor. Leaders need to be quiet, but that doesn't mean that they need to be passive. One of the best ways to practice *active listening* is to restate what someone else has said. By restating, then asking the person if the restatement is correct, leaders can check their understanding. Active listening also has the side benefit of contributing to strong relationships with others.

Asking for clarification takes time. But in the end, it saves time. Sometimes leaders don't say much because they assume that they understand the employee's point and immediately disagree with it. They do not ask for more details or for clarification because they just want to move on. But this just makes people feel that they aren't being listened to, so rejected employees end up repeating their points over and over again in different ways. This is time consuming and counterproductive.

3. WHAT IF LEADERS HELP THEIR TEAMS IDENTIFY KEY WORDS THAT ARE OFTEN MISINTERPRETED?

If leaders had their teams identify the words and phrases that were at high risk for being misinterpreted, those words could become a signal. Whenever people heard those words, they could ask for clarification. One leader, for example, often used the "royal we." For example, he would say, "We need to make sure that this request is routed through accounting first." His people, failing to hear a direct request, did nothing. The leader felt that he had made a clear request but his people thought he was just making a comment. His requests often fell through the cracks. The leader later wondered why no one took care of the matter, and in return he heard, "You didn't tell us to do that." Next time the leader says "we," the team should, in turn, ask, "Who exactly should do this?"

Here are some other words that often have at least two possible interpretations:

"Day" as in, "We need to implement this within ten days." But how are we counting days? Calendar days, business days, workdays (within a certain number of eight-hour shifts)?

"**Results**" as in, "Give me your results from last month." But which results? Results can pertain to nearly anything, from financial results, to employee satisfaction results to sales figures.

"**Summary**" as in, "Get me a summary of the sales results." But a summary in what time frame? Daily, monthly, quarterly, year-to-date?

"**My people**" as in, "Let my people know about this development." But which people? Direct reports, everyone in the organization, those whom the leader usually tells this kind of information to, members of the leadership group, only people at a supervisory level?

"**Management**" as in, "We want to make sure management knows this." But does that mean just those who have a manager title, those who supervise others, or those above a certain level in the organization?

4. WHAT IF LEADERS ENCOURAGE SLOWER-PACED COMMUNICATION?

Leaders can show that they would like to see people take a bit more time before responding to one another rather than shooting from the hip. What if leaders experimented by imposing more silence? For example, what if leaders proposed that for just fifteen minutes of a meeting, everyone would pause for two seconds after every comment or question? Team members would learn how they react to silence. Does silence make them impatient or uncomfortable? Do they use the time to see if they understood what was said? Or do they use it to think about what to say next? Team members might even realize that this additional time led them to change how they otherwise would have responded.

NOTES

1. Robert Burton, *On Being Certain: Believing You Are Right Even When You're Not* (New York: St. Martin's, 2008), pp. 74–77.

2. John Medina, *Brain Rules: 12 Principles for Surviving and Thriving at Work, Home, and School* (Seattle: Pear, 2008).

3. Benjamin Libet, *Mind Time: The Temporal Factor in Consciousness* (Cambridge, MA: Harvard University Press, 2004).

4. Burton, *On Being Certain*, p. 75.

5. David Stauffer, "Yo, Listen Up: A Brief Hearing on the Most Neglected Communication Skill," *Harvard Management Update*, (July 1998): 3.

6. Ibid.

7. Ibid.

Section III

CULTURE

Chapter 10

THAT'S NOT FAIR!

WHAT'S THE STORY?

Evolutionary biologist Keith Jensen apparently has a mischievous side. During his work with chimpanzees at the Max Planck Institute for Evolutionary Anthropology in Leipzig, Germany, Jensen set up a sliding table laden with food. He placed the table just outside the chimps' cages. Chimps could slide the table toward their own cages, sometimes pulling the food out of the reach of other chimps. Each chimp also had a rope which—if tugged—would collapse the whole table and send the food crashing to the floor.

What happened when one chimp essentially stole another chimp's food by pulling the table out of reach? The victims of such thefts were clearly incensed. The offended chimps collapsed the whole table to get revenge at least half the time. "It's extraordinary how angry the chimps would get when food was stolen from them—they just became exploding black balls of rage," researcher Jensen said.[1] The act of collapsing the table was clearly vindictive—aimed at punishing the thief. Those same chimps did not send the food flying when they were simply barred from reaching it themselves, despite seeing other chimps enjoying the feast.

Other research with capuchin monkeys shows that even more subtle experiences of unfairness can trigger anger. Monkeys in adjacent cages were trained to hand over small granite rocks to researchers in exchange for slices of cucumber. As long as the monkeys saw that their neighbors also received cucumbers, the monkeys happily traded rocks for food. But

Figure 10.1. When monkeys get rewards that seem unfair, they throw them away!

what happened when the researchers favored some of the monkeys with juicy grapes, a much-preferred treat? The slighted monkeys reacted. "They would literally take the cucumber from me and . . . throw it on the ground, or when I offered it to them they would simply turn and refuse to accept it," psychologist Sarah Brosnan commented.[2] Ultimately, the monkeys who felt insulted were less willing to continue the exchange. This was even more evident when they saw other "slacker monkeys" getting grapes for *doing nothing*.

Human beings hate unfair treatment, too. We want to punish people who treat us unfairly. Researchers often use the *Ultimatum Game* to demonstrate this. In this game, you have a partner who has been given money—say, $20—to share with you. Your partner has one chance to offer you a portion of this money, and you have one chance to either accept or reject that offer. If you reject it, you both go home with empty pockets. For example, if the partner offers you a mere $1 and you reject that offer, both of you receive nothing. Economists are famous for pointing out that logic states you should take the dollar, since financially you will gain more by accepting it than by refusing it. But what makes logical sense does not always make psychological sense, and people in these studies routinely turn down insultingly small offers.[3]

Like the monkeys who toss the cucumber aside, people retaliate when they feel they have been treated unfairly. People will retaliate even when it means that they themselves get nothing. In one study, participants turned down lowball offers in the Ultimatum Game even when offered an amount equivalent to three months' income![4] The desire to express our displeasure at unfair treatment can apparently trump our own economic interests. Moreover, there seems to be a biological basis for our reactions. Neuroeconomists Ernst Fehr and Bettina Rockenbach recap a number of studies in this area. These studies show that lowball offers activate the *insula* on both sides of the brain. The insula is involved in negative emotional states such as disgust and pain. In fact, the stronger the response in the insula to an unfair offer, the more likely that a participant will reject the offer.[5]

Neuroscience research also shows that revenge is sweet. Neurons in the brain's reward center are active when someone who has betrayed us is punished.[6] Like the chimps that retaliated by collapsing the table of food, we too take delight in getting revenge on someone who has treated us unfairly. Given the chance, we will sacrifice our own gains in order to reduce the earnings of a greedy partner.[7]

The natural desire for justice is so strong that we will even sacrifice our own gains on behalf of *someone else* who has been treated unfairly. In research using "third-party punishment" games, a "giver" starts with a sum of money to be shared with a "receiver" who has no money. A third party witnesses how generous the giver is, and then decides whether to punish selfish givers. But there is a cost attached to doing so. Witnesses have to spend some of their own money to "pay" for taking punitive action. Despite this personal cost, more than half of the witnesses punish givers who fail to give half of their funds to the players who are penniless. Moreover, the lower the amount of funds transferred by the giver, the harsher the punishment issued for that stingy person.[8]

People are similarly willing to give up some of their money to punish group members who don't pitch in their fair share toward a group project.[9] In one startling demonstration, players could choose one of two game scenarios. In the first scenario, players could financially punish "slackers" who didn't pull their weight. In the second scenario, no such punishments were allowed. Initially, about two-thirds of the players chose the "no sanctions" scenario. But players could change their choice at the beginning of each new round of play. Over time, nearly every player shifted to the scenario that allowed freeloaders to be punished. People prefer to interact in a setting where cooperation prevails. Having the ability to punish slackers is apparently a key to achieving that cooperation.

INTERESTING, BUT SO WHAT?

HOW CAN I USE THIS INFORMATION AS A BUSINESS LEADER?

Brosnan, the Georgia State University psychologist whose monkeys disdainfully tossed those cucumber slices aside, finds that her research resonates with people. She writes, "All of us have had those experiences where something seems good enough until we found out that someone else had a higher salary or a better start-up package."[10] Leaders often have to make decisions about who gets the larger raise, the promotion, or the choice assignment. They also have to deal with the repercussions if people feel they have been treated unjustly.

When we feel mistreated, we sometimes behave like the chimps that sent the food flying—we retaliate. In a discussion titled "Why It's So Hard to Be Fair," Joel Brockner describes a study from the mid-1990s involving nearly one thousand business people. All the participants had been recently terminated from their positions.[11] Researchers found that participants who felt the termination process was fair were far less likely to sue their companies for wrongful termination. As a result, these companies saved substantial legal fees.

Petty retaliation in the form of stealing also escalates when people feel that they have been treated unfairly. Brockner describes a study that compared the aftermath of across-the-board pay cuts in two different companies. The president of one company announced the cuts at a meeting. He explained why the cuts were needed and discussed other options he had considered, such as layoffs. The alternatives discussed were deemed even more damaging to employees than the pay cuts. The president also extended the meeting to answer people's questions, talking with them for ninety minutes. In the second company used for this study, the task of delivering the bad news was delegated to a vice president. He spent a mere fifteen minutes meeting with employees, and failed to mention that other options had been considered. He also didn't stay long enough to answer everyone's questions. The result? At this company, employee theft was almost 80 percent higher during the ten weeks after the pay cuts.

When leaders fail to make impartial decisions, productivity and engagement can suffer as well. In one setting, a leader was promoted to a very senior-level position. Many employees felt that this leader was unqualified. They noted that attrition in his division had been very high because people did not want to work for him. Employees felt the promotion was based on favoritism rather than merit. The decision initially reduced productivity as people neglected their work and allowed themselves to be drawn into bitter gripe sessions. The employees knew they would pay a price for putting off their project work, but their anger over the apparent injustice overrode their better judgment. Even a year later, employees cited the promotion as a reason for lower engagement scores.

Feeling unrecognized for our efforts or having others steal the credit for our work can also trigger resentment. This resentment can significantly reduce employee engagement. If pervasive enough, it can cause people to leave an organization. Feelings of resentment can even occur because of unintentional oversights. It is easy to forget to mention a colleague's contribution when discussing a project. Or a leader might simply accept a compliment on a presentation, giving the impression that she did the work herself. This is a small matter to the overtaxed leader who was simply delivering a passing update on the project. But employees who feel discounted may retaliate. For example, they may be less willing to work overtime or to volunteer to help orient a new trainee. Leaders who take credit for others' work may eventually find that they no longer have followers to do the work.

Finally, the research showing how angry we get at slackers also speaks to how leaders deal with poor performers. Take the case where a poor performer seems to receive similar pay and opportunities as high performers. Viewing the situation as unfair, team members may take matters into their own hands and find ways to punish the slacker. For example, they might withhold information or refuse to help the person meet an important deadline. Such actions, of course, reduce the overall productivity of the team. Leaders know that team members may retaliate when fairness seems violated, but these leaders often fail to act on what they know. The neuroscience research reminds leaders how important it is to deal with slackers.

In looking at fairness, it is also important to distinguish *fairness* from *equality*. Fairness implies that leaders apply the same set of rules to everyone. Equality involves treating everyone identically. When everyone gets a 5 percent raise, regardless of performance, that's an example of equality. When raises vary by performance rating, that's more about fairness. When employees mistakenly interpret "fair" to mean "equal," leaders will need to clarify the distinction between the two.

WHAT IF ... ?

1. WHAT IF LEADERS TREAT THEIR PEOPLE UNEQUALLY IN ORDER TO BE MORE FAIR?

In *Getting to Yes*,[12] authors Patton, Ury, and Fisher provide an example that illustrates why solutions based on equality are not always the best solutions to implement. Two people are arguing over an orange. They decide that an equitable solution is to cut the orange in half so each gets an equal portion. The authors point out that while this is equitable, it may not be a good solution. Here is why: Imagine that the first person discards the peel and eats the fruit, and that the second person discards the fruit and uses the peel in a recipe. Although equitable, the solution is poor because the two people have different needs. In contrast, giving one the peel and one the fruit might have been better for both of them. Was it really fair for the person who wanted to eat the fruit to see half of it discarded?

In work settings, it is not uncommon for leaders to impose equal solutions in the name of fairness. To many leaders, equality means treating everyone the same. But people, departments, customers, and shareholders have differing needs. Treating them equally is not necessarily fair, nor is it necessarily the best solution.

This idea can be applied to the way leaders treat high performers. If a leader is having the same type of conversations with her high performers that she has with her low performers, something is wrong. She might be treating them equally. But because they have different needs, she may not be treating them fairly. High performers need to hear about the future and how to get there. Low performers need to hear about the present and how to continue to be a part of it. Instead, what if leaders focused their discussions with each person on his or her specific needs? What if they rewarded high performers with more time and sponsorship? That's fair—they have earned it.

The same is true for organization-wide decisions. For example, across-the-board budget cuts are equal, but they unfairly penalize groups who already manage their budgets well or who already operate as a lean organization. What incentive does a leader have to come in below a budget target in one quarter when he knows that if his peers overspend, everyone (including him) will get hit with budget cuts in the following quarter? What if leaders took the time to understand which departments were performing well and which were inefficient? They could then set fair budget targets accordingly. What if leaders reward managers who meet their goals instead of forcing them to subsidize those who do not?

Sometimes leaders try to be fair by creating one program that works for everyone. Instead, leaders could have suites of programs varied enough to meet different individual needs. For example, an organization could create work-at-home, part-time, and job-share programs to benefit workers with families. They could also create flexible schedules and volunteer abroad programs designed to suit the interests of unmarried workers—all with the goal of improving work-life balance. The fair solution is the one that meets people's individual needs, not the one that can be applied to everyone in the same way.

Fairness is about consistency—but it is also about applying a consistent *process*. As long as leaders give equal, unbiased consideration to each person's or department's needs, they are being fair. The final results or actions taken might be very different for each person or department. In fact, if leaders are leading effectively, they should be.

2. WHAT IF LEADERS ACTIVELY MANAGE SLACKERS WITHOUT MICROMANAGING TEAM PROCESSES?

Leaders can consider allowing team members to have some input into the performance evaluations of their peers. However, this kind of strategy needs safeguards so that one disgruntled team member doesn't wield undue power over others. But peer input could act as a sanction for people who are not doing their fair share. As the research showed, groups work together most cooperatively when slackers are forced to be accountable.

People are more likely to feel as though they are treated fairly if they participate in determining the way that they are evaluated. Depending on how the process is managed, letting employees be involved in their own evaluation can be an option. For example, what if organizations supplemented the traditional performance management processes with a process that included team input? Team members could provide input into how the members of that team would be held accountable and the consequences of failing to meet expectations.

3. WHAT IF LEADERS USE TRANSPARENCY AND EMPATHY TO IMPROVE EMPLOYEE PERCEPTIONS OF FAIRNESS?

Leaders need to make sure that they are evenhanded in their dealing with employees. But just being fair is not enough. Leaders also have to make sure that employees *perceive* their decisions and actions to be fair. This perception is not based solely on the actual fairness of the leaders' decisions. It is also influenced by two other factors—transparency and empathy. One manager, for example, found that her team felt it was unfair to rank one person against another during the annual performance evaluation. The team members had little knowledge of the ranking process and how it was actually implemented. Once the manager made the process more transparent, members could see how much care and effort went into evaluating each person's performance. The result was that even employees with lower ratings came to view the process as fair.

When leaders are genuinely willing to listen to and treat employees' concerns with respect and empathy, those employees are far more likely to feel that they have been treated fairly. For example, employees who are passed over for a promotion are more apt to see the judgment as fair when they understand the basis for the decision. This may include explaining the ways in which the selected candidate was more qualified (transparency). But the employee who was not promoted will be even more likely to feel fairly treated if the leader also helps him or her to become a more viable candidate for the next promotion. This could include helping that person gain the needed expertise or giving the employee an overseas or other stretch assignment.

4. How can leaders demonstrate that they understand and consider people's needs?

Leaders sometimes act as if employees judge fair treatment only in terms of money. But employees are often looking more for empathy than for other costlier forms of support. Brockner discusses one company in which the managers were overwhelmed by changes that they were being called upon to implement. The leaders met with the managers, expecting them to demand more resources to deal with the required changes. However, what the harried managers really wanted was for upper-level executives to "recognize their plight."[13] Leaders who listen carefully to the perspective of their employees, remain open to their ideas, and genuinely empathize with their concerns are more likely to be perceived as fair.

Unfortunately, leaders are not always astute at recognizing how they come across to others. For example, consider the statement "When managing change, I make extra efforts to treat people with dignity and respect." In Brockner's change management seminars, managers tend to rate themselves significantly higher on this item than their groups rate them. This is another area in which 360-degree feedback may be helpful, though there are indirect measures that can also be used.

As a unique example of an indirect measure, Brockner describes a well-respected electrical engineering firm that had teams brainstorm ideas to improve the company. After the brainstorming session, the leaders of these teams streamed into a room filled with the company's executives. The team leaders were told to approach whichever executives they preferred and sell their ideas to those individuals. As Brockner puts it, the team leaders "swarmed like bees to honey" to the executives who had a reputation for being good listeners and being open to ideas, while other leaders stood around with nothing to do. [14]

Another way to identify which leaders are perceived as approachable is to simply survey employees about whom they would go to, given the opportunity to talk with upper-level leaders. Provide employees with a list of people at similar levels of authority, and see if there are a handful of people who are consistently selected, while their counterparts are rarely chosen.

The behaviors discussed in this chapter are played out on a daily basis in the hallways of companies all over the world. People retaliate against perceived unfairness by sabotaging others. Group members seek vengeance on slackers. How should leaders deal with the need for fairness? Hard-nosed leaders who go by the numbers might be tempted to use money as the sole basis of fairness. For example, they might assume that they can establish fairness through equitable raises or severance packages. But both research and personal experience indicate otherwise. The calculation of fairness also involves the less tangible factors of transparency and empathy.

NOTES

1. Charles Q. Choi, "The Bright Side of Spite Revealed," *Live Science* (July 16, 2007), http://www.livescience.com/animals/070716_spite_chimps.html (accessed September 22, 2008).

2. Jeanna Bryner, "Monkeys Fuss over Inequality," *Live Science* (November 12, 2007), http://www.livescience.com/animals/071112-monkey-treats.html (accessed September 22, 2008).

3. Daria Knoch et al., "Diminishing Reciprocal Fairness by Disrupting the Right Prefrontal Cortex," *Science* 314, no. 5800 (2006): 829–32.

4. Lisa A. Cameron, "Raising the Stakes in the Ultimatum Game: Experimental Evidence from Indonesia," *Economic Inquiry* 37 (1999): 47–59.

5. Ernst Fehr and Bettina Rockenbach, "Human Altruism: Economic, Neural, and Evolutionary Perspectives," *Current Opinion in Neurobiology* 14 (2004): 784–90.

6. Dominique DeQuervain, "The Neural Basis of Altruistic Punishment," *Science* 305, no. 5688 (2004): 1254–58.

7. Tania Singer and Ernst Fehr, "The Neuroeconomics of Mind Reading and Empathy," *American Economic Review* 95, no. 2 (2005): 340–45.

8. Fehr and Rockenbach, "Human Altruism."

9. Ibid., p. 785.

10. Bryner, "Monkeys Fuss over Inequality."

11. Joel Brockner, "Why It's So Hard to Be Fair," *Harvard Business Review* (March 2006): 1–10.

12. Roger Fisher, William L. Ury, and Bruce Patton, *Getting to Yes: Negotiating Agreement without Giving In* (New York: Penguin, 1991).

13. Brockner, "Why It's So Hard to Be Fair."

14. Ibid., p. 4.

Chapter 11

RULES OF ENGAGEMENT

WHAT'S THE STORY?

Imagine you are a participant in a study involving gambling. Four decks of cards, marked A, B, C, and D, are sitting on the table. Your job is to continually pick a card from any of the four decks in hopes of winning money. "Pick a card, any card," says the researcher. So you turn over a card that says "plus $1," meaning you have won $1. Or maybe it says "minus $3," meaning you have lost three bucks. Over a series of picks, you begin to choose more often from the C and D decks and less often from the other two. It turns out that this strategy increases your overall winnings.

What is surprising is that you are choosing as if you knew the odds—but you are not consciously aware of them!

This example is based on an actual study where decks A and B were riskier. They contained bigger wins but also much bigger losses. The participants in the study were unable to explain why they chose more often from the C and D decks.[1] They just "had a feeling" when they would reach for the riskier A and B decks. So they often shifted their choice to the C and D decks. Where did this "feeling" come from? During the study, the participants' palms were monitored to detect small changes in their perspiration. It turned out that when a person considered choosing a card from one of the riskier decks, that person perspired more. This increase, a sign of anxiety, was too small for the participants to consciously notice. Yet their brains apparently recognized the pattern of gains and losses, calculated the odds of losing more with the high-risk decks, and triggered anxiety when they reached for those decks. That anxiety expressed itself in clammy palms.

Neuroscientist Timothy Wilson describes this research and discusses the part of the brain that was involved—the *ventromedial prefrontal cortex*, located in the region of the brain just behind the bridge of the nose.[2] The researchers knew that this area of the brain was responsible for influencing people's choices because they also tested patients with neurological damage to this area. When the brain-damaged patients played the gambling game, they were unable to make winning choices. Instead, they took greater risks and lost money. Their palms also remained dry when they contemplated choosing a card from the riskier decks. Based on this and other related research, Antonio Damasio and his colleagues concluded that the prefrontal cortex enables the brain to learn from experience—without our awareness. It influences the choices we make without our conscious knowledge by producing a gut feeling.[3]

In the gambling game, the brain seems to come up with a simple rule of thumb. The rule is to avoid decks A and B and instead choose from decks C and D. Psychologist Gerd Gigerenzer, director of the Center for Adaptive Behavior and Cognition at the Max Planck Institute for Human Development in Berlin, argues that all of our gut feelings are based on such rules of thumb. Through life experience, we implicitly learn what pays off.[4] For example, in one study Gigerenzer and his associates asked German students at the University of Salzburg a set of what were considered to be easy questions. These were questions about German cities, such as "Which city has more inhabitants, Munich or Dortmund?" They also asked the German students similar geography questions that the researchers anticipated would be much more difficult. These were questions about cities in the United States. To their surprise, the German students did slightly *better* in stating whether Detroit or Milwaukee had more inhabitants than they did in knowing about German cities. Yet it was clear that, in general, the students knew a great deal more about German than US cities. Gigerenzer concluded that the students were following a simple rule of thumb when they answered questions about US cities. That rule is, "if you recognize something—if it seems familiar—it is probably the right answer."

Apparently our brains compute the odds of getting rewarded and create rules of thumb to guide us to the biggest payoffs—all without our conscious awareness.

INTERESTING, BUT SO WHAT?

HOW CAN I USE THIS INFORMATION AS A BUSINESS LEADER?

Leaders influence the rules of thumb that employees learn. In *Gut Feelings*, Gigerenzer argues that an entire culture can shift when enough people implicitly learn what the leader values. Based on the leader's behavior, the culture can become "more or less open, more or less inclusive, more or less formal."[5] Those effects "tend to become absorbed into the organizational bloodstream, where they may linger long after the leader moves on."[6] As a simple example, Gigerenzer points out that if an executive shows she is annoyed when she gets too many e-mails, an employee who is unsure about whether to include her in an e-mail distribution will play it safe and leave the peeved leader out. Over time, such decisions may influence the overall pattern of communication in the organization.

Leaders know that their behavior impacts others, but many leaders fail to realize that they are probably conveying rules of thumb without being aware of what they are doing. Leaders leave hundreds of subtle cues about their expectations, likes, and dislikes. Because they are communicating norms without being aware of it, leaders can unknowingly establish norms that they would never intentionally promote.

One norm that has a tremendous impact on a culture is the degree to which it is acceptable to question the thinking and decisions of the organization's leaders. The story of the crash of Air Florida Flight 90 (also discussed in chapter 16) shows how reticent employees can become about confronting people in authority. The captain of that doomed flight had one last chance to avoid the crash. In the conversation captured in that little black box, we hear the copilot tell the pilot: "God, look at that thing. That doesn't seem right, does it?"

And then he repeats, "That doesn't seem right, does it?"[7]

Presumably the copilot saw an anomaly with the instrument readings or the throttle position when he made his remarks. But the captain ignored him. Why? Probably because in that era many captains arrogantly viewed themselves as "gods of the skies" whose judgment was not to be questioned. This copilot, even as he recognized the odd reading, still yielded to the captain's authority.

The Air Florida crash became a textbook example of what can go wrong when a culture discourages honesty. The incident also became a catalyst for change. Today, instructors at Embry-Riddle Aeronautical University play a tape of those haunting words, "That doesn't seem right, does it?" to drive home the point that copilots need to be more forceful. One instructor tells his students, "You say: 'Captain Smith, I have a concern. . . . Do you agree with me?' You push for an answer." Today, many airline pilots actively encourage their crews to talk to them. As one captain says, "If anybody sees any red flags, something they are uncomfortable with, bring it to my attention."[8]

These airline lessons have now spread to a completely different industry plagued by a similar culture—hospital care. The "physician as god" persona, like the pilot as "god of the skies," made it difficult for others to question a doctor's judgment or decisions. But hospitals came to recognize that this reticence contributed to medical errors. Sometimes these errors were fatal for the patients involved. For example, in the article "Silence Kills," the authors observe that "each year one in twenty inpatients at hospitals will be given a wrong medication, 3.5 million will get an infection from someone who didn't wash his or her hands or take other appropriate precautions, and 195,000 will die because of mistakes made while they're in the hospital."[9]

There seems little doubt that some of these errors would have been prevented if employees spoke up when they believed physicians were making poor decisions. When 1,328 nurses and other clinical care workers at thirteen different hospitals were surveyed, 34 percent said that they were concerned about a physician's competence.[10] This doesn't mean that they viewed 34 percent of the doctors as incompetent. Rather, in many cases, the same physician was the cause of many people's concern. The survey also showed how reluctant people were to confront these doctors. Less that 1 percent of those responding said they had "spoken with the physician and shared their full concern." Yet 19 percent felt that the physician in question did something dangerous at least once a month, and 8 percent believed that the physician's actions had harmed a patient during the preceding year.

It is not hard to understand how someone devoted to patient care might still back down from confronting a physician. Consider how some doctors react when they are questioned. One nurse who was a member of a focus group in the study related this story:

> A group of physicians went right into the patient's room without gowns or masks or gloves. This was a patient who was supposed to be in isolation. We didn't confront them because that cardio surgeon has a reputation. He belittles nurses by saying things like, "Do they have any nurses on this unit who aren't stupid?" If you question him, he starts yelling, and turns it into a war.[11]

The "Silence Kills" report makes it clear that people with less authority are not the only ones who have a hard time confronting others. Nurses found it hard to challenge doctors, but in many cases nurses were also reluctant to talk to peers about their concerns. Some doctors even hesitated to confront nurses. This only reinforces how important it is to nurture an entire culture in which speaking up is encouraged at all levels. Leaders are pivotal in setting that tone. Moreover, as Gigerenzer observed, oppressive rules of thumb can continue to influence people—sometimes even years after the leader who introduced them has left the scene.

What If . . . ?

1. What if Leaders Make a Conscious Effort to Discover the Rules of Thumb That They Are Conveying to Employees?

There are many rules of thumb people won't be able to report because they aren't explicitly conscious of them. Still, employees are aware of many such unwritten rules. A freewheeling discussion (without the leader present) may bring those to the surface. Think of what leaders might learn if they asked employees to compile a list of "hints about the boss" that they would have appreciated knowing when they were first hired.

Here are some items that might appear on that list:

- "No surprises. This guy hates to be taken unawares! If anything is going wrong, let him know on day one. Wait—make that minute one."
- "He really hates it when you come into his office really chipper in the early morning. Wait until he has had at least two cups of coffee and don't act cheerful until after lunch."
- "She'll tell you that she wants you to innovate. But if you go even $1 over budget because you tried something new, you're toast."

Leaders can read these comments and ask themselves, "Are these the rules of thumb I want to be conveying?"

2. WHAT IF LEADERS PAY MORE ATTENTION TO SUBTLE WAYS IN WHICH THEY CONVEY THEIR LIKES AND DISLIKES?

The behaviors that leaders reward or punish will determine the rules of thumb that employees acquire. The rewards can be subtle. If a leader takes a personal interest in Joe's report but delegates the review of Mary's report, Joe feels rewarded and Mary feels slighted. Simply showing more interest by asking a follow-up question when an employee makes a comment can be significant. What was it that captivated the leader about that comment? The style in which she made it? The slant she took on the problem? The area that was being addressed? Without employees being aware of it, their brains calculate the odds of getting a reward based on how their leader reacted in the past. In a sense, every interaction an employee has with a leader is like choosing a card from one of those four decks in the beginning example. Employees soon learn which "decks" to avoid.

Organizations and leaders try to make employees explicitly aware of the vision and core values of the company. But what is explicitly taught and what is implicitly rewarded are not always in alignment. When the two diverge, employees have to choose which norm to follow. They are likely to choose the high-payoff alternative, even when that violates the publicly endorsed policy.

3. WHAT IF LEADERS ARE MORE AWARE OF HOW THEY RESPOND TO EMPLOYEES?

Leaders can intimidate employees by reacting to suggestions with outrage or ridicule. Sometimes leaders make fun of ideas that are too far out of the status quo. Yet ideas, in and of themselves, pose no hazard. Idea generation should be the safest time to take risks. But when leaders ridicule, just speaking out can be a risk. Employees quickly learn to keep their suggestions within a very narrow boundary of acceptable ideas in order to decrease their risk.

4. WHAT IF LEADERS ENCOURAGE RISK-AVERSE EMPLOYEES TO SPEAK UP?

Like the pilots who urge copilots and flight attendants to voice their concerns, leaders can intentionally invite people to share divergent ideas. Having expressed their own opinions, leaders can pose questions like the following:

- Does anyone have a different answer to that question?
- Is there a different perspective that we might be missing here?
- Would someone play "devil's advocate" here and help us think through the likely objections to this proposal?

When people have been staying under the radar for a long time because of a punitive CEO or other top executive, a new leader who enters that culture faces a great challenge. Employees are going to be wary of speaking out—they have learned the rules of thumb, and they cannot easily unlearn them.

One reason these employees cannot easily break the rules of thumb is because, in a sense, the new leader is asking them to take a card from that high-risk deck. Eager to establish a more collaborative culture, the new leader urges them to speak out. He assures them that is what he wants. But for the employees, there is only one way to find out if the odds have truly changed. That is to take a risk and do the very thing that they have learned to fear. How can leaders encourage employees to take that risk?

Figure 11.1. Actions speak louder than words in driving organizational culture.

For line and project managers, leaders can try having an open discussion about what the previous culture was like. They can contrast that with a different vision. It is useful to find a metaphor that powerfully captures the old way and contrast that with a new image. For example, in healthcare the old metaphor was the "master-servant" metaphor. The physician was the master, and the nurse was to be the obedient servant, following directives without question. Hospital cultures did not begin to change until nurses drew attention to this metaphor and protested the behavior associated with it.

In the corporate world, there is a different metaphor that might help leaders who are trying to encourage employees to speak up. This metaphor is based on what psychologist Margaret Donaldson calls "the classroom question."[12] Donaldson notes that the purpose of a classroom question is exactly the opposite of normal questions. In everyday life, people normally ask a question because they don't know the answer. But teachers always know the answers to the questions they pose in the classroom. Students quickly grasp that what the teacher really wants is for them to match the answer that she has in her head.

Leaders can talk to their teams about the difference between classroom questions and everyday-life questions. Then they can use that metaphor the next time they get no response when they ask, "So what do you think?" Leaders can talk about whether the team members are acting as if this is a classroom question. Do they think they are supposed to guess the right answer—the one that is in the leader's mind? That is a risky business. Leaders can declare outright, "This is not a classroom question. I want and need to know what you really think about this." Of course leaders who press for candid responses must really mean what they are saying. If they punish honest answers, however subtly (with a frown, a raised eyebrow, a bored look), employees will quickly revert to low-risk behavior.

With their senior leadership team, leaders may need to adopt a more forceful strategy if other approaches fail. One new CEO tried everything he could think of to encourage his fifteen direct reports to tell him what they really thought. But because they had previously worked under an autocratic leader who publicly reprimanded people, the leadership team would not speak up. The new CEO found it nearly impossible to draw them out. Despite all his efforts, including sharing his own vulnerability with the team to encourage mutual trust, nothing changed. So this leader decided to alter the odds in the decks. He decided to make reticence riskier than speaking up. One morning he told his team, "If you are in this room, then I expect you to speak up and tell me what you are thinking. If you have nothing to contribute to this discussion, why should you be here at all? Why should you hold your position at all?" His confrontational method was effective because it forced people to choose what had been the riskier deck. He also followed up the confrontation with active listening and careful consideration of his team's viewpoints. Over time, they learned that the odds had truly changed.

NOTES

1. A. Bechara, H. Damasio, D. Tranel, and A. R. Damasio, "Deciding Advantageously before Knowing the Advantageous Strategy, *Science* 275 (1997): 1293–95.

2. Timothy Wilson, *Strangers to Ourselves: Discovering the Adaptive Unconscious* (Cambridge, MA: Belknap Press of Harvard University Press, 2002).

3. Antonio R. Damasio, *Descartes' Error: Emotion, Reason, and the Human Brain* (New York: Penguin Putman, 1994).

4. Gerd Gigerenzer, *Gut Feelings: The Intelligence of the Unconscious* (New York: Viking, 2007).

5. Ibid., p. 77.

6. Ibid., pp. 76–77.

7. Del Quentin Wilber, "A Crash's Improbable Impact: '82 Air Florida Tragedy Led To Broad Safety Reforms," *Washington Post*, January 12, 2007, p. A1.

8. Ibid.

9. "Silence Kills," *Vital Smarts*, 2005, http://www.silencekills.com/Download.aspx (accessed December 21, 2008).

10. Ibid., p. 7.

11. Ibid., p. 10.

12. Margaret Donaldson, *Human Minds* (New York: Penguin, 1993).

Chapter 12

THINK GLOBALLY
AND LOCALLY!

WHAT'S THE STORY?

Imagine that you are the president of a company that is in financial trouble. To make the company profitable again, you decide that you must lay off 15 percent of your employees. Afterward, an interviewer asks you two questions. First, how many people do you think your decision will affect? Second, how responsible do you feel for the effects of the downsizing?

Researchers posed this hypothetical scenario to Japanese and American university students. The students' answers reflected a deep cultural difference. Japanese students saw more people being affected. They thought about how the layoffs would affect not only the workers themselves and their immediate families but also the community as a whole. The Japanese students also felt more responsible for the repercussions of their decision. Many said they would feel some responsibility even for indirect repercussions. For example, they would feel somewhat responsible if crime in the area rose after jobs were lost.

Why would Japanese students and American students react so differently? As psychologist Richard Nisbett describes in *The Geography of Thought: How Asians and Westerners Think Differently*, Asians see events as more interconnected.[1] They are more likely to notice a broader context. For example, psychologist Taka Masuda showed people underwater film scenes and then asked them, "What did you see?" Japanese and Americans were equally likely to recall the large, striking fish in the scenes. But the Japanese made 60 percent more references to the broader context, mentioning background features like plants.[2]

The basic finding in a number of psychological studies is that, on average, Asians are more aware of context, whereas Westerners focus on individual elements. There are obviously exceptions to generalizations of this sort, but brain research has recently confirmed this general pattern. Researchers studied areas in the *frontal* and *parietal* brain regions that are known to be associated with controlling attention. These areas are more active when we have to concentrate harder. The participants in this study completed two tasks. One required participants to pay attention to context. In the other, they needed to ignore context. The brain activity showed that it was hard for the Asians to *ignore* context, while it was hard for the Westerners to *pay attention* to context.[3]

Because they are more sensitive to context, Asians see the effects of their actions as more far-reaching. Nisbett points out that Japanese managers may resign when things go wrong. This happens even though they personally had no direct hand in the problem. Why? The managers might assume that a decision they made years earlier was part of a cascade of events that ultimately resulted in a business loss. To the Asian mind, responsibility goes far beyond one's most immediate actions simply because the world is a complex place where events are subtly interconnected.

The Asian view of time also reflects the idea that everything is connected. For example, the Chinese view time as cyclical. To them: "Nothing is lost, gained, or surpassed, but only repeated. . . . The past is ever present, and the present is everything that has come to pass. The future, no matter how far away, results from actions in the present, no matter how small."[4] In fact, in the Chinese languages there are no tenses to express past and future. Instead, "the three dimensions of time are always present and can be distinguished only through context."[5]

Chinese people have to pay attention to context in order to know whether another person is referring to past, present, or future. Asians may be more aware of context than Westerners partly because of language differences like this one. In *A Whole New Mind*, bestselling author Daniel Pink points out a similar need to notice context in languages like Arabic and Hebrew. Those languages are often written without vowels, so the reader has to "fill in" the right word based on the context. As Pink writes, "If you read the equivalent of 'stmp n th bg,' you'd fill in different words depending on whether the phrase appeared in a pest control manual ('stomp on the bug') or a short story about a trip to the post office ('stamp in the bag')."[6] This requires you to pay a lot of attention to context!

Neuroscientist V. S. Ramachandran notes that when a blood vessel spasms due to a migraine headache, it may temporarily disable a patch of visual cortex. This creates an empty spot in the visual field. If the person with the headache is facing a clock on a wall when the spasm occurs, the clock will disappear if it is in the blind region. But the migraine sufferer doesn't see a void there. Instead, the person sees "a normal-looking wall with paint or wallpaper . . . [because the brain fills in] . . . the region corresponding to the missing object . . . with the same color of paint or [pattern of] wallpaper."[7]

Culture is like that wallpaper. Culture is a broad context that the brain uses to "fill in" meaning. As one example, most people from Western cultures value individualism. In contrast, most people from Asian cultures value collectivism. Research shows that Western cultures encourage people to place their own needs above others' needs,[8] while the opposite is true of Asian cultures.[9] Asians are more concerned about sustaining harmony in the group. Northwestern University professor Joan Chiao and her associates found that these differences in people's values were reflected in their brain activity. When asked questions about themselves, people's brain activity differed depending on which they valued more—individualism or collectivism.[10]

But the results of Chiao's research also held a surprise. Not all Asian participants in the study were collectivists and not all Westerners were individualists. This finding is a vivid reminder that people within a cultural group are not identical. Culture influences how we think, down to the inner workings of the brain. But individuals within any given culture will vary. When researchers performed a meta-analysis in which they merged findings from numerous studies, they found that native Japanese people were not always more collectivistic than Caucasian Americans.[11] Similarly, Chinese people living on the mainland of the People's Republic of China will differ from one another. Chinese in Hong Kong may differ from Chinese on the mainland—as well as from one another.

INTERESTING, BUT SO WHAT?

HOW CAN I USE THIS INFORMATION AS A BUSINESS LEADER?

In our global economy, leaders are very aware of cultural differences. However, many business leaders are most sensitive to important, but superficial, cultural customs. For example, a business traveler to Thailand is warned not to cross his legs in such a way that the sole of his shoe is exposed. In Thailand, exposing one's sole to another person expresses contempt. It is crucial for business leaders to have this information, but it is not enough. Leaders need to grasp how cultural differences divide us at a deeper level.

As one example, the Asian sense of interconnectedness means that relationships are very important to them. Global business leaders are aware that relationships are important in Asian business. But they may not grasp just how important relationships are. Ming-Jer Chen, founder-director of the Wharton School's Global Chinese Business Initiative, describes a Chinese company that decided to create a database of its suppliers.[12] Someone objected. What if a competitor broke into the system and got their hands on this list? But the president of this company wasn't worried. His attitude was, "So what if they get the list?" All they would have is a list. They would not have the relationships that the company had been building for ninety years with the people on the list. Without those, the list would be worthless.

Because relationships are so important, Asians value spending time to build those relationships. Westerners can spend two weeks in China and leave feeling that they got nothing done. To Western minds, getting something done means making some measurable progress—not simply meeting and talking. But to Asians, spending time to develop a relationship *is* getting something done. As Chen writes, "It is critical for Western firms to recognize . . . relationships are not incidental accessories to business strategy but the strategic *starting point* for doing business in a Chinese context."[13]

The differences between Asian and Western cultures tend to be very dramatic. But cultural differences can lead to conflict in multicultural teams of any makeup. Jeanne Brett, director of the Dispute Resolution Research Center at Northwestern University's Kellogg School of Management, describes a number of examples in her book *Negotiating Globally*.[14] She and her coauthors also recount examples in an article, "Managing Multicultural Teams"[15]:

1. One manager talked about how her Mexican traditions worked against her. "In Mexican culture," she commented, "you're always supposed to be humble. So whether you understand something or not, you're supposed to put it in the form of a question. You have to keep it open-ended, out of respect. I think that actually worked against me, because the Americans thought I really didn't know what I was talking about."[16] Similarly, in India, team members do not want to disagree with anyone in authority. As a result, sometimes other team members or leaders equate their deference with lack of knowledge.

2. The American and French members of a multicultural team had different styles of problem solving. The Americans accused the French of always focusing on what could go wrong and analyzing problems forever—"analysis paralysis." The French accused the Americans of being overly optimistic and acting without giving matters enough thought. The French described the American approach as, "start, realize after 3 months that it's not working, stop, change approach, and start over."[17]

3. The "in-your-face, argumentative style" of the Israelis on his team shocked one American engineer.[18] From the American's perspective, the discussions he heard were arguments, sure to disrupt the team's functioning. It took some time before he understood that confrontation was a natural style among the Israelis and that it didn't prevent them from working well together.

4. One American manager had trouble understanding the more indirect communication style she encountered in Japan. As she noted, "In Japan, they want to talk and discuss. Then we take a break and they talk within the organization. They want to make sure that there is harmony in the rest of the organization. One of the hardest lessons for me was when I thought they were saying yes but they just meant 'I'm listening to you.'"[19]

5. One Latin American team member at a call center was taking twice as long with her calls. The North American team members resented having to make up for her low call rate. When they discussed the issue, the Latin American woman admitted she had trouble ending calls politely. In her culture, chitchat was the norm. In this case, the team worked out a short-term solution. They broke in when she felt trapped. They would interrupt, apologize to the customer, but then say that her services were urgently needed elsewhere. The team also worked out a long-term solution by helping her get better at ending calls on her own.

All of these examples show how easily conflict can arise because of cultural differences. Global leaders need ways to proactively address cultural differences in ways that promote genuine understanding.

WHAT IF . . . ?

1. WHAT IF LEADERS HELP GROUPS TO OPENLY DISCUSS CULTURAL NORMS AND VALUES?

"Can't we all just get along? We're all human beings with similar wants and needs." Some leaders place an emphasis on our shared humanity and common values. For example, people in every culture want to connect with others. Relationships are important to everyone. The problem is that even when people share similar values, their cultures may weigh those values differently. What happens when two values conflict in a particular situation? Which value takes priority? For example, an American manager rushes to be on time for an important meeting. He cuts short a conversation with a colleague he happens to meet along the way. In this situation, efficiency and promptness take precedence over "small talk." But as the earlier example of the person at the call center illustrates, someone from Latin America or India might choose to be late rather than act in a way that her culture considers rude.

What is cultural can become personal. In one of the situations mentioned above, Brett discusses a conflict between French and American team members that did become personal. The French managers took the position, "Our way is best because we do it right and we get the right answer." The American managers took the position, "Our way is best because there is no single, right answer and we don't waste time looking for it."[20] When the conflict becomes personal, Brett says, leaders often step in and impose a solution. This strategy usually backfires, however, because team members do not learn how to resolve conflict on their own. They increasingly involve the leader in every decision and dispute.

What if leaders encourage their teams to have an open dialog at the beginning of each multicultural project? The team could discuss not only cultural norms and values but their relative importance to each culture and even to each team member. Rather than the leader telling the team how to behave, the team members can talk in detail about how they will work together.

This seems logical. But when it comes right down to it, resolving cultural differences is harder than it appears. "The devil is in the details" when it comes to the way cultural values actually drive people's behavior. Leaders should expect to help team members revisit their "rules of engagement" as issues arise. One way to do this is to have everyone on the team identify specific situations in which they have recently felt conflict or discomfort. Then the team can work through these scenarios together and figure out solutions. Some solutions may require a change in behavior. But sometimes the discussion itself causes a shared understanding that eliminates the problem altogether. It is often the dialogue itself that makes the difference.

2. WHAT IF DIVERSITY INITIATIVES FOCUS ON THE WAY PEOPLE *THINK*?

Many effective diversity programs include similar elements: "Make the business case for diversity," "Overcome stereotypes in the workplace," and "Listen and communicate more effectively with people who are different from you." In contrast, some programs seem to focus more on cultural customs, such as different holidays, food, and clothing. Multicultural training usually includes basic historical information about different countries and behaviors to adopt or avoid. All of these programs can make people more aware of others who are different from themselves. This is a good thing, of course.

But leaders should take a hard look at their diversity and multicultural programs. While the elements listed above are helpful, they may not be enough. Leaders should ensure that their programs also address differences in the way people think. What makes people tick at a deeper level? How might deeply ingrained differences affect the way individuals behave? Open dialogue about these differences could spur a deeper level of understanding. This dialogue helps people appreciate those who think differently and enables them to recognize valuable ideas that will enrich the business. That's the real business case for diversity.

3. WHAT IF UPPER-LEVEL MANAGEMENT GIVES GLOBAL LEADERS MORE FREEDOM?

When a company goes global, it often tries to use its corporate culture as a unifying force. Executives in the corporate office want leaders in every country to adhere to the company's core values. But this does not mean that all countries must have identical practices. What if global leaders adopted the corporate culture but were allowed to adapt it locally as well? For example, the corporate culture might support rewarding top performers. In the United Kingdom, this might involve performance-based compensation. But in some countries, individually focused reward strategies don't work as well. Giving leaders the flexibility to reward top teams or divisions instead might alleviate the problem. Organizations need to give their geographic leaders the freedom to find the most effective way to adhere to organizational expectations and outcomes within the context of their unique culture.

Of course, there may be some elements of corporate culture that a company may not be willing to compromise. Multinational organizations are often held accountable to specific regulations, regardless of where they do business. For example, some companies may have policies that prohibit the use of kickbacks, gifts, or favors in exchange for new or continued business opportunities. In some cultures these are an acceptable (and even expected) way of doing business. Yet employees must resist these practices and adhere to the corporate policies.

Global leaders recognize that cultural differences can either help or hinder the success of multicultural teams. What the recent brain research adds is the realization of just how hardwired cultural differences can be. Employees who succeed in adapting to another culture are changing how they think and how they perceive the world. To some extent, they are changing their very identities. One Chinese employee confided that she had so fully adapted to the culture of her American company that she no longer felt she fit in with her own family. Leaders who ask global workers to embed themselves in a different culture need to realize the full significance of this request.

NOTES

1. Richard Nisbett, *The Geography of Thought: How Asians and Westerners Think Differently* (New York: Free Press, 2003).

2. T. Masuda and R. E. Nisbett, "Attending Holistically versus Analytically: Comparing the Context Sensitivity of Japanese and Americans," *Journal of Personality and Social Psychology* 82 (2001): 922–34.

3. Trey Hedden et al., "Cultural Influences on Neural Substrates of Attentional Control," *Psychological Science* 19, no. 1 (2008): 12–17.

4. Ming-Jer Chen, *Inside Chinese Business: A Guide for Managers Worldwide* (Boston: Harvard Business School Press, 2001), p. 94.

5. Chen, *Inside Chinese Business*, p. 94.

6. Daniel Pink, *A Whole New Mind* (New York: Penguin, 2006), p. 21.

7. V. S. Ramachandran and Sandra Blakeslee, *Phantoms in the Brain* (New York: Harper Perennial, 1998), p. 89.

8. Geert Hofstede, *Culture's Consequences: Comparing Values, Behaviors, Institutions, and Organizations across Nations* (Thousand Oaks, CA: Sage, 2001).

9. B. Morling, S. Kitayama, and Y. Miyamoto, "Cultural Practices Emphasize Influence in the United States and Adjustment in Japan," *Personality and Social Psychology Bulletin* 28 (2002): 311–23.

10. Joan Y. Chiao et al., "Neural Basis of Individualistic and Collectivistic Views of Self," *Human Brain Mapping (forthcoming)*, http://www.interscience.wiley.com/.

11. D. Oyserman, H. M. Coon, and M. Kemmelmeier. "Rethinking Individualism and Collectivism: Evaluation of Theoretical Assumptions and Meta-analyses," *Psychological Bulletin* 128, no. 1: (2002): 3–72.

12. Chen, *Inside Chinese Business*.

13. Ibid., p. 64.

14. Jeanne Brett, *Negotiating Globally: How to Negotiate Deals, Resolve Disputes, and Make Decisions across Cultural Boundaries* (San Francisco: Jossey-Bass, 2007).

15. Jeanne Brett, Kristin Behfar, and Mary C. Kern, "Managing Multicultural Teams," *Harvard Business Review* (November 2006): 1–11.

16. Brett, "Managing Multicultural Teams."

17. Brett, *Negotiating Globally*, p. 182.

18. Brett, "Managing Multicultural Teams," p. 1.

19. Ibid., p. 3.

20. Brett, *Negotiating Globally*, p. 184.

Chapter 13

MOOD CONTAGION

Can Everyone Be Having a Bad Day?

WHAT'S THE STORY?

In his breakthrough book *Emotional Intelligence*, Daniel Goleman tells an amazing story of what happened in the middle of heavy fighting during the Vietnam war. As American troops and Viet Cong soldiers were shooting, six monks suddenly came into the line of fire. They walked with utter calm along a ridge through the middle of the battle. Not one shot was fired at them from either side. In fact, no one issued another shot after the monks had passed safely through. The American soldier who recalled this incident said that something changed in him after watching the monks. He said it was as if "all the fight was out of me. I just didn't feel like I wanted to do this anymore, at least not that day. It must have been that way for everybody, because everybody quit. We just stopped fighting."[1]

Goleman uses this extraordinary story to illustrate the power of a phenomenon called *emotional contagion*. This idea is not new; in fact, over fifteen years ago, Elaine Hatfield, John T. Cacioppo, and Richard L. Rapson published a book called *Emotional Contagion*. The authors tell us that people unknowingly communicate their moods to others: "When we are talking to someone who is depressed it may make us feel depressed, whereas if we talk to someone who is feeling self-confident and buoyant we are likely to feel good about ourselves."[2] Many later studies validated this finding. Reviewing research on the emotional con-

143

tagion phenomenon, neurologist Richard Restak concluded, "Emotions are infectious . . . you can catch the mood of other people just by sitting in the same room with them."[3]

Part of the reason this happens is a result of the way the brain is wired to help us understand emotion. As a general principle of brain function, it seems likely that we understand someone else's feelings—and even their thoughts and actions—by using the same brain networks we use for coding our own feelings, thoughts, or actions. As discussed in chapter 8, one study demonstrated that just *watching* someone in a film reach for a cup of coffee activates the same brain area as when we ourselves actually reach for a cup to take a sip.[4] In this cleverly designed study, the researchers even discovered that this only happens when the cup is being lifted for the *purpose* of drinking from it. When the participants undergoing the brain scans observed a clean-up crew in the film picking up the same cup with the same exact motion, these brain regions did not activate.

The same type of mirroring causes us to unconsciously mimic both the facial expressions and moods of the people around us. As Restak notes, we all know people we would rather avoid. Just being with them drains us. Maybe they are chronically depressed or cynical or angry. Without our awareness, our facial muscles imitate theirs. Our very physiology, in fact—heart rate, respiration, even our hormone levels—can come into attunement with others.[5] For example, when someone else yawns, it is contagious. Similarly, we find ourselves unintentionally mimicking the gestures of other people. We may lean forward during a conversation just after they do, or imitate their nod without realizing that we are doing so.

One classic study shows that just being in the same room with another person can shift your mood to match theirs. Imagine that a researcher asks you to fill out a "mood" form that indicates your frame of mind. Then you enter an empty room with the instructions to remain silent. Another participant joins you a moment later, with the same instructions. The two of you silently sit in the room for the next few minutes. Then the researcher returns with a clean set of forms and asks you both to record your mood again. Would either of you really change your mood in that brief time? The answer is yes, and the nature of the change is remarkable. One of you–the one with more expressive nonverbal

behaviors–will influence the other. It may be the person who is more visibly euphoric. It may be the person who is more visibly depressed. Good
or bad, the more expressive individual will cause a mood shift in the
other person . . . all due to just a few silent minutes together.[6]

INTERESTING, BUT SO WHAT?

HOW CAN I USE THIS INFORMATION AS A BUSINESS LEADER?

Are moods contagious in work groups? Research shows that moods of
group members converge within two hours. Both group members themselves and independent observers found this convergence when they
rated the mood of seventy different work groups during meetings.[7] Even
a single individual can influence the mood of an entire group—to the
point of affecting how well the group functions. Yale researcher Sigale
Barsade videotaped student teams working on a typical leadership task.[8]
During the task, each student played the role of a manager who was
responsible for a team of employees. The managers had to work together
to decide how to allocate a limited pool of bonus money. Each manager
had to obtain the largest bonus possible for his own employees, while
keeping the overall health of the organization in mind. There was also
pressure to come to a decision. If the managers were unable to come to
a consensus within the allotted time, none of the employees would
receive a bonus.

In one version of this research, an actor (unbeknownst to the others)
played the role of one of the managers. In some groups, he portrayed a
positive mood during the discussion while in others he portrayed a negative mood. The goal was to see whether the actor's mood would influence the group. Did it? Absolutely. One of the clearest findings from the
study was the distinct improvement in the group's mood when the actor
was playing the positive role. Not only did the group's mood improve but
the group also became more cooperative and experienced less conflict.
Although the mood data was originally self-reported, independent
coders later confirmed the results as well. Video-coders watched tapes

and rated both the moods of the members and various aspects of the group process. The results still held true.

Barsade concludes that people "do not live on emotional islands but, rather, group members experience moods at work, these moods ripple out and, in the process, influence not only other group members' emotions but their group dynamics and individual cognitions, attitudes, and behaviors as well."[9]

So it is clear that a single individual can impact the mood of an entire group. And who is more likely than the leader to influence a work group's mood and so impact their productivity? Studies have shown that when leaders and managers maintain positive moods, the performance of employees is higher.[10]

One of the ways that leaders influence the mood of the organization is through their sense of humor and ability to be lighthearted. And the leader reaps personal benefits as well. In his article, "Laughing all the way to the bank," Fabio Sala points out that leaders who introduce levity

Figure 13.1. Moods can spread like a virus.

into discussions are more likely to be promoted and to earn more money than their more serious counterparts.[11] As Adrian Gostick and Scott Christopher describe in their book, *The Levity Effect*, as a result of creating a lighter tone so that people have fun at work, employee loyalty and retention increase.

Beyond creating a lighthearted atmosphere at work, humor can improve group dynamics as well, as long as it is not sarcastic. Gostick and Christopher describe a study in which meetings of six different management groups were videotaped. Each meeting began negatively with complaints, adversarial comments, and sarcasm in response to dissimilar points of view.[12] But the mood changed after non-sarcastic humor was introduced in the discussion, and the group made more progress. The humor facilitated "a transition from . . . tension and defensiveness to . . . relative safety and playfulness. This shared comic vision created a bond."[13]

The guru of emotional intelligence, Daniel Goleman, would not be surprised. He consistently urges leaders to recognize the pivotal role that they play in determining the shared emotions of groups.[14] Leaders talk more, are listened to more carefully, and are watched more closely than anyone else in a work group.[15] In addition, the way that leaders react to and interpret information influences the meaning that others assign that information.[16] As proponents of emotional intelligence note, "for better or worse, leaders' moods affect the emotions of the people around them."[17]

WHAT IF . . . ?

Since positive moods are so beneficial, what can a leader do to decrease negativity and sustain a more positive culture?

1. WHAT IF LEADERS MEET COMPLAINING AND NEGATIVITY HEAD-ON?

Most leaders accept that it is not possible to achieve 100 percent scores on employee surveys. So they set targets below 100 percent. For example, they may decide that having 80 percent of employees "engaged" is acceptable. But the mood contagion research suggests that the 20 percent who are not engaged could be having a major impact on the overall organization. Leaders cannot make everyone happy. But they may want to discover how the unhappy employees are impacting their teams and take action. Leaders need to address valid complaints. But when employee negativity stems from a habitual attitude, it might be time to simply call people on it. What if a leader decided to no longer put up with the cynicism and complaining that can drag down the mood and productivity of an entire team? Leaders can say something as simple as "Let's take this off-line" to interrupt a complaining team member. Won't the cynic then sit back in the chair, sullen, arms folded across the chest? Maybe so, but even this might be a considerable improvement. Since the research indicates that it is the more intense and emotionally expressive person whose mood is most likely to get "caught" by others, silencing negative voices might go a long way in letting the mood of more enthusiastic individuals dominate. Once the leader is behind closed doors with the cynical employee, she can discuss the impact the cynicism and complaints are having on the entire team and put a stop to the behavior.

2. WHAT IF LEADERS CONSIDER MOOD OR "ATTITUDE" WHEN HIRING, EVALUATING, AND TERMINATING EMPLOYEES?

Leaders can go further than simply trying to squelch griping as it occurs. Imagine a hiring process in which the first person to encounter a prospective employee—say the receptionist—is charged with greeting the candidate and then recording the candidate's response? This is just one of the suggestions made by professional speaker Steve Gilliland in his analysis of workplace negativity.[18] He notes that most job candidates are likely to appear bright-eyed and energetic during the interview itself. But what if moments earlier they snarl at the receptionist or treat the security guard with disrespect?

This type of rudeness can have a profound impact on the mood and productivity of coworkers. A University of North Carolina Business School study found that more than half of the workers surveyed had lost time worrying about irate or rude people in the office.[19] In addition, 32 percent cited the rudeness of coworkers or clients as a major source of stress.

In his own business, Steve Gilliland regularly evaluates his employees on "attitude." Gilliland points out that the vast majority of his clients indicate that negativity, complaining, and cynicism are major difficulties. This isn't surprising, as Gilliland's clients bring him in to help with these kinds of problems. Then he asks how many members of the organization are the *source* of the complaints and negativity. Typically, the answer is very few— sometimes only one in a small setting. So, Gilliland concludes, the mood of a handful of people can infect an entire organization. What if leaders had the courage to identify and, if necessary, terminate these people?

3. WHAT IF LEADERS CREATE A CULTURE IN WHICH FUN IS THE NORM?

Some companies, like Scripps Networks, include "humor" as one of their core values. Southwest Airlines encourages its employees to come to work with a "Warrior Spirit, Servant's Heart, and Fun-Loving Attitude."[20] Southwest has leveraged these values to achieve a success that its competitors have tried in vain to replicate.

Leaders don't need to be comedians to make this work. Even if they are not naturally funny, they can still encourage a sense of fun in the workplace, often through very simple and low-cost initiatives. For example, factory workers at Ben and Jerry's take home a couple of pints of ice cream a week. Intuit employees have potluck breakfasts and play their own version of Jeopardy. Members of Microsoft design groups sign up to take responsibility for boosting energy daily, often by things as simple as belting out a song midday. Boston Pizza employees send one another Golden Banana awards for "having fun while being the best."

Another classic example comes from Herb Kelleher, CEO of Southwest Airlines. Southwest and Stevens Aviation were in a dispute over rights to a marketing slogan. Instead of going to court, the CEOs decided to have some fun. They opted to settle the dispute in a two-out-of-three arm wrestling competition. Renting out a stadium, they turned it into a giant spectacle for their employees.[21] Although there were certainly costs to rent the stadium, both companies avoided legal fees and other costs that would have come with an extended dispute. And by using friendly, funny competition in place of legal action, the CEOs demonstrated the kind of levity necessary to increase the overall functioning of a company—they led by example.

Creating a culture that encourages fun also pays off in increased employee engagement. Research from the Great Place to Work Institute shows that employees who agree with the statement, "This is a fun place to work," are significantly more likely to say they work for a great company.[22] The BlessingWhite organization studies employee engagement around the world. Their North America Employee Engagement Report 2008 states that engaged employees "are **'enthused' and 'in gear'** [original emphasis] using their talents and discretionary effort to make a difference in their employer's quest for sustainable business success."[23] The report goes on to note, "There is a clear correlation between engagement and retention, with 85 percent of engaged employees indicating that they plan to stay with their employer through 2008."[24] So, by engaging employees and promoting a lighthearted, and perhaps humorous, workplace culture, leaders can increase the productivity and loyalty of their teams. And they can have fun doing it.

NOTES

1. Daniel Goleman, *Emotional Intelligence: Why It Can Matter More Than IQ* (New York: Bantam Books, 2006), p. 114.

2. Elaine Hatfield, John T. Cacioppo, and Richard L. Rapson, *Emotional Contagion* (Cambridge, MA: Cambridge University Press, 1993), back cover.

3. Richard Restak, *The Naked Brain: How the Emerging Neurosociety is Changing How We Live, Work, and Love* (New York: Three Rivers Press, 2007), p. 103.

4. Ibid., p. 59.

5. Daniel Goleman, Richard Boyatzis, and Annie McKee, *Primal Leadership: Learning to Lead with Emotional Intelligence* (Cambridge, MA: Harvard Business School Press, 2004), p. 7.

6. Ellen Sullins, "Emotional Contagion Revisited: Effects of Social Comparison and Expressive Style on Mood Convergence," *Personality and Social Psychology Bulletin* 17, no. 2 (1991): 166–74.

7. Caroline A. Bartel and Richard Saavedra, "The Collective Construction of Work Group Moods," *Administrative Science Quarterly* 45, no. 2 (2000): 197–231.

8. Sigal Barsade, "The Ripple Effect: Emotional Contagion in Groups,"

Yale School of Management Working Paper Series, OB-01 (August 2001) http://papers.ssrn.com/abstract=250894 (accessed November 7, 2008).

9. Ibid., p. 42.

10. J. M. George and A. P. Brief, "Feeling Good-Doing Good: A Conceptual Analysis of the Mood at Work-Organizational Spontaneity Relationship," *Psychological Bulletin*, 112 no. 2 (1992): 310–29.

11. Fabio Sala, "Laughing all the way to the bank," *Harvard Business Review*, September, 2003, http://hbr.harvardbusiness.org/2003/09/laughing-all-the-way-to-the-bank/ar/1 (accessed October 8, 2008).

12. Adrian Gostick and Scott Christopher, *The Levity Effect* (New Jersey: Wiley, 2008), pp. 45–46.

13. C. M. Consalvo, "Humor in Management, No Laughing Matter," *Humor: International Journal of Humor Research*, 2 (1989): 285–97.

14. Goleman, Boyatzis, and McKee, *Primal Leadership*.

15. Anthony Pescosolido, "Emotional Intensity in Groups," (unpublished doctoral dissertation, Department of Organizational Behavior, Case Western University, 2000).

16. Howard Gardner, *Leading Minds: An Anatomy of Leadership* (New York: Basic Books, 1995).

17. Daniel Goleman, Richard Boyatzis, and Annie McKee, "Primal Leadership: The Hidden Driver of Great Performance," *Harvard Business Review* (December 2001): 46.

18. Steve Gilliland's official Web site, http://www.stevegilliland.com (accessed March 10, 2009).

19. M. Wolfe, "Stand Up to Desk Rage–and Rude People at Work," *AOL Find a Job* series (August 5, 2008), http://jobs.aol.com/article/_a/stand-up-to-desk-rage-and-rude-people-at/20080723151509990001 (accessed September 4, 2008).

20. Kevin Freiberg and Jackie Freiberg, *Nuts! Southwest Airlines' Crazy Recipe for Business and Personal Success* (New York: Random House Broadway Books, 1998).

21. Ibid.

22. Gostick, p. 13.

23. BlessingWhite, "Employee Engagement Report 2008," *BlessingWhite Intelligence* (April/May 2008), http://www.blessingwhite.com/EEE__report.asp (accessed March 20, 2009).

24. Ibid.

DECISION MAKING

Chapter 14

OFTEN WRONG, BUT NEVER IN DOUBT?

WHAT'S THE STORY?

Do you remember where you were when you learned about the terrorist attacks on September 11, 2001?

We all can give detailed answers to questions about where we were when we learned about a traumatic historical event, such as 9/11, the *Challenger* explosion, or the assassination of John F. Kennedy. We can give a full account, often in vivid detail. And we are certain that we remember.

But do we?

In *On Being Certain*, neurologist Robert Burton recounts research conducted by psychologist Ulric Neisser.[1] The day after the *Challenger* explosion, Professor Neisser asked his class of 106 students to write down the circumstances they were in when they heard about the tragedy. The students recorded where they were, what they were doing, who they were with, how the news came to them, and how they felt. Neisser collected their answers, waited two and a half years, and then interviewed the students to have them once again recount their experiences when they learned about the *Challenger* tragedy.

How accurately did the students remember? How closely did their interview answers match what they themselves had written the day after the event, more than two years earlier?

Here were Neisser's results:

- 25 percent had dramatically different accounts.
- More than half of the others had some details wrong.
- Less that 10 percent remembered the circumstances exactly as they had previously described them.

Burton's point in describing this research is not so much to point out the frailty of our memories but to emphasize the power of our brains to create a feeling of knowing—a sense of certainty that we are correct in what we know. Most of the interviewed students felt sure that their memories were correct—until they were shown their original journals. And *even then* many expressed a high degree of confidence that their memories were more accurate than the contradictory evidence. As one student insisted, "That's my handwriting, but that's not what happened."[2]

We have all experienced what Burton calls "the feeling of knowing." It is the feeling we have when we say, "It's on the tip of my tongue." We can't bring the answer to mind but we know that we know it. That sense of certainty—that sense of knowing something for sure, even though we can't prove it at the moment—is at the heart of neurologist Robert Burton's book *On Being Certain.*

How do we know that the feeling of being right is a creation of the brain? One strong indicator is that neurological conditions can exaggerate this sense of being certain so much that we cling to beliefs that we ourselves know cannot be true. Burton describes what happened when a friend of his, an art collector, suffered a stroke that appeared so minor that he was only kept overnight in the hospital. But upon returning to his apartment the next day, the collector phoned Burton in a panic. He told Burton that the antique table in his apartment, which he used as a desk, had been stolen during the night and replaced with a cheap reproduction. As Burton writes, this piece "was a massive eighteenth century Italian refectory table that took up most of his den." It would take several men to lift it; it would require removing the French doors to get it through the doorway. Burton pressed his friend to realize how impossible his allegation was. The art collector admitted that it was physically impossible that the desk had been replaced. Still, he insisted that it had. "You have to take my word for it," he persisted, "I know real when I see real, and this desk isn't real." Despite running his hand along the grain and fingering some prominent wormholes, the art dealer could not shake his certainty that this desk was fake. "It's funny," he said, "these are exact replicas of the holes in my desk. But they don't feel the least familiar. No, someone must have replaced it."[3] As this example illustrates, the feeling of knowing can be so strong that it trumps logic and leads us to accept beliefs that we ought to be questioning.

Some other neurological conditions also lead patients to cling to illogical claims. Individuals afflicted with the condition of *anosognosia*, for example, will deny suffering from an illness. This syndrome can result from a stroke in the right hemisphere, in which case there may also be paralysis of part of the left side of the body. However, a patient with anosognosia may vehemently deny that her left arm or leg is paralyzed. When these patients are asked to demonstrate that they can still move the paralyzed limb, they claim that they just do not feel like moving it, or they give other far-fetched reasons for not doing so.

Neurologist V. S. Ramachandran describes a case in which he attempted to prove to such a patient that she could not move her left arm. He asked if she could clap her hands. When she assured him that she could, he challenged her to do so. The patient "proceeded to make clapping movements with her right hand, as if clapping with an imaginary hand near the mid-line."[4] Then she insisted, "I am clapping." Even more bizarre, patients suffering from *Cotard's syndrome* are adamant that they have died, despite logical arguments against this assertion and evidence of life, such as listening to their own heartbeat. In yet another example of how our brains create a false sense of certainty, patients with *Capgras syndrome* cling to the bizarre claim that their loved ones have been replaced by imposters.

Having a brain that creates a mental sensation, "I am sure this is right," can be a great advantage. It keeps us going when we are in the middle of long projects. A scientist who is developing a theory and a novelist writing a book need the feeling that they are on the right track to continue their work.

But our brains attach that feeling of certainty to many thoughts that arise in our minds—the dazzling and the foolish, the well-founded and the unlikely. Consider John Nash, the brilliant economist who received a Nobel Prize for his Game Theory and whose life—and mental illness—

Figure 14.1. Sometimes we don't let the facts interfere with our certainty.

were depicted in the film *A Beautiful Mind*. Nash once stated that he could not accept a full professorship at MIT because, "I am scheduled to become emperor of Antarctica." When he was asked by a colleague, "How can you believe such a crazy idea?" Nash answered that his brilliant ideas and the notion that he was to become emperor came to him in the same way—both "felt right," both were accompanied by a "feeling of knowing" that what he believed was true.[5]

INTERESTING, BUT SO WHAT?

HOW CAN I USE THIS INFORMATION AS A BUSINESS LEADER?

Business leaders make decisions based on what they believe to be true. Sometimes their insights are astute, as when Bill Gates knew that the personal computer would be the wave of the future. Sometimes those insights couldn't be more wrong. In the 1980s, the film industry was fearful that video rental stores would undermine its profits from movie theaters. So it used the copyright laws of the time to try to outlaw home ownership of VCRs. Had these film industry leaders succeeded, they would have lost the revenue from video rentals, which constitutes a significant portion of their profits today.[6]

As *New Yorker* financial columnist James Surowiecki notes in his book *The Wisdom of Crowds*, people whose professions range from engineers to entrepreneurs consistently believe that they know more than they actually do. One study of foreign exchange traders showed that they were not even aware of just how inaccurate their predictions actually were. "In other words," Surowiecki writes, "it wasn't just that they were wrong; they also didn't have any idea how wrong they were."[7] We are often more confident than our expertise justifies, maybe because the "feeling of knowing" assures us that we are right.

In general, Surowiecki is arguing that leaders place too much faith in "superhero" experts. In *The Wisdom of Crowds*, he cites research suggesting that given the choice of following the advice of one expert or pooling advice from a number of different experts, most people "try to pick the best expert rather than simply average across the group."[8] Instead, leaders would do better to trust "the wisdom of crowds."

In fact, Surowiecki contends that it's not possible to find experts in the areas where leaders most need guidance, like decision making and strategic planning. The fact is that skills like "decision making" and "strategic planning" are so broad that it is simply not possible to become "expert" in these areas. It's possible to become a master in more defined areas of expertise, such as facilitating a strategic planning session or creating a product marketing strategy. But skills like decision making involve a wide range of abilities, including the difficult challenge of predicting which of many possible scenarios will actually occur.

So the words "I just know" should raise a red flag to leaders. People make many different statements as if they were definitely true: "This new product would be a great addition to our line!" "We should adopt a different software system—this one is easy to learn and would save the company a ton of money," and "Kristin's mind just hasn't been on her work lately—I'm sure she's interviewing for that open vice president job with our competitor." Statements like these should alert the leader to ask two crucial questions. First, leaders need to ask, "How do we know that?" They should encourage people to articulate the basis for their beliefs so that they can see what evidence supports their claims. Is the evidence strong? Nonexistent? Anecdotal? Does this claim need to be investigated further?

Second, leaders should actively seek evidence that is *counter* to the stated belief. Is there any research that shows the opposite or fails to support this idea? Are there are counterexamples? Are there other observations that aren't consistent with this belief?

Surowiecki recommends taking this one step further by intentionally creating teams in which opposing viewpoints will be present. He points out, for example, that a major contributor to the Bay of Pigs fiasco was that the Kennedy administration made decisions without consulting anyone who was skeptical about the proposed plan. In fact, neither the CIA nor the Cuban desk of the State Department was even consulted about the idea. As Surowiecki puts it, "The people who planned the operation were the same ones who were asked to judge whether it would be successful or not."[9] Given our inclination to believe we are right, this is a recipe for disaster.

It is one thing to question employees, but it's the rare business leader who is truly able to question himself or herself. Most successful business leaders would not have achieved their high status had they not been right much of the time. This makes it easy for successful leaders to become arrogantly sure of themselves. Leaders who have an arrogant style discourage employees from bringing up contradictory ideas or information, which only reinforces a leader's conviction that if he is sure of something, then it must be right.

Sometimes high-achieving business leaders believe that they must exude certainty to show that they are self-confident. These leaders think that self-confidence—even at times whopping self-confidence—is what makes success possible. However, that's not what Jim Collins found at the companies he describes in *Good to Great*.[10] Instead, his research showed that most of the leaders of the companies with a "great" status had personal humility. They combined that humility with a professional resolve to do whatever it took to get the job done. Personal humility leads executives to recognize and encourage the talents of those around them instead of acting as if their own superstar abilities will save the department or company. In an article on "Leadership Run Amok," Scott Spreier and his coauthors note that it was only after a pharmaceutical executive at AstraZeneca "tamed his overbearing achievement drive" that "his previously frustrated team won recognition for being the first to attain market leadership with three top-selling drugs."[11]

WHAT IF … ?

People often feel more certainty than they can objectively justify. Knowing this, leaders can encourage employees to take a closer look at the basis for their beliefs before taking action. Here are some ways in which leaders can encourage people to communicate not only their ideas but also the reasoning behind those ideas.

1. WHAT IF LEADERS ENCOURAGE PEOPLE TO QUANTIFY THE ODDS THAT THEY ARE RIGHT?

Greg Risberg is a funny motivational speaker who urges his audiences to communicate more honestly with one another. Risberg suggests that people use a letter system to answer the question "How are you?" Instead of the ubiquitous "fine," Risberg suggests, "Why not say 'A+' if you're having a great day, or 'C-' if things are tough?" Risberg uses this shorthand system to communicate more information without taking up much more time.

What if employees used a shorthand system to communicate just how sure they were about the ideas they were proposing? Imagine that an employee said, "This product will sell great on the Internet," or "It would be a lot more efficient if we did it this way," or "That will never work." What if the leader then asked, "How sure are you about that?" and pressed the person to give a percentage? Imagine how a discussion might change if someone said, "I'm 70 percent sure that at least half of my current accounts will sign up for this new service," instead of, "My current accounts are really going to go for this new service!" While questions like this don't remove the need for hard data, they encourage a culture of thinking more deeply about decisions.

2. WHAT IF LEADERS DESIGNATE PEOPLE TO PLAY "DEVIL'S ADVOCATE" AND "FACT-CHECKER"?

What if, as Edward de Bono suggested decades ago, we thought about six different thinking hats that team members might wear?[12] In de Bono's system, the negative "Black Hat" searches for the flaws and the drawbacks to proposed plans. What if team members took turns wearing the Black Hat, playing devil's advocate with ideas, so that everyone would practice spotting potential weaknesses? Team members could also take turns wearing the neutral "White Hat." This person is a fact-checker, always asking, "Is that really true?" and "What data supports that idea?" Both the White and Black Hats push team members to recognize that their sense of certainty may outstrip the evidence.

The US military has taken this one step further by institutionalizing this idea. In her article, "To Battle Groupthink, the Army Trains a Skeptics Corps," Anna Mulrine describes an army program called "Red Team."[13] Red Teamers are trained to be skeptical and challenge the status quo. After intensive training on critical thinking and communication, they are deployed to the field. Their "mission" is simple. Question decisions, regardless of who is making them. According to Greg Gontenot, the program director, "This is having someone inside [who] says, 'Wait a minute, not so fast.'"[14]

What if leaders went even further and adopted a policy of not moving forward on a decision until they have found at least one valid counterargument? Some people might fear that this will lead to "analysis paralysis." However, by limiting the time devoted to analysis and requiring people to look at alternative sources, leaders can mitigate the risk of analysis paralysis.

3. WHAT IF LEADERS RELY MORE ON "THE WISDOM OF CROWDS"?

It is difficult to project into the future, yet this is what leaders often must do. Leaders want to predict future sales or anticipate future trends in the industry, or even accurately estimate the resources needed to complete a project. To do this, leaders often rely solely on themselves. Or they rely on a single team member whose expertise they respect, or an outside consultant for advice.

In *The Wisdom of Crowds*, James Surowiecki claims that we keep looking for the super-expert instead of averaging estimates from a group of knowledgeable people because we associate "averaging" with dumbing down or compromising. [15] Yet in a room full of different department heads, for example, the pooled estimates of projected sales during the upcoming retail season will nearly always be more accurate than the estimate of any individual. What might leaders learn if they kept a record of both individual estimates and a group-estimated average? They could see which projections turned out to be more accurate.

4. DO LEADERS REALLY NEED TO ACT LIKE THEY ARE SURE OF EVERYTHING IN ORDER TO GAIN PEOPLE'S CONFIDENCE?

Some leaders fear that unless they act sure of themselves, the people they lead will lose confidence in them. They believe that they will lose credibility unless they pretend to be omniscient. There is a different way to look at this issue. Leaders can be more *conditional* about what they believe and still act *decisively*.

- *"To get respect, leaders need to be decisive."*

  True. In many organizations, business leaders who aren't decisive won't be respected. But being more conditional means that leaders examine their sense of certainty, not that they are indecisive. Once leaders have looked at opposing perspectives, questioned assumptions, and exhausted other alternatives, they can act decisively based on the information they have gained. The key is to consider the alternatives in a timely manner, rather than falling into analysis paralysis.

- *"At some point leaders have to act; there is no way to be 100 percent sure of things like a future trend."*

    True. At some point leaders do have to act, usually without 100 percent certainty. Again, the issue here isn't that leaders need to become 100 percent sure of things before they act. The idea is that leaders can shoot for a reasonable level of certainty before they act.

- *"People can make statistics say anything they want. Research doesn't guarantee success."*

    True. Research doesn't guarantee success, and research that misleads may be worse than no research at all. But this doesn't mean we should consign research to the trash bin. It means that leaders need to be careful to ensure that the research they are depending on is trustworthy.

- *"Research isn't always right. Sometimes your personal experience contradicts the data on the spread sheets and your personal experience turns out to be right."*

    True. Personal experience can be a great source of information. What if leaders assume that there is some validity to both personal experience *and* the research that seems to contradict it? If both are at least partially true, then leaders can hunt for factors that might explain the discrepancies. Did the research fail to consider an important element? Are the leader's personal experiences based on a different set of assumptions? Asking both of these questions can help increase the accuracy of decision making.

In *On Being Certain*, Burton tells a story about the brilliant mathematician Srinivasa Ramanujan. Ramanujan filled a notebook with concepts that he was certain were accurate but that he had not yet been able to prove. After his death, some of these theorems were found to be correct. But others turned out to be "dead wrong."[16] This, Burton concludes, is why it is crucial to examine the basis of our beliefs. We need to take a hard look at the evidence that supports our claims and the reasoning that supports our conclusions. By itself, "I know I'm right" is a better measure of arrogance than of accuracy.

NOTES

1. Robert Burton, *On Being Certain: Believing You Are Right Even When You're Not* (New York: St. Martin's Press, 2008).

2. Ibid., p. 11.

3. Ibid., pp. 16–17.

4. V. S. Ramachandran and Sandra Blakeslee, *Phantoms in the Brain* (New York: Harper Perennial, 1998), p. 129.

5. Burton, On *Being Certain*, pp. 13–14.

6. Tim Dirks, "The History of Film: Film History of the 1980's," *AMC Filmsite*, http://www.filmsite.org/80sintro.html (accessed August 6, 2009).

7. James Surowiecki, *The Wisdom of Crowds* (New York: Doubleday, 2004), p. 34.

8. Ibid., p. 36.

9. Ibid., p. 37.

10. Jim Collins, *Good to Great: Why Some Companies Make the Leap—and Others Don't* (New York: HarperCollins, 2001).

11. Scott W. Spreier, Mary H. Fontaine, and Ruth L. Malloy, "Leadership Run Amok," *Harvard Business Review*, http://harvardbusiness.org/product/leadership-run-amok-the-destructive-potential-of-o/an/R0606D-PDF-ENG (accessed August 6, 2009).

12. Edward de Bono, *Six Thinking Hats* (Boston: Back Bay Books, 1999).

13. Anna Mulrine, "To Battle Groupthink, the Army Trains a Skeptics Corps," *U.S. News & World Report*, May 15, 2008, http://www.usnews.com/articles/ news/world/2008/05/15/the-army-trains-a-skeptics-corps-to-battle -groupthink.html (accessed March 31, 2008).

14. Ibid.

15. Surowiecki, *The Wisdom of Crowds*, p. 36.

16. Burton, *On Being Certain*, p. 151.

Chapter 15

THE HALO EFFECT

Blinded by the Light

WHAT'S THE STORY?

I magine that it's just before the 2004 presidential election and you are shown a statement supposedly made by incumbent George W. Bush. In this statement, President Bush is praising executive Kenneth Lay for his fine leadership at Enron. Moments later, you are shown a statement claiming that Mr. Bush "now avoids any mention of Kenneth Lay and is critical of Enron when asked."

How might you react to this apparent about-face? You might think that your response would be objective and rational. You'd be wrong.

In fact, your reaction would most likely depend on your political allegiance. Staunch Republicans would probably justify the change as reasonable in light of the Enron debacle. But loyal Democrats would likely consider the change a sign of President Bush's poor judgment or lack of candor.

Research such as the study conducted by political scientist Charles Taber and his colleagues shows that most of us reject or ignore information that contradicts what we believe about our political favorites.[1] In contrast, we gleefully embrace information that reveals the flaws of their opponents. Aware of this research, clinical psychologist Drew Westen of Emory University wondered what was happening in our brains during this process. To find out, Westen and his colleagues scanned the brains of thirty men as they read and thought about situations like the one about President Bush's sentiments regarding Enron and Kenneth Lay. Half of the thirty participants were committed Republicans and half were committed Democrats. How would they react when a candidate appeared to change his position in ways that made him seem unreliable, if not outright deceitful? Would the participants' reactions be different when they favored the candidate?

Westen created a series of contradictory statements. He then falsely attributed some to President Bush and others to John Kerry.[2] For example, in addition to the Lay statement above, participants read statements that made it seem as if Kerry first wanted to raise the retirement age and then later switched positions and pledged to never support such a measure. The results of this research were summarized by *New York Times* reporter Benedict Carey, "The Republicans in the study judged Mr. Kerry as harshly as the Democrats judged Mr. Bush. But each group let its own candidate off the hook."[3]

How did the participants make these decisions? "Everything we know about cognition suggests that, when faced with a contradiction, we use the rational regions of our brain to think about it," said Westen. "But that was not the case here," he continued. "We did not see any increased activation of the parts of the brain normally engaged during reasoning. None of the circuits involved in conscious reasoning were particularly engaged. Instead, it appears as if partisans twirl the cognitive kaleidoscope until they get the conclusions they want."[4] When participants read the statements, it was the "emotional" areas of the brain that became active, not the more "rational" regions. In addition, when participants decided that they could reject the information that implied their candidate was less than ideal, the "reward centers" in their brains were aglow.[5]

Nearly one hundred years ago, psychologist E. L. Thorndike first introduced the term *halo effect*. The halo effect describes how our perception of one desirable trait in a person can cause us to judge that person more positively overall.[6] If people are likable, for instance, we often perceive them as more honest and intelligent as well. The neurological research on political candidates described earlier shows the halo effect in action. But it goes even further. It suggests that we are willing to keep those halos shiny by denying, overlooking, or forgiving negative characteristics. We let our analytic brain networks take a vacation while our emotional brain networks take over.

INTERESTING, BUT SO WHAT?

HOW CAN I USE THIS INFORMATION AS A BUSINESS LEADER?

Thorndike first discovered the halo effect by studying employee ratings. Human resource managers have been sensitive to this potential bias ever since. Leaders who evaluate their teams recognize this pitfall and try to counterbalance it. But this turns out to be more difficult than they might think. People are often unaware just how much the halo effect can cloud their judgment.

Most leaders are also aware of classic research showing that physically attractive people tend to be rated more positively on numerous traits, such as talent and honesty.[7] Nonetheless, awareness of the information doesn't seem to prevent leaders from being influenced by attractiveness. Researchers report that "good-looking" individuals earn 12 to 14 percent more than their less attractive colleagues.[8] In research on

Figure 15.1. Sometimes a single, memorable event sticks to you forever.

recruiting, interviewers felt sure that grooming had little effect on their judgment but they were wrong. In these studies, attractiveness was manipulated by having the same person appear well groomed in some interviews and poorly groomed in others. People who were "hired" tended to be in the well-groomed group.[9]

As the political research showed, people don't judge information dispassionately. When we hold strongly positive or negative feelings toward the group that someone belongs to, we are not always objective. Instead, our emotional brain circuits may dominate our thinking.

Furthermore, we can be influenced by implicit beliefs about groups even when we reject those beliefs on a conscious level. In his bestseller *Blink*, author Malcolm Gladwell describes a test that is publicly available on a Harvard University Web site.[10] The Implicit Associations Test, or IAT, measures the extent to which individuals associate various characteristics, such as race, sexual preference, or weight, with positive or negative attributes. The test reveals that even when people consciously reject a notion—such as the idea that white people are superior to black people—they respond in ways that reveal their unconscious biases. Gladwell himself is part black—his mother is Jamaican—and he rejects racial stereotypes of white superiority. Yet he found his own test responses showed a moderate "pro-white" attitude.

Could a person decide to change his score on this test to correspond more closely to his own conscious beliefs? Research cited on the IAT Web site indicates that this may not be easy to do. Gladwell himself retook the test four times in an attempt to change his score, but he was unable to do so. Is it even possible to offset our implicit biases? It is—but it is more indirect than gritting our teeth and trying to force the emotional brain to conform to our rational thoughts. We can weaken our implicit associations by exposing ourselves to experiences that contradict our stereotypes. Even just *reminding* ourselves of more positive associations can diminish the impact of negative associations. For example, if just before taking the IAT individuals view a series of photos of respected people of color, such as Martin Luther King Jr., Oprah Winfrey, and Barack Obama, their automatic responses to the test are likely to shift in a more positive direction. It takes effort, but we can learn to quiet the emotional part of our brain when judging others.

The most obvious area where the halo effect directly impacts leaders is in their treatment of employees. This includes decisions in recruiting, promoting, and even doling out coveted assignments. Consciously or not, leaders' decisions in these situations are likely to be influenced by characteristics like physical appearance, gender, and race. In *Blink*, Gladwell cites a curious fact about male CEOs—58 percent of the CEOs from Fortune 500 companies are six foot two or taller. Yet in the United States as a whole, only 3.9 percent of males are that tall. No one consciously says, "Hmmm, which of these candidates for promotion is taller?" No one believes that height is a logical predictor of leadership performance. But the halo effect is powerful. A single vivid characteristic—good or bad—can color our entire response. Yet we cling to the belief that we are being reasonable and evenhanded.

Finally, another form of bias is the "shadow effect." This is the halo effect in reverse. Leaders who fall under the shadow effect may view people through the lens of the "One Big Mistake." Although the mistake may have happened years earlier, the story has been retold so many times that it overshadows any future successes. To overcome this bias, a leader can ask himself, "What would I do now if I hadn't heard that Joan lost our biggest account last year? How can I look more objectively at what she has accomplished since then?"

Just as biases influence leaders as they deal with individuals, they also influence leaders' attitudes toward organizations. Phil Rosenzweig, a professor at the International Institute for Management Development in Lausanne, Switzerland, works with leading companies on questions of strategy. In his recent book, *The Halo Effect: How Managers Let Themselves Be Deceived*, Rosenzweig argues that our judgments about companies—like our reactions to individuals—are subject to the halo effect bias.[11]

"In business," Rosenzweig notes, "a company's overall performance—usually defined by tangible financial results—shapes our evaluation of other things that are less tangible. . . . When times were good, Cisco Systems and ABB were both admired for their customer focus, efficient organizations and charismatic CEOs; but when performance slipped, they were criticized for the exact same things."[12] Rosenzweig points out that once a company has been deemed successful, researchers and business authors make the assumption that those "less tangible" factors caused excellent financial performance. Then they offer a success formula based on those factors.

What's the problem with that approach? An analogy proposed by writer Steve Miller in his interview with Rosenzweig helps clarify this concern.[13] What would happen if a baseball manager decided to study the Chicago Cubs during a winning streak to learn from the team's success? The manager might decide to use a comparable system for incentives, training, coaching, and organizational structure. Yet those same factors were in place when the Cubs were losing dismally! In fact, as Miller points out, when the Cubs were losing, the media were quick to point out the overpaid, arrogant players; the unwieldy organizational structure; the bungling farm system; and the manager past his prime. But when the team had a winning streak, suddenly its management was seen as shrewd, its farm system productive, and its players selfless and committed.

The point is that the team's overall performance—that is, whether the Cubs were winning or losing at the time—dictated how all the other factors were evaluated. Rosenzweig argues that business researchers make the same mistake when they study high-performing companies. In these studies, researchers attribute a company's success to the current leadership style or the latest business strategy. Bathed in the glow of the halo effect, the leadership style is seen as "visionary" and the business strategy is "brilliant." But the supporting evidence is based on the conditions present during the company's heyday. Equally problematic in Rosenzweig's view is the exclusive focus on winning companies. He believes that in some bestsellers, such as *In Search of Excellence* and *Blue Ocean Strategy*, the focus on winning companies prevents the important comparison of how they differ from less successful ones.

Rosenzweig advises leaders to do something different. Instead of being swayed by powerful stories of successful companies, he urges leaders to follow more rational methods for analyzing performance. A simple example is to look for *unsuccessful* organizations that have the same attributes as the successful organizations. If such organizations exist, then the corresponding attributes probably aren't what drove success. This approach is similar to de Bono's suggestion discussed in chapter 14 that at times leaders wear the "White Hat" and the "Black Hat" in order to look not only at what supports an idea but also what undermines it. Rosenzweig outlines what leaders can do to avoid not only the halo effect but other biases that lead to poor leadership decisions as well.

WHAT IF . . . ?

Biases are not all bad. In fact, people would have a hard time making decisions without them. Neurologist Antonio Damasio argues that the emotional brain circuits that lead us to have favorable or unfavorable feelings about different options are crucial to decision making. For example, Damasio describes one patient who had brain damage that interfered with his ability to make decisions: "He had the requisite knowledge, attention, and memory; his language was flawless; he could perform calculations, he could tackle the logic of an abstract problem. [But his neurological disease left him] with a marked alteration of the ability to experience feeling. . . . [The result was] a profound defect in decision making."[14] When the man in question tried to decide when to make his next appointment, he spent thirty minutes weighing reasons for and against each of two possible dates. As this patient's dilemma shows us, emotion-based biases are often very helpful for making decisions. But problems occur when leaders allow those biases to go unchecked.

1. WHAT IF LEADERS USE THEIR BIASES TO DRIVE QUESTIONS RATHER THAN ANSWERS? WHAT IF LEADERS LEARNED TO HARNESS THEIR BIASES TO *INFORM* DECISIONS RATHER THAN ALLOWING THEIR BIASES TO *DICTATE* THOSE DECISIONS?

Leaders who treat their biases as facts get into trouble. Instead, leaders should step back and ask themselves why they believe something to be true. "Why do I think that Bob is such a great salesman?" "Why do I believe that the market for middle-aged people is diminishing?" Once the leader identifies the criteria that she is using to make decisions, she can then gather data to confirm or refute her initial bias. In addition, she can use the same process to assess new people or opportunities in a less biased way.

2. WHAT IF LEADERS RECOGNIZE THAT EVEN QUANTITATIVE, "OBJECTIVE" MEASURES MAY STILL CONTAIN BIAS?

Leaders often make the mistake of confusing something that is quantifiable with something that is objective. For example, metrics aren't always objective. Why? Because often a metric just represents one person's opinion of what constitutes a valid measure of performance. For example, to gauge employee productivity, one company might measure the number of calls each employee handles per hour. Another company might measure the number of problems resolved. Both measures are quantifiable and fact-based. However, the metrics themselves are subjective because they reflect a subjective opinion of what indicates "good performance."

Similarly, an "objective" goal can be set in a subjective way. How often do companies set targets based on the prior year's performance? That is a subjective decision. Often this decision is not based on an objective assessment of what is realistic for a given year. For example, a sales target may be set at 15 percent over last year. But rather than an objective assessment of what is possible, that 15 percent may be nothing more than a subjective wish. Yet once the target is published and people become accountable for reaching it, everyone forgets that the target might have just been made up in the first place. Because it is quantified, the target is now viewed as "objective." But in reality, the target itself is not objective—only the measurement of that target is objective.

3. WHAT IF LEADERS PUT THEIR BIASES ON THE TABLE AND ENCOURAGE OTHERS TO DO SO AS WELL?

From early on, leaders are taught to be objective and unbiased in their decision making. But as recent brain research repeatedly demonstrates, that is nearly impossible. Since they can't achieve pure objectivity, leaders sometimes try to mask their biases. This generally leads to more problems. Instead of trying to cover up their biases, leaders should put them on the table. Doing so is the first step toward dialogue and understanding. By revealing their biases, leaders encourage open discussion about how the business works, how success should be defined, and how the business should be run. Through such discussion, the team may come to a better consensus about what they are trying to accomplish. Just as important, they might discover that they are barking up the wrong tree!

4. What if Leaders Put Their Biases to the Test?

Most major symphony orchestras adopted the practice of *blind auditioning* sometime during the 1970s and 1980s. Auditioning musicians play behind a partition so that knowledge of information such as the person's gender, or whom the person studied under, will not influence the evaluators. This practice prevents the halo effect. After a dramatic increase in female hires, one analysis of eleven major symphony orchestras, such as the Boston Symphony orchestra and the New York Philharmonic, concluded that 25 percent of this increase was due to the switch to blind auditions.[15] In this analysis, the researchers compared how many female musicians were hired before and after blind auditioning was implemented in each of the orchestras. Even after controlling for other factors, such as increases in the numbers of female musicians who auditioned, they found that the practice of blind auditioning was a significant factor in increasing the number of females hired. In a business environment, leaders can't put people behind a partition to hide the irrelevant characteristics that might influence their decisions. What if leaders pay special attention to the critical features they are searching for in a new employee? What if they try to intentionally discount other factors? Organizations do this when they make an extra effort to ensure that women or minority candidates are represented on lists for recruiting or promotion. This doesn't mean that a lesser-qualified candidate gets the post. But it does ensure that, for example, a promotion isn't just awarded to the "best buddy" of the hiring executive without a fair search.

How will leaders know when they are successful at overcoming these biases? Formal tracking of hirings, promotions, ratings, salaries, and even special job assignments can provide the data needed to uncover bias. Leaders can also seek 360-degree feedback about how others perceive them. Do team members accuse them of favoritism? Leaders are often unaware when they show signs of favoritism. The signs can be as subtle as using more attentive body language when listening to a particular person's ideas. Leaders show favoritism when they interrupt some people or acknowledge some remarks with an indifferent nod, while listening to others more carefully.

As the aforementioned brain research shows, decisions based on the "emotional brain" can be biased. But the solution is not to eliminate emotion—which would be an impossible goal in any case. Rather, the solution is to recognize potential sources of bias and address them.

NOTES

1. Charles S. Taber et al., "The Motivated Processing of Political Judgments," *Social Science Research Network* (2008), http://papers.ssrn.com/sol3/papers.cfm?abstract_id=1274028 (accessed August 7, 2009).

2. Drew Westen et al., "Neural Bases of Motivated Reasoning: An fMRI Study of Emotional Constraints on Partisan Political Judgment in the 2004 U.S. Presidential Election," *Journal of Cognitive Neuroscience* 18 (2006): 1947–58.

3. Benedict Carey, "A Shocker: Partisan Thought Is Unconscious," *New York Times*, January 24, 2006, http://www.nytimes.com/2006/01/24/science/24find.html?ex=1190260800&en=345d50dbc467f552&ei=5070 (accessed July 8, 2008).

4. Ibid.

5. Westen, "Neural Bases of Motivated Reasoning."

6. E. L. Thorndike, "A Constant Error on Psychological Rating," *Journal of Applied Psychology* 82 (1920): 665–74.

7. A. H. Eagly et al., "What Is Beautiful Is Good, but . . . : A Meta-analytic Review of Research on the Physical Attractiveness Stereotype, *Psychological Bulletin* 110 (1991): 109–28.

8. D. Hammermesh and J. E. Biddle, "Beauty and the Labor Market," *American Economic Review* 84 (1994): 1174–94.

9. D. Mack and D. Rainey, "Female Applicants' Grooming and Personnel Selection," *Journal of Social Behavior and Personality* 5 (1990): 399–407.

10. Malcolm Gladwell, *Blink: The Power of Thinking without Thinking* (Boston: Little, Brown, and Company, 2005). Project Implicit, Implicit Associations Test (IAT), https://implicit.harvard.edu/implicit/ (accessed March 9, 2009).

11. Phil Rosenzweig, *The Halo Effect: How Managers Let Themselves Be Deceived* (New York: Free Press, 2009).

12. Phil Rosenzweig, "From Halo to Hell," *Chief Executive* (June 4, 2007), http://www.chiefexecutive.net/ME2/dirmod.asp?sid=&nm=&type=Publishing&mod=Publications%3A%3AArticle&mid=8F3A7027421841978F18BE895F87F791&id=88A15F4EFD1C40279AC05827677F79EF&tier=4 (accessed March 27, 2009).

13. Steve Miller, "Interview with Phil Rosenzweig, Author of *The Halo Effect*," *BeyeNETWORK* (July 31, 2007), http://www.b-eye-network.com/view/5649 (accessed January 5, 2009).

14. A. R. Damasio, *Descartes' Error* (New York: Avon, 1994), p. xii.

15. Claudia Goldin and Celia Rouse, "Orchestrating Impartiality: The Impact of Blind Auditions on Female Musicians," *American Economic Review* 90 (2007): 715–41.

Chapter 16

CAN I HAVE YOUR ATTENTION PLEASE?

WHAT'S THE STORY?

Imagine that you are on a plane and you are able to overhear your pilot and copilot running through the preflight checklist. The copilot reads out the next item on the list, "anti-ice." This refers to a mechanism, an "anti-icer," that prevents the icing of critical gauges in the engine. If they are frozen, these gauges can give a false reading of crucial information, such as the thrust needed for takeoff. When the copilot says "anti-ice," the pilot responds, "off." To your surprise, they both continue on to the next point without missing a beat. Yet from your window seat in 17A you can see the snow drifting past and you know that the temperature outside is only 20 degrees.

Unfortunately, this conversation isn't hypothetical. The cockpit recording of Air Florida Flight 90, a plane that crashed into Washington, DC's 14th Street Bridge on January 13, 1982, documents this conversation. The plane plummeted into the Potomac moments after takeoff, killing seventy-eight passengers, motorists, and crewmembers.

How could this happen? Both pilot and copilot were apparently on automatic pilot themselves when they skimmed through that checklist. They checked items off by rote. But how could they fail to notice the freezing weather as they noted that the anti-ice mechanism was "off"? The most likely answer is that both the checklist itself and the answer "off" were very familiar to the crew of an Air Florida flight. They had probably answered "off" to that question innumerable times in the balmy climate of Florida. The sheer familiarity of both the checklist and their answers probably lulled the pilots into not paying attention.

In a sense, the pilots were betrayed by their own brains. The way that brains decide what people will notice contributed to the Flight 90 tragedy.

We usually think that we consciously decide what we will pay attention to and what we will ignore. But one of the lessons of neuroscience research is how often this decision is made below our level of awareness. For example, imagine yourself at a noisy cocktail party, deep in conversation with a small group, supposedly oblivious to the surrounding chatter. Yet if someone ten feet away mentions your name, you will notice. You will perk up and try to locate the source of the gossip so that you can figure out what they are saying about you.

The question is: How do we do that?

It's tempting to imagine that there is a little person inside our brains, a miniature replica of ourselves, who somehow listens (as we do when we are consciously paying attention) and then alerts us when our name is spoken. But we know, of course, that there is no such little person. There are only neurons—brain cells—and their connections with other neurons, that are able to "pay attention."

In his book *Strangers to Ourselves*, Harvard neuroscientist Timothy Wilson uses this classic cocktail party example to point out how the brain determines, without our conscious awareness, what is important enough to cause us to pay attention. To hear our name above the hubbub, on some level the brain has to be taking in all that surrounding chatter.[1] It is as if the sounds around us register in a holding area of the brain below the level of consciousness. The neurons in this holding area decide that the babble isn't worthy of our attention. So they let us be aware of it only as vague background noise. Like a watchful sentry, the brain lets us consciously attend to the conversation in our group. Meanwhile, the "sentry" takes over the job of monitoring the surrounding noise. Noticing our name, the sentry decides that this information might be important to us. It alerts us so that we now become conscious of hearing our name. The brain alerts us to other things as well. It knows what we are currently concerned about. If we are considering getting a new garage door or taking a trip to Mexico, our brain might alert us when someone at the party mentions "garage door" or "Acapulco."

How do our brain cells "know" what is important to us? The brain knows what interests us partly based on what we have paid attention to in the past. For example, the odds are pretty high that we will be interested in a conversation about ourselves. But we can't possibly consciously pay attention to every conversation at once. So the underground sentry monitors the conversations around us and alerts us when our name is spoken at the party.

The pilots of Air Florida Flight 90 were failed, in a sense, by that underground sentry in their own brains. With both the checklist and their answers appearing rote and familiar, the sentry was lulled into complacency. It ignored the snow falling softly outside the cabin.

INTERESTING, BUT SO WHAT?

HOW CAN I USE THIS INFORMATION AS A BUSINESS LEADER?

The lesson of the Air Florida Flight 90 crash is a lesson about attention. The crash shows why people should never let the sentry below the level of consciousness totally determine what is worthy of their attention. Instead, people need to consciously influence what they pay attention to. They need to ensure that they focus on the right things.

Leaders need to make sure that employees pay attention to the right things, too. What are the "right things" in a business setting? At a macro level, leaders want employees to direct their attention to activities that will most benefit the organization. Many leaders use methods like SMART goals to focus their employees' attention. But as we discuss in detail below, SMART goals often fail to direct attention to goals that really make a difference to the organization. In fact, they can divert attention away from what is truly important.

At a micro level, leaders also want employees to pay attention to small details when these are crucial. The aim of the preflight checklist is to make sure that pilots pay attention to critical elements. Obviously, the checklist failed to do this in the Air Florida disaster. Leaders can use checklists to vastly improve employee performance, as the examples presented below illustrate. But leaders need to understand what it takes for a checklist to be effective. How checklists are designed and implemented determines whether they will be successful.

1. MACRO LEVEL—SETTING GOALS AS A WAY OF DIRECTING ATTENTION

Leaders often ask managers to identify their goals for the coming year. Here are some typical responses.

- Finance: Submit monthly financial reports within one week of each month's close.
- Customer Service: Increase by 15 percent the number of customers who complete our customer satisfaction survey.
- Marketing: Increase the viewers of our new advertising by 20 percent.

All of these are SMART goals.[2] The acronym SMART has different variations but is often represented as Specific, Measurable, Achievable, Relevant, and Time-based. Unfortunately, SMART goals aren't always good goals. The SMART system is excellent in the sense that it makes sure that goals are actionable and measurable. But it does not determine whether a goal is worthwhile in the first place.

Are the goals listed above worthwhile? Maybe. But the problem with these goals is that all of them could be achieved without impacting the business. For example, 20 percent more people may view the new advertising material. But do they have a more favorable impression of the company's brand? Do they purchase more of the company's products or services? If not, then employees are making a commitment to a meaningless activity. Their time might be better spent in activities that improve the brand or increase sales, because these are the outcomes that are important to the business.

The same ideas apply to the other goals listed. In each case, the goal focuses on an activity. But what is the reason for doing that activity? It should always be in the service of a larger goal—a desired outcome for the organization. For example, the reason for trying to increase the number of customers completing surveys is to use that information to improve customer satisfaction. It is this outcome that leaders want employees to focus on when setting goals. It is very different for an employee to say that her goal is to "improve customer satisfaction by 5 percent" than for her to say she will increase the percentage of customers completing a form.

SMART goals are appealing to leaders because it is easy to observe whether employees are doing the activities they promised to do. But this focuses the employee's attention simply on doing the activities. "Did I go to all the meetings?" "Did I revamp the questionnaire?" However, what leaders really need to do is to direct employees' attention to the outcomes that the organization values. They can do this by requiring employees to develop outcome-based goals.

One leader, for example, described a manager who came to him with a long list of activity-based goals. One goal had to do with developing new training materials. The purpose of the new materials was to improve client service. In particular, the company wanted new hires to have fewer client complaints and to lose fewer accounts. The leader encouraged the manager to put her goal in those terms. As she did so, she said, "Wow, that's big. That's hard. It's sort of scary." She understood that outcome-based goals increase accountability.

2. MICRO LEVEL—USING CHECKLISTS AS A WAY OF DIRECTING ATTENTION.

Checklists are a second way of directing attention. They can be very effective. So why didn't the preflight checklist for the Air Florida flight help? Checklist items should direct people's attention to the critical factors that should influence their actions. The question "Is the anti-icer on or off?" focuses attention not on the critical factor—the temperature outside—but on the position of a switch. Had the list item read "Is the temperature below freezing?" the outcome might have been different.

Author Malcolm Gladwell describes a checklist that achieved impressive results at Cook County Hospital in Chicago.[3] Brendan Reilly, the head of the Department of Medicine, wanted to create a checklist to help doctors distinguish higher-risk cardiac patients from people who were moderate or low risk. This would allow the hospital to place lower-risk patients in units that were less expensive to run than the cardiac intensive care unit. To come up with a list, Reilly drew on the work of Lee Goldman. Decades earlier, Goldman had analyzed data about cardiac patients, such as their symptoms upon admission to the cardiac unit and the eventual outcome. Goldman was surprised to discover that the answers to four questions reliably predicted the patient's risk level:

> Is the patient's ECG (*electrocardiogram*) normal?
> Is the patient's pain *unstable angina*?
> Is there fluid in the patient's lungs?
> Is the patient's *systolic* blood pressure below 100?

Goldman's list directed the doctor's attention to these four crucial factors. The list then dictated what action the physician should take. For example, doctors placed patients with normal ECGs who were positive on the other three factors in intermediate care. They put patients with abnormal ECGs who were positive on only one of the remaining factors in mild observation.

Reilly found that the checklist led to more accurate diagnoses than the individual physicians' judgments. The checklist method was 70 percent better than doctors at identifying patients who were not actually having a heart attack. It accurately identified high-risk patients more often as well, succeeding 95 percent of the time, compared to the physicians who were accurate between 75 percent and 89 percent of the time.

An experience in a different hospital teaches another crucial lesson about checklists. Dr. Peter Pronovost designed a checklist to reduce the number of infections that result from the insertion of intravenous lines. Intensive care units frequently use intravenous lines to deliver medication to patients. Without proper precautions, these lines easily become infected. *New Yorker* writer and author Atul Gawande notes that 4 percent of the five million lines placed in patients each year become infected, affecting eighty thousand people annually in the United States.[4]

Pronovost instituted a simple, five-item checklist at Johns Hopkins Hospital to reduce this rate of infection. The list included directives such as washing your hands with soap and washing the patient's skin with chlorhexidine antiseptic before inserting the line. All five of the required steps were no-brainers based on common knowledge about averting infection. But the results of consistently implementing these steps were "so dramatic that (the researchers) weren't sure whether to believe them: the ten-day line-infection rate went from eleven per cent to zero [in the following 15 month period]. . . . Only two line infections occurred. . . . In this one hospital, the checklist had prevented forty-three infections and eight deaths, and saved two million dollars in costs."[5]

The list worked. The challenge was how to ensure that physicians would follow it religiously. Pronovost put nurses in charge of monitoring the physicians to make sure they complied. They also ensured that the hospital administration unequivocally supported the nurses in this matter. Doctors had to sign a document testifying that they had carried out each of the steps—a document countersigned by the nurse. Pronovost also learned that it was vital to bring senior hospital executives into the units so that they could see firsthand how their decisions affected the implementation of the checklist policy. For example, executives visiting intensive care units in Michigan discovered that the chlorhexidine soap needed to wash the patient's skin was available in fewer than a third of the units—a situation that the leaders had the power to rectify.

As is clear in the above examples, by setting goals and creating checklists to direct employees' attention, leaders can increase productivity, curtail problems, cut costs, and prevent disasters.

WHAT IF . . . ?

What if leaders required outcome-based goals? Outcome-based goals direct employees' attention to the most important organizational outcomes. They also increase accountability because it is no longer enough for employees to simply carry out activities. They have to demonstrate that their efforts have made a difference.

1. HOW CAN LEADERS TELL IF A GOAL IS OUTCOME-BASED?

Outcome-based goals are goals that, if accomplished, would have a positive impact on the overall functioning of the business. Leaders should ask employees, "Can this goal be met *without* producing a positive change in the organization?" If the answer is yes, then that goal is probably not outcome-based. Imagine, for example, that a marketing department sets goals such as "We will implement a new marketing strategy," or "We will reach ten thousand additional prospects." Is it possible to accomplish these goals without having a positive impact? Sure. There is no positive outcome unless the new marketing strategy results in increased sales. An outcome-based goal, in contrast, would measure positive growth. One example could be "The marketing department will increase sales of the new product line by 12 percent."

There is a straightforward way to convert activity-based goals into outcome-based goals. Simply ask, "Why are we doing this activity"? That "why" is the outcome. Sometimes leaders can't come up with a good "why" for an activity. (It's surprising how often people can't!) In this case, maybe the leader should scratch that activity.

2. AREN'T OUTCOME-BASED GOALS HARDER TO MEASURE THAN ACTIVITY-BASED GOALS?

In adopting outcome-based goals, leaders might have to trade measurability for meaningfulness. Activity-based goals are easily measured. That's one reason they have great appeal. But that appeal can take an organization off target. For example, a public affairs department measured the number of programs provided, program participants, and volunteer hours. Department members tracked this data meticulously. Over time, their goals began to reflect the number of programs, participants, and volunteer hours they had. But what they really wanted to do was improve the company's image in the community. By focusing more and more on activity-based goals, they let their existing metrics drive their goals and they lost sight of their primary responsibility. At times it might be more difficult to measure some outcome-based goals. But rough measures of the right results can be better than "tight" measures of the wrong ones. At the very least, measures of the right objective keep the focus on what is important.

3. WHAT IF LEADERS ASKED WHERE CHECKLISTS MIGHT BE HELPFUL IN THEIR ORGANIZATION?

Checklists are humble little devices. They don't grab headlines. What leader wants to be noticed because "she sure introduced a lot of checklists into the organization"? It sounds much more impressive to introduce hightech solutions to problems. In his article on line infections, Gawande notes that hospitals "spent tens of millions of dollars" on expensive, high-tech, antimicrobial catheters, despite the fact that they reduced infections only slightly." In contrast, when Michigan hospitals adopted the checklist for an eighteen-month test period, "line infections were virtually eliminated, saving the hospitals an estimated $175 million, because they no longer had to treat the associated complications . . . and saved about 1,500 lives."[6]

Leaders can overlook checklists because they are such simple devices. But properly designed checklists, which must aim at a crucial aspect of the business, can be invaluable. Here are some guidelines to help leaders construct useful checklists.

Guidelines for Developing Checklists:

1. Make sure that the recommended actions on the list are valid. The cardiac patients' list was based on an analysis of thousands of records of other cardiac patients and the accuracy of the list was then tested out at Cook County Hospital itself. If leaders have no access to preexisting data, then their first step must be to gather the information they need to develop the list. Sometimes the people who will eventually use the list can be a great resource in creating it.
2. Make sure that the items on the list direct attention to the *conditions* that matter ("Is it snowing outside?"), and not just on the actions that should be taken ("Is the anti-icer on?").
3. Keep the list simple by including only the essential items. People will ignore rather than follow a twelve-page set of required steps.
4. Demonstrate that following the list results in positive outcomes. If possible, involve employees in testing the effectiveness of the

required actions. The physicians at Cook County Hospital would not have deferred to the guidelines for admitting cardiac patients had they not seen for themselves that the list led to more accurate diagnoses.

5. Make sure that employees have what they need in order carry out the prescribed actions. This may involve tangible resources, such as supplies. But in many cases it may involve subtler resources, such as time. Is the system set up so that employees can implement the required actions?

NOTES

1. Timothy Wilson, *Strangers to Ourselves: Discovering the Adaptive Unconscious* (Cambridge, MA: Belknap Press of Harvard University Press, 2002).

2. Brad Kolar, "When SMART Goals Are Dumb," *Brad Kolar Associates* (2007), http://www.kolarassociates.com/articles/When%20SMART%20goals%20are%20dumb.pdf (accessed February 1, 2009).

3. Malcolm Gladwell, *Blink: The Power of Thinking without Thinking* (Back Bay Books, 2007).

4. Atul Gawande, "The Checklist," *New Yorker Magazine*, December 10, 2007, p. 1, http://www.newyorker.com/reporting/2007/12/10/071210fa_fact_gawande?currentPage=1 (accessed on December 17, 2008).

5. Ibid.

6. Dan Heath and Chip Heath, "Heroic Checklists: Why You Should Learn to Love Checking Boxes," *FastCompany.com Magazine* 123 (February 14, 2008), http://www.fastcompany.com/magazine/123/heroic-checklist.html (accessed October 27, 2008).

Chapter 17

SEEING IS BELIEVING?
NOT ALWAYS.

WHAT'S THE STORY?

W hen she was in her midtwenties, Debbie argued with her parents about a statistic she had brought to their attention. "And I said, by way of proof, that it could not have been 'seventy' and had to be 'forty' because it was a red number with a warm feel."[1] Debbie's parents looked at her as if she had lost her mind. For the first time, Debbie understood that not everyone experienced the world as she did.

Neuropsychologist Jamie Ward describes Debbie's case in *The Frog Who Croaked Blue*, a discussion of *synesthesia*. Synesthesia is the strange condition that caused Debbie to experience various colors in association with numbers and letters. A person with synesthesia experiences two sensory modalities, such as sight and sound, as intertwined—not in a metaphorical sense but literally. A person listening to guitar music may experience the sound (as we do) but also feel a blowing sensation on her ankles. Another person might have a taste in his mouth when he hears certain words. Still other people with synesthesia see words, numbers— even time—projected "out there" in space rather than in their minds. One person, for example, saw words literally tumbling out of people's mouths into the air when they spoke—in full Technicolor. Another saw the months of the year as a Hula-hoop around her body.

What causes such strange experiences? The answer is still a mystery, but we do know that these experiences depend on discrete areas of the cerebral cortex that have distinct functions. For example, there is an area in the temporal lobe that is typically devoted to recognizing letters and numbers. It happens that this area is adjacent to a region called *V4*, which is involved in our perception of color. V4 is more active, for instance, when we look at bright colors than when we look at shades of gray. Many neuroscientists believe that in people with synesthesia, these two normally separated areas have somehow become intertwined.

We would like to believe that those who do not experience synesthesia have the correct or accurate perception of the world, while the person with synesthesia does not. But neuropsychologist Chris Frith argues that it doesn't make sense for either party to claim that they see how the world "really" is.[2] If everyone had the crosswired brains of the synesthete, we would all "know" that letters and numbers have the property of color. Some philosophers take the extreme position that there is no objective reality. Frith is not saying that. But he is saying that what we believe reality to be is based on what our brains tell us.

Sometimes the brain fills in or infers an inaccurate representation of the world. This is what happens in optical illusions, like the one illustrated in figure 17.1. If we measure the two horizontal lines in the picture, we see that they are exactly the same length. Even though we know this, we continue to perceive the two lines as unequal. Our brain tells us they are unequal based on the context of the other lines in the drawing.

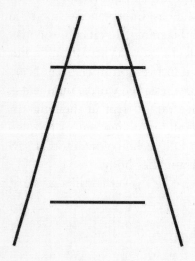

Figure 17.1. Even when we *know* that the two short lines are the same length, we still have the illusion that one is longer than the other.

The brain *constructs* meaning from the information that it receives. Perhaps most important, the brain fills in what psychologists call "causal patterns." For example, when we are watching a pool game, we don't see the movement of the balls as a series of disconnected events. We see causation. The cue ball hits the nine ball and propels it into the pocket. We think of this causation as existing somewhere "out there." But causation is a perceived relationship, a pattern that the brain discerns. For example, if people watch a film in which a billiard ball appears to cause a patch of light on the pool table to move, they will have the strong sensation that the ball really did cause the light to move. They intellectually know this isn't possible. Nonetheless, it will seem to them as if the ball moved the light because the timing perfectly imitated the pattern they would see when billiard balls collide.

Yale University psychologist Brian Scholl and his colleagues have spent years studying just what leads the brain to decide that one event has caused another. Often these researchers create videos of little geometric objects moving in different ways, and then play with various factors to see how they affect our perception of causality. For example, timing matters. We won't think that the cue ball caused the nine ball to move if it touches the nine ball and then nothing happens for the next ten seconds—even if at that point the nine ball propels itself toward the pocket.

The tendency to see causality is very strong. It can even be observed in babies as young as seven months old. Yet just as the brain can lead us astray in its perception of optical illusions, our inferences of causality can also be wrong. As Scholl and his colleagues write, "We can see—and can barely avoid seeing—causality in some situations even when we are certain it does not exist (as when a real billiard ball appears to cause a patch of light to move), but we will fail to perceive causality in many other situations when we know that it does exist."[3]

INTERESTING. BUT SO WHAT?

HOW CAN I USE THIS INFORMATION AS A BUSINESS LEADER?

People with synesthesia experience the world very differently from the rest of us. But in less dramatic ways, each of us sees the world differently to some extent. We all "fill in" meaning. We all interpret what is going on in different ways.

This has two major repercussions in the business world. First, different interpretations can be a source of conflict. In business settings, for example, leaders are frustrated when their employees don't "get" what seems obvious to the leader—and vice versa. Second, the fact that we don't know "reality" directly, but rely on the brain to interpret reality, is a source of error. We all recognize that optical illusions can fool the brain. But we sometimes forget how easily the brain can also be fooled by illusions of causality. This can have serious repercussions. Leaders can sometimes make poor decisions if they are wrong about which variable is causing which result.

1. WHY IS IT SOMETIMES HARD TO "GET" WHAT THE LEADER WANTS?

Neuroscientist Gregory Berns describes what happened in the 1970s when Silicon Valley engineer Nolan Bushnell invented a video game called Computer Space. Although it would be considered rudimentary by today's standards, this game was revolutionary at the time. It was a hit with Bushnell's engineer friends when they tried it out. But when the game was installed alongside other video games in bars, it flopped. People just didn't "get it." They did not understand what they were supposed to do. They would put their quarter in and then just stand there waiting for something to happen. As Berns writes, "What happened was, the flying saucer flew over and zapped their spaceship."[4]

People didn't "get it," because at the time they couldn't relate what they were seeing to anything that was familiar. Computer Space was not like the other video games in the bar, and people did not have a familiar context to help them "fill in" the meaning of the game. In contrast, Bushnell's next attempt was Pong, the first video game designed for home use. Unlike Computer Space, Pong succeeded because everyone understood its context: Ping-Pong.

When leaders want employees to do something new, they need to think about how unfamiliar the new agenda is. If it is too unfamiliar, employees will have trouble understanding what they are expected to do. As one example, think of the leadership drive to "flatten" the organization and reduce hierarchy in decision making. This requires a significant shift in thinking for many employees. They are used to doing exactly what the leader tells them to do, or at least asking for permission before they act. In a flattened organization, leaders still want to provide their input. But they don't want employees to automatically take their input as a directive.

Sometimes it is hard for employees to understand this. One team was discussing what the company should do for Employee Recognition Day. Hearing about some of the pressures employees had recently been under, the leader remarked, "Everyone here should get a medal!" This was not a directive. It was an offhand comment made in the context of a collaborative discussion. So the leader was astounded when three cases of medals arrived at the door the following week. When questioned, the team members admitted that they didn't think giving out the medals was a good idea. But they thought that they were required to incorporate the leader's suggestion into their plans.

It is hard for people to grasp new approaches that are very different from what they have done in the past. This doesn't mean that leaders should give up on changes. It does mean that leaders need to appreciate how hard it might be for employees to understand what each change requires.

2. WHY DO WE MAKE MISTAKES ABOUT "WHAT'S CAUSING WHAT"?

The brain is terrific at inferring causal patterns. Often this serves us in good stead. But the downside, as Nassim Nicholas Taleb warns us in *Black Swan*, is that the brain is adept at finding meaning, even in random data.[5] Taleb illustrates this idea with what happened when Saddam Hussein was captured in December 2003. *Bloomberg News* flashed two different headlines. The first headline noted a rise in US Treasuries and implied that Hussein's capture had caused the rise. Thirty minutes later, US Treasuries fell. The second headline connected the *fall* with Hussein's capture.

Undoubtedly the rise and fall were part of the normal market fluctuations that occur during the course of a day. But the media seem compelled to come up with a "reason" for every market fluctuation, and they can always find one. This is how our brains work. When we try to find reasons for whatever is happening, we can almost always come up with something—even when what is happening is random.

Business leaders also see random events as meaningful. When random fluctuations occur—in sales, in employee performance, in the outcome of an advertising campaign—the brain is all too ready to identify a culprit . . . or a hero. Leaders who mindlessly embrace the explanations that the brain offers can make big mistakes. For example, a leader might eliminate an otherwise useful program because a meaningless fluctuation in results showed it had little impact on one group. Conversely, a leader might adopt a program whose successful pilot was a matter of sheer luck.

Leaders often focus on the most recent events to explain any change that has occurred. This is also how the brain works. Remember what happens when people watch films of little geometric figures moving around? If a blue cube hits a red circle, which then starts to spin, the brain assumes that the cube caused the circle to spin. This assumption works well with simple, physical events—like the movements of billiard balls. But in complex systems the belief "whatever happened most recently is the cause of what I see now" can lead us astray.

WHAT IF . . . ?

What if leaders keep in mind that causality is something the brain perceives—sometimes wrongly? Leaders who pay attention to this potential pitfall can make better decisions. To avoid the pitfall, leaders can ask themselves the following questions:

1. IS THE INFORMATION ACCURATE?

The first question that business leaders should ask when they see data is "Is the information accurate?" Leaders often accept numbers on a report as indisputable facts. Instead of questioning the numbers, they jump to trying to explain them. As a small example, in one survey, managers had to indicate on a scale from 1 to 5 how much they agreed with statements like "My direct reports are often not aligned with my vision." They then correlated the results with the performance level of the managers. For example, in this case they would predict that team members of high-performing managers would be strongly aligned with that manager's vision. Instead the results showed that high-performing managers had *fewer* people aligned with their vision. It turned out that this happened because the statement was written in the negative. For this statement, we would expect a low number—meaning that the managers disagreed with the statement—to correlate with high performance. But the team analyzing the results didn't catch this. Instead, they misinterpreted the numbers to mean that *high-performing* managers had *fewer* people aligned with their vision. This result was improbable. But the team wrote four paragraphs explaining why this might be the case. They didn't catch the error until a higher-ranking person questioned the data.

Leaders who understand their business should have a rough idea of what they are expecting to see. They should ask themselves "Does this data make sense, based on what I know?" If they see something unlikely, they should explore it further. Especially with strategic or risky decisions, questioning the data makes good business sense. Make sure the data itself is accurate before trying to explain it, or worse, acting upon it.

2. AM I CONFUSING IMMEDIACY, FAMILIARITY, OR REPETITION WITH CAUSALITY?

In trying to explain events, the brain is likely to offer up one of two alternatives. Either the brain will point to a vivid factor—like a huge economic shift—as the cause of the change. Or the brain will latch on to the event that immediately preceded the change. The closer in time the two events occurred, the stronger our feeling that the first caused the second.

Remember how strongly timing affects the brain's perception of causation. The brain perceives the billiard ball as moving the patch of light because it moved the instant after the ball touched it.

Consider a classic training exercise called "The Beer Game." Jay Forrester at the Massachusetts Institute of Technology developed the Beer Game in the 1960s. In the game, some players represent a company that manufactures beer. Others represent the retailers who stock it. The exercise is set up so that there is a sudden spike in the demand for beer in the second week. Players typically react to this spike in ways that have a snowball effect. The ultimate result is that the company ends up with so much overstock it has to halt production and lay off employees.[6]

The problem is due to misunderstanding causality. In the Beer Game example, when demand increases, the retailer sees his stock dwindling, so he places a larger order than usual. This pattern continues for several weeks. Due to the lead time in receiving the larger orders, the retailer eventually sees his inventory run out entirely. Then, the larger orders start arriving week after week. The retailer suddenly switches from being sold out to having major overstock.

The reason for the problem is that the players believe that increased demand is causing their dwindling inventory. In fact, with the exception of the spike in the second week, demand stays the same throughout the game.

Leaders can counter errors of causality in two ways. First, they should review data for the entire system. Instead of simply reacting to a sudden change in one part of a system, leaders should step back and review data on all of the parts of the system. Looking at historic trends might provide an alternative explanation. Second, leaders should take feedback loops into consideration when developing measurement tools. For example, instead of measuring customer satisfaction on a weekly basis, leaders might take monthly or quarterly snapshots. This will allow time for decisions and programs to fully kick in before another measurement is taken (and acted upon).

3. IS THIS JUST A FLUKE?

Once business leaders are sure that the data is reliable, the next question they should ask is "Could this be a fluke?" The brain is very clever in generating ideas about causality. But as earlier examples emphasize, it is all too easy for the brain to think that Hussein's capture made US Treasuries rise—and fall. It is too easy for the brain to see causality where none exists.

Jonah Lehrer provides a vivid example of this in his book *How We Decide*.[7] Lehrer describes a study in which a rat would be placed in a T-shaped maze. The rat started at the bottom of the T. The researcher would put food in either the upper right or the upper left corner of the T. The placement of the food was essentially random, although 60 percent of the time the food was placed on the left side. The rats soon "learned the odds" and automatically went to the left side. Researchers later did the experiment with Yale students instead of rats. But the students could not accept that the placement was essentially random. Instead, they tried to figure out the pattern so that they could better predict where the food would be each time. As Lehrer writes, "The problem was that there was nothing to predict; the apparent randomness was real." In fact, the students' efforts to discover a pattern that would pay off led them to be *less* successful than the rats. The students found the food only 52 percent of the time while the rats found it 60 percent of the time.

Just raising the question "Could this be a fluke?" can help leaders avoid this type of problem. Leaders can determine whether they need to gather more information to answer that question. They also need to identify recurring cycles in their industry so that they don't overreact to routine ups and downs.

4. AM I LOOKING AT THE DATA IN A BROAD ENOUGH CONTEXT?

The Beer Game shows how the reactions of decision makers caused a major problem. It illustrates the "systems thinking" that Jay Forrester introduced. Although they may now seem commonplace, Forrester's ideas were revolutionary at the time of their inception. He emphasized that cause and effect are interwoven in any feedback system. For example, the thermostat detects a drop in temperature and triggers the furnace to go on. The furnace raises temperature and causes a change in the thermostat. As Art Kleiner puts it in his discussion of Forrester's work, systems models show that "there is no single cause-and-effect; the effect always influences the cause."[8] This is a much more sophisticated view of causality than the one the brain typically perceives.

Dr. Peter M. Senge, the founding chairperson of the Society for Organizational Learning, spread Forrester's ideas about systems thinking.[9] Influenced by Senge, many leaders now accept the thermostat feedback analogy as obvious. But leaders often ignore one powerful implication of this basic idea. As Kleiner writes, "Most problems that corporate leaders . . . face aren't caused by outside forces: competitors, market trends, or regulation. Problems tend to derive from the unintended consequences of the leaders' own ideas and efforts."[10] Leaders most often look to outside causes. But that's like the homeowner trying to explain why the heat is going on solely by looking at the outside temperature. The outdoor temperature does influence the furnace. But the settings on the thermostat do as well. Even when there is no change in the temperature outside, the heat will go on and off because of the way the feedback system is structured.

In businesses, leaders control how that feedback system is structured. They also influence the feedback system every time they react to changes. Leaders need to ask, "In what ways are my own responses to these events fueling the very problems I am trying to solve?"

5. HAVE I THOUGHT ABOUT THE "UNTHINKABLE"?

Past events are the best predictors of what will happen in the future. But as Taleb emphasizes in *Black Swan*, there are some events that no one would ever predict based on what happened earlier. Leaders cannot know for sure what these "unthinkable" futures might involve. What leaders can do is to actively entertain the possibility that there are alternatives that they would never predict based on past experience.

Scenario planning is a technique that can help leaders do this. Leaders can create possible future scenarios, both similar to and different from anything that they expect to happen. Quite likely, none of these specific scenarios will occur exactly as imagined. But by thinking about the factors that might create such scenarios, leaders can recognize the triggers they should watch for. They can also create plans that will help them deal with the unthinkable, should it occur. For example, in 1979 a meltdown at the Three Mile Island nuclear power plant seemed imminent. In the midst of the crisis, the city officials of Harrisburg, Pennsylvania, realized that there was no evacuation plan. No one had bothered to create one because the power plant builders had been certain that a meltdown could never happen.

Once business leaders become aware of the fact that different people perceive reality differently, and that their very own brains can misinterpret data to determine causality, then leaders can work to create more effective plans, whether it be to flatten the hierarchy of an organization, to determine the variables behind market trends, or to prepare for the unforeseeable future.

NOTES

1. Jamie Ward, *The Frog Who Croaked Blue: Synesthesia and the Mixing of the Senses* (New York: Routledge, 2008), p. 4.

2. Chris Frith, *Making Up the Mind: How the Brain Creates Our Mental World* (Malden, MA: Blackwell Publishing, 2008).

3. G. E. Newman et al., "The Origins of Causal Perception: Evidence from Postdictive Processing in Infancy," *Cognitive Psychology* 57, no. 3 (2008): 262–91.

4. Gregory Berns, *Iconoclast* (Boston: Harvard University Press, 2008), p. 31.

5. Nassim Nicholas Taleb, *The Black Swan: The Impact of the Highly Improbable* (New York: Random House, 2007).

6. Peter Senge, *The Fifth Discipline: The Art and Practice of the Learning Organization* (New York: Doubleday Business, 2006), pp. 25–51.

7. Jonah Lehrer, *How We Decide* (New York: Houghton Mifflin Harcourt, 2009).

8. Art Kleiner, *The Age of Heretics: A History of the Radical Thinkers Who Reinvented Corporate Management* (San Francisco: Jossey-Bass, 2008).

9. Peter Senge, *The Fifth Discipline.*

10. Kleiner, *The Age of Heretics*, p. 176.

Chapter 18

BLINK OR THINK?

When Should You Go with Your Gut?

WHAT'S THE STORY?

In his book *Blink: The Power of Thinking without Thinking*, Malcolm Gladwell describes an incident in which a Cleveland firefighter ordered the men under his command to retreat from a burning house. As they were shooting water into the kitchen, the lieutenant was suddenly overwhelmed with anxiety. He shouted, "There's something wrong. Get out, now!"[1] Seconds later, the living room floor that the men had been standing on collapsed.

Months later, an interviewer urged the lieutenant to try to remember what might have alerted him to a problem. He recalled a feeling of being surprised at how hot the fire was, how quiet it was. The reason that the living room was so hot and the fire was so quiet was because the fire was not solely in the kitchen as he had initially supposed. It was centered in the basement, just below the living room floor.

Yet while in that stifling house, the lieutenant was not consciously thinking about these factors and weighing them. He didn't say to himself "this fire is too quiet" or "this fire is so hot." In fact, he had to think long and hard after the fact to even recognize that he had had these fleeting impressions of "too quiet" and "too hot." His brain, below the level of his conscious awareness, noticed the elements that didn't seem right and alerted him to the danger.

What happens when people "know" something without being con-

202 SECTION IV: DECISION MAKING

scious of what they know? They may feel that some mysterious force is guiding them. In fact, the fire lieutenant who saved his men from disaster initially believed that he must have had ESP. How else could he have known that they were in danger? Only after reflecting on his experience did he recall the clues that led his unconscious mind to decide that something was wrong.

The idea that our brains can perform sophisticated analysis and decision making without consulting *us* (our conscious minds) is one of the most unexpected realizations to emerge from the field of neuroscience. This insight feels like both a gift and a threat. It feels like a gift when we have a lifesaving impulse unaccompanied by any apparent thought or effort. But it is threatening because it's disconcerting to realize how often our brains are making up our minds for us! In his book *The Brain Has a Mind of Its Own*, neurologist Richard Restak notes that people often assume that conscious knowledge is the only "real" knowledge. Information and ideas that are stored below the level of consciousness don't "count" as real knowledge. But, Restak objects, "Modern brain research suggests that knowledge involves dynamic, evolving patterns that are stored at multiple levels in the nervous system. This exciting, scary insight explains such things as intuitions [and] hunches. . . . We all know more than we can say."[2]

What are these "patterns" that are stored in the nervous system? Much of what we are doing when we develop expertise is learning to recognize patterns. A clear example of this is what happens when a physician sees a patient. The doctor listens to the patient's complaints and then tries to see if the symptoms and test results form a pattern that fits a diagnosis. The patient may say that he recently had an odd experience in which he briefly felt as if he were tipsy and disoriented—yet he had not been drinking. As he is speaking, the physician realizes just by looking at him that his thyroid gland seems prominent. She asks a question, "Have you experienced any pain in your calves recently?" The patient looks up, startled, "Why yes, I didn't think anything of it, but I've been having some cramps on and off." The ensuing exam confirms the physician's hunch that the patient has an enlarged thyroid gland, and she further verifies that hunch with a blood test.

What she is doing is looking at a collection of symptoms and trying to match that to the hundreds of patterns she has in her mind—templates of different diseases. Many symptoms can be part of any number of different disorders. The trick is to match a set of symptoms with the right template, the correct diagnosis. And how do physicians typically do this? Apparently not through painstaking analysis! Robert Hamm at the University of Colorado's Institute of Cognitive Science argues that expert clinicians usually develop an initial hunch about what is wrong with a patient within twenty seconds. This is too quick for them to be reasoning their way to a conclusion. Instead, these experts rely on pattern recognition. Recognizing a pattern can occur within seconds. In experts, it occurs "largely without any conscious analysis . . . or linear, step-by-step combining of cues."[3]

In some studies of expert diagnosticians, researchers made the puzzling discovery that less-experienced physicians performed about as well as the experts.[4] This was in sharp contrast to other research in which physicians who were recognized as superior diagnosticians outperformed less-experienced doctors. What made the difference? It turned out the average physicians performed about as well as the experts when the sets of cases they were given to diagnose included only common diseases. But the experts shone when the cases included some rare diseases. If we think of the brain as a "matchmaker" that notices patterns, we can make sense of these findings. The average physician does a good job diagnosing routine cases because, in routine cases, the match is usually correct. The obvious answer is the right one. But superior diagnosticians do better with unusual cases because they have acquired more patterns. They are more sensitive to small details that indicate a case does not quite fit the "usual" template.

INTERESTING, BUT SO WHAT?

HOW CAN I USE THIS INFORMATION AS A BUSINESS LEADER?

Historically, there have been recurring debates about how business leaders should make decisions. Advocates of *rational* management approaches advise leaders to create what are essentially detailed decision trees. In rational management, leaders solve problems by following a logical series of steps from problem definition to action plans based on the root cause they have identified. More intuitive, seat-of-the-pants decision-making approaches are in sharp contrast to this kind of effortful thinking.

As psychologist Richard Wagner notes, acceptance of the rational method of management has declined.[5] Why? "The downfall of rational approaches," Wagner writes, "is the growing belief that they just do not work as effectively as alternative approaches actually used by managers on the job."[6] Research shows that, on the job, managers "typically grope along with only a vague impression of the problems they are dealing with, and with little idea of what the ultimate solution would be until they found it."[7] Rather than planning ahead, managers take an action. Then they consider what happened as they decide their next step.

Like the physician making an on-the-spot decision and the firefighter intuitively knowing that the situation is dangerous, many managers base their decisions on tacit knowledge. Tacit knowledge is knowledge that people possess but often find hard to articulate. Their years of experience have taught leaders a great deal and they are successful partly because they allow this tacit knowledge to guide them. Research shows that measures of tacit knowledge reliably distinguish experienced managers from MBA students. Tacit knowledge is also related to leaders' success. For example, researchers surveyed participants in a leadership development program at the Center for Creative Leadership. The results showed that the managers with greater tacit knowledge enjoyed higher salaries, greater success in generating new business, and were more likely to work for a company nearer the top of the Fortune 500 list.[8]

Some leaders look at research like this and conclude that managers should let their implicit knowledge guide them. They should just follow their intuitions. But it is not quite that simple. As psychologist and researcher Gary Klein points out, people make good gut decisions when, like the expert diagnosticians, their brains have stored "very large repertoires of patterns acquired over years and years of practice."[9] Klein believes that leaders can get better at making intuitive judgments. But to do so, they need more than just experience. They need to intentionally learn from experience so that they can refine that database of patterns. They need to make tough decisions and thoughtfully review their mistakes. Klein describes specific exercises to help leaders do just that.

But how willing are business leaders to engage in this kind of review? Nobel Prize–winning psychologist Daniel Kahneman argues that most leaders shy away from such an analysis. Kahneman remarks, "The thing that astonishes me when I talk to businesspeople in the context of decision analysis is that you have an organization that's making lots of decisions and they're not keeping track. They're not trying to learn from their own mistakes. . . . So there is a lot of curiosity [about my ideas], and I get invited to give lots of talks. But the idea that you might want to appoint somebody to keep statistics on the decisions that you made and a few years later evaluate the biases, the errors, the forecasts that were wrong, the factors that were misjudged, in order to make the process more rational—they won't want to do it."[10]

Even leaders who routinely hold post-project debriefs often fail to focus on the information that might lead to better decisions in the future. Instead, the analysis typically focuses on a simple outcome, such as "did we make the right decision, or not?" Or it focuses on specific actions that contributed to the fiasco, such as realizing that "we should have talked first with the other project team to see if we would be able to coordinate our efforts." Rarely do leaders make the thought processes themselves the center of attention. Rarely do they focus on what people were thinking or assuming that led them to fail to talk with the other project team.

To hone intuition, we need to think more about what caused people to make poor decisions. A team member might realize, for example, "We assumed that the quality of the vendor's materials wouldn't have changed and the reason we assumed that was because . . ." Identifying the "because" is key. That information will modify the database the team is relying on. This kind of postmortem analysis refines the templates the team is using. Ultimately, refining the database will lead to better intuitive decisions.

Gary Klein is careful to insist that no one should rely solely on intuition. In many situations, it would be ludicrous to "go with your gut" instead of gathering basic information and analyzing it before making a decision. Nevertheless, Klein does advise leaders to "start with intuition, not analysis."[11] He suggests this because he believes that thinking analytically can squash the subtle intuitions people might otherwise notice. So begin with first impressions, Klein says, and then—if necessary and possible—verify them using more analytical methods.

No one is arguing here that people should rely solely on intuitive judgments, or that careful reasoning has no value. In fact, much of this book is dedicated to understanding the science behind the intuition, that is, the neurological research that explains the decisions the brain makes without our conscious knowledge. It would be silly, for example, to try to solve certain types of problems through "intuition." If you need to know which major capital expenditure would pay off in the long run, it makes sense to gather information and analyze it in a methodical way. In fact, the more complex the decision is—the more elements that you need to take into account—the more likely that you need to supplement your hunches with investigation and analysis. But realizing that the brain is a maestro at recognizing patterns reminds you to respect your intuition as well.

WHAT IF . . . ?

Leaders can help themselves and their people make better intuitive judgments. Here are some specific approaches that leaders can take to do that:

1. WHAT IF LEADERS ANALYZE DECISIONS THAT ARE DIFFICULT FOR PEOPLE?

When Gary Klein consults with groups, he sometimes asks them to identify a decision that is hard for people to make. As one example, a project manager might say that it is hard for her to estimate how long it will take to complete a project or how much it will cost. Then Klein asks, "If this is an important judgment, and one that is difficult to make, how do you train for it?"[12] Leaders and team members consider just what makes that judgment hard. For example, is it hard to estimate the time required because team members are inexperienced and really have little idea about how long each step takes? Or is it because the leader needs to get better at anticipating potential glitches? Or that the leader misses early signs that team members are going beyond the original scope of the project? First team members should identify what often goes awry. Then they can intentionally search for opportunities in which they can practice the target skill and get useful feedback on how they are doing.

2. What if leaders discuss past mistakes to build up a database of rarely occurring situations?

In his book *How Doctors Think*, Jerome Groopman describes several master diagnosticians.[13] What they had in common was that they paid great attention to odd cases. They also paid attention to the times when they were wrong. For example, one highly esteemed cardiologist meticulously recorded every mistake he had ever made and reread this log often, especially when he was trying to figure out baffling cases.

To become more expert, we need to add the outlier cases to our brain's database. Because they occur so rarely, these cases are difficult to acquire and hard to bring to mind. They may also be the situations in which we are most likely to err. That is why keeping a special database of errors, from our own experience and from the experience of others, is so valuable. Klein also suggests having teams engage in simulation exercises involving rarely occurring scenarios so that they can attain experience about circumstances that only occur once in a blue moon.

3. What if leaders recognize that employees might not make the "obvious" connections?

Expertise gives leaders an edge. Experienced leaders have a storehouse of patterns to draw on that their employees simply don't have. Sometimes leaders assume that their employees will see the same patterns that are obvious to them. But that is unlikely. For example, a leader might be thinking, "What is the matter with her? She is going on with her presentation as if she is reading a script. Why doesn't she see that she is losing the client's attention?" The truth is she may not notice the pattern of nonverbal communication that is so clear to her superior. Experienced salespeople will have a host of templates for how different clients might respond. If the client appears impatient, confused, eager, or irritated, they adjust what they saying—once again drawing on a set of templates or patterns that they have acquired. The inexperienced person who is oblivious of the client's cues, or fails to adjust to them, needs more training and experience—and understanding from her superiors.

The inability of employees to grasp what seems obvious to leaders can be a frustrating obstacle during times of change. Sometimes leaders think that all they need to do is let employees in on all the current information. To the leader, this information makes the need for change undeniable. But employees may not interpret the information in the same way because they lack the broader context that the leader has. Without this context, the employees just don't see the urgency of the situation. In these circumstances, it takes careful thought and planning to communicate why change is necessary. One leader spoke with a small group of relatively inexperienced team leaders about some changes that were being considered. She used the team leaders as a kind of pilot group to test her thinking. Based on their reactions, she was better able to position the change with the rest of her employees.

4. WHAT IF LEADERS DON'T JUST EXPLORE THE RIGHT PATH, BUT EXPLORE THE WRONG PATH AS WELL?

Gary Klein suggests that leaders rely not only on "postmortem" sessions to learn from past mistakes, but on "premortem" sessions to avoid future mistakes. These premortem sessions take place during the early phases of project planning. Klein begins the premortem session by telling a team, "I'm looking into a crystal ball and, oh no, I'm seeing that the project has failed. It isn't a simple failure either. It is a total, embarrassing, devastating failure."[14] Then Klein asks, "What could have caused this?" The team members spend three minutes writing down all the possible factors that could cause such a failure. They do this silently so that each person will initially draw on his individual intuitions based on his own set of templates. Klein then draws on the collective experience of the group by consolidating these lists. Ultimately, the group identifies the most problematic factors and designs strategies to avoid or minimize these pitfalls.

Leaders should recognize that the old question "Should I go with my gut or should I think analytically?" is a false dichotomy. The gut may be extremely valuable – but it can only be as good as the experience that informs it. Leaders should hone their intuitions by reflecting on and analyzing their past experiences.

NOTES

1. Malcolm Gladwell, *Blink: The Power of Thinking without Thinking* (Boston: Little, Brown, and Company, 2005), p. 122.

2. Richard Restak, *The Brain Has a Mind of Its Own* (New York: Crown Trade Paperbacks, 1991), p. 153.

3. Jerome Groopman, *How Doctors Think* (New York: Mariner Books, 2007), p. 34.

4. K. Anders Ericsson, "The Acquisition of Expert Performance: An Introduction to Some of the Issues," in *The Road to Excellence: The Acquisition of Expert Performance in the Arts and Sciences, Sports and Games*, ed. K. Anders Ericsson (Mahwah, NJ: Lawrence Erlbaum Associates, 1996), pp. 1–50.

5. Richard K. Wagner, "Smart People Doing Dumb Things: The Case of Managerial Incompetence," in *Why Smart People Can Be So Stupid*, ed. Robert J. Sternberg (New Haven, CT: Yale University Press, 2003), pp. 42–63.

6. Ibid., p. 45.

7. Ibid.

8. Ibid., p. 52.

9. Gary Klein, *The Power of Intuition* (New York: Doubleday, 2003), p. 6.

10. Michael Schrage, "Daniel Kahneman: The Thought Leader Interview," *Strategy + Business*, January 7, 2009, http://www.dailygood.org/more.php ?n=3556 (accessed January 9, 2009), p. 3.

11. Klein, *The Power of Intuition*, p. 80.

12. Ibid., p. 39.

13. Groopman, *How Doctors Think*.

14. Klein, *The Power of Intuition*, p. 99.

PERSONAL EFFECTIVENESS

Chapter 19

MULTITASKING

Asset or Liability?

WHAT'S THE STORY?

T here is a striking video used to demonstrate what cognitive psychologists call "selective attention." In this video, a group of young adults are dribbling a basketball in a hallway. They pass the ball to their teammates. When this video is used in seminars and workshops, viewers are instructed to count how many times the team in the white shirts passes the ball. At the end of the clip, the viewers are asked how many passes they observed. They spout off various numbers—the white-shirted team passed the ball nine times, or eleven, or thirteen times.

The facilitator then asks if they noticed anything unusual. This question is often met with puzzled expressions. It turns out that in the middle of the video, a person in a gorilla suit marches right through the basketball players. He stops at one point to pound his chest. The gorilla is in full view during this display of dominance. Yet typically, at least half the viewers fail to see the gorilla at all. They are stunned when the clip is replayed. This time—undistracted by the request to count the number of passes, they cannot help but see the gorilla in the midst of the game.

Were these viewers *inattentive*? Or were they simply so focused that they were bound to miss something? Neurologist Timothy Wilson notes that our eyes alone receive and send over ten *million* signals every second. This estimate is based on a count of both the receptor cells in our retinas that are stimulated by light waves and the nerves that go from these cells to the brain.[1] Of course, we cannot be consciously aware of all these signals. We mainly notice the signals related to our areas of focus, such as "Is the white team passing the ball now?" We ignore other competing stimuli, like the gorilla. And we also ignore tons of information that is theoretically available from other sensory systems—like the color of the walls or the texture of the chair we are sitting on.

Magicians, in fact, depend on our hardwired selective attention to fool us. They intentionally misdirect our attention so that we won't notice what they are really doing. *New York Times* science writer George Johnson describes his experiences onstage with magician Apollo Robbins at the 2007 *Magic of Consciousness* symposium in Las Vegas: "Apollo, with the pull of his eyes and the arc of his hand, swung around my attention like a gooseneck lamp, so that it always pointed in the wrong direction. When he appeared to be reaching for my left pocket he was swiping something from the right. At the end of the act the audience applauded as he handed me my pen, some crumpled receipts and dollar bills, and my digital audio recorder, which had been running all the while. I hadn't noticed that my watch was gone until he unstrapped it from his own wrist."[2]

On the Web you can see demonstrations of how magicians capitalize on our narrow focus of attention.[3] In one example, a magician seemingly transforms an entire set of blue cards into red cards. This trick illustrates what is known as "change blindness." In change blindness, we miss noticing that a significant feature of a scene has changed in some way. And this does not happen only when we are at the mercy of magicians! In a study of Harvard University students, a researcher posed as a disoriented visitor to the campus. He stopped lone students and asked for directions. In the middle of each student's reply, two additional researchers carried a door and walked between the two. While the student's view was blocked by the door, a different person took the place of the person asking for directions. What happened? Half of the students noticed the change—but half did not![4]

Selective attention explains why, with the exception of drunk drivers, cell phone users are involved in more car accidents than any other group. Research comparing attentive drivers with drivers using cell phones shows that, in addition to slowing down your reaction time, talking on the phone substantially reduces the number of visual cues you notice.[5] In fact, as microbiologist John Medina notes, any activity that distracts you from driving increases the risk of an accident.

INTERESTING. BUT SO WHAT?

HOW CAN I USE THIS INFORMATION AS A BUSINESS LEADER?

Many business leaders believe they are talented multitaskers and are proud of this ability. They rely on it to help them get things done, and they appreciate employees with similar skills. But what is really happening when we multitask? Are we actually giving our attention to two or more tasks at the same time?

The answer to that question is a resounding "No!" As John Medina puts it, when applied to the idea that we can simultaneously attend to more than one thing at a time, he says, "multitasking is a myth."[6] So what is going on when we multitask? Sometimes when we multitask we are simply carrying out actions that are so habitual they do not require any conscious attention. For example, when we type an e-mail, we do not have to think about which fingers to move; we can pay attention to the message we want to convey. We can drive halfway home without noticing how we got there because we are so well practiced that we can drive on autopilot. This frees our mind to think about other matters.

But when we are engaged in multiple activities that cannot be done on autopilot, something different is going on. At these times, multitasking involves a split-second shifting of our attention from one task to another. This is what we are doing when we text a colleague at a meeting while listening with half an ear to the discussion. We believe that we are thinking about what we are texting and simultaneously taking in the discussion. But, in fact, we are shifting our attention back and forth between these activities.

This means that normally when we multitask we are working in a stream of interrupted time. We have to stop what we have been doing, however briefly, in order to turn our attention to another task. Think of what happens in a meeting when we are distracted for a minute, and then

Figure 19.1. We think we are good multitaskers because we don't notice what we are missing.

hear a burst of laughter. "What's so funny?" we wonder, realizing that we have no idea what was just said. Or we make a note to follow up on a great idea that just occurred to us, only to find ourselves lost when we rejoin the discussion because we have totally missed that the group has moved on to another topic.

Sometimes the information that we hear is quite repetitive. For example, we listen to a colleague who drones on, making the same point in four different ways. We may be able to divide our attention in this case without a problem. But, sometimes, crucial information is coming at a fast pace or the situation is particularly difficult and requires more focus. When this happens, we need to stop multitasking and pay attention. In general, jumping from one activity to another, or shifting our attention from one input to another, has a price tag. Medina argues that research shows it takes substantially longer to complete interrupted tasks and we make more errors as we carry them out.[7] Multitasking can cause a significant productivity hit, even though it is a "skill" we tend to admire.

Selective attention can impact customer service as well as productivity. In one example, a customer service representative was surveying clients to see how easy it was for them to use a new Web site. She reported that many clients told her they had been unable to find a crucial link. "Did you show them how to find it?" her supervisor asked. The representative was embarrassed. "No, it didn't occur to me to do that. . . . I was focused on getting their feedback about navigating the Web site." She had been so focused on capturing the feedback that she forgot to help the customers find the information. The selective focus of her attention made her miss an obvious need.

If something vivid is capturing our attention—like a spike or dip in sales for the current month—we may fail to notice other more gradual changes, such as a slowly building increase in customer satisfaction. This is not only true of internal information but of our awareness about the industry overall. Leaders should think about where the attention of the organization as a whole is directed and make sure that the focus is not too narrow. Like people, organizations can have "selective attention." They can stay so focused on a few elements that they miss something as big as the gorilla pounding his chest. In his book, *Why Smart Executives Fail*, Sydney Finkelstein tells a classic story about Rubbermaid.[8] During the 1990s, Rubbermaid continued its focus on innovation, an area in which it had achieved significant success. What it failed to notice was that its customers had become more cost-conscious. Consequently, Rubbermaid lost significant market share to other companies that developed cheaper products.

WHAT IF … ?

What if leaders considered the costs of constantly shifting attention from one task to another? Instead of encouraging multitasking, leaders could emphasize the importance of uninterrupted time as a way to increase productivity. To erase barriers to uninterrupted time, leaders can start by asking the following questions:

1. DOES THE ORGANIZATIONAL CULTURE MAKE IT HARD TO PROTECT BLOCKS OF TIME?

Some organizational cultures demand a high degree of responsiveness. Blackberries are required for senior leaders. Instantaneous responses to e-mails become the norm. The culture then trickles down throughout the organization. In the end, people in these organizations may not have a single, solid hour of concentrated time in their workday. Instead, leaders can ask, "How can we be responsive *and* protect some time for uninterrupted work?" Simple, low-cost ideas can help. Schedule preparation time into daily calendars. Call for "Meeting-free Monday Mornings." Establish rotating "on call" schedules to handle customer issues.

In one hospital, an employee found a quiet area in the hospital's library. He posted a note on his office door letting people know when he would return. He indicated where they could find him if their business was urgent. To his surprise, in a year's time not a single person made the trek to the library. This gave him two hours a day of productive time. Leaders who carve out productive time for themselves will find that their employees do too. This increases productivity across the organization and also reduces the risk of errors in work.

2. DOES THE PACE OF CHANGE IN THE ORGANIZATION MAKE IT HARD FOR PEOPLE TO FOCUS THEIR ATTENTION?

Change initiatives often require people to shift attention between "keeping the lights on" and learning completely new ways of doing things. Now multiply that across departments. The finance department has a new reporting system. Sales has a new customer contact system. Human Resources has a new compensation process. Employees need to learn their part in contributing to all of these new processes while simultaneously keeping their customers happy and handling their regular workload. Leaders need to balance the schedule and pace of change so that people can focus their attention. This improves productivity and allows change to happen more quickly and effectively in the long run.

3. ARE LEADERS FOCUSING THEIR OWN ATTENTION ON THE RIGHT THINGS?

Sometimes leaders focus too much attention on operations and miss strategic opportunities. Leaders can miss important information because they live in a distracting, information-rich world. Finkelstein, who is also a professor of management at Dartmouth's Tuck Business School, gives a high-stakes example.[9] The Xerox Corporation had a research center in Palo Alto that "created dozens of 'killer app' products." Very few of these ever made it into production. Why? Few senior leaders had the vision to see what could be done with them. As Finkelstein writes, "When its Palo Alto Research Center invented the products of the future, it had no one in the company to tell."[10] While a continued focus on operations is essential, leaders also need to ensure that strategic ideas get the attention they deserve.

Finkelstein also argues that critical information failed to reach upper-level management at Palo Alto because the company lacked communication channels to bring strategic ideas to leaders' attention. He suggests that leaders trace the trail of information from the first person who receives it to the ultimate decision maker to see where vital information might go astray. Leaders can make sure that vital information is flagged so that it doesn't get lost in day-to-day operations.

4. DO LEADERS NEED TO PROACTIVELY DISCOURAGE MULTITASKING IN YOUNGER EMPLOYEES?

Many organizations today struggle to assimilate new college grads. As students, these young adults spent their time texting, listening to iPods, doing homework, eating, and watching TV—all at the same time. As these young adults start their first jobs, they bring their work habits with them. They may work with their headphones on, respond to instant messages continually, and take cell phone calls throughout the day. Younger adults may be able to juggle all this a bit better than older employees. They have had more practice, their working memory is probably a little larger, and they may be able to shift their attention back and forth more quickly.

Nevertheless, they are losing productivity. David E. Meyer, director of the Brain, Cognition, and Action Laboratory at the University of Michigan, notes that it takes us much longer to accomplish tasks when we have to shift our attention back and forth. "The toll in terms of slow-down is extremely large—amazingly so," Meyer states in a *Time* magazine interview.[11] Meyer often tests members of the Millennium generation in his research. He finds that when younger people are bombarded by interruptions, their work declines just as much as that of older people.

Research outside the laboratory confirms Meyer's observations. Microsoft researcher Eric Horvitz and University of Illinois doctoral candidate Shamsi Iqbal teamed up to study multitasking in a corporate environment. They observed Microsoft employees while they performed demanding tasks such as writing computer code or preparing reports. On average, they found that it took employees fifteen minutes to return to these tasks after they had stopped to respond to instant messages or e-mail. Often the interruption caused the person to go off track, answering other e-mails or browsing Web sites unrelated to their jobs.

Younger employees are used to multitasking and may resent suggestions that they limit it. Cutting younger people off from all distractions might even cause some to quit. But given the loss in productivity, imposing some restrictions might be worth the risk.

5. What if leaders focused less on distributing information and more on creating meaning from information?

Leaders have hectic schedules and competing priorities. It is very easy to just pass along facts. As a result, many leaders sacrifice meaning and instead send along information without context. These leaders simply become conduits (upward and downward) through which information passes. Leaders, their bosses, and their employees need more than facts to make good decisions. Leaders should use their business understanding to add the context and perspective that can make information meaningful. It might take a bit longer up front to provide this, but on the back end, it will save time. Leaders who simply pass along information create a bottleneck.

Leaders often value the apparent efficiency of multitasking. Yet the research presented in this chapter shows that it is more likely to cause productivity losses than gains. The key is to use selective attention to your advantage, rather than letting it take advantage of you.

NOTES

1. Timothy Wilson, *Strangers to Ourselves: Discovering the Adaptive Unconscious* (Cambridge, MA: Belknap Press of Harvard University, 2002), p. 24.

2. George Johnson, "Sleights of Mind," *New York Times* Science Section, August 21, 2007, http://www.nytimes.com/2007/08/21/science/21magic.html?_r=1 (accessed October 16, 2008).

3. Brandon Keim, "Magic Tricks Reveal Inner Workings of the Brain," July 23, 2008, http://blog.wired.com/wiredscience/2008/07/the-science-of.html (accessed September 12, 2008).

4. Daniel J. Simons and Daniel T. Levin, "Failure to Detect Changes to People during a Real-World Interaction," *Psychonomic Bulletin and Review* 5 (1998): 644–49.

5. Joel Cooper, Frank Drews, and David Strayer, "What Do Drivers Fail to See When Conversing on a Cell Phone?" (proceedings of the 48th Human Factors and Ergonomics Society Annual Meeting, New Orleans, LA, September 20–24, 2004): pp. 2213–17.

6. John Medina, *Brain Rules: 12 Principles for Surviving and Thriving at Work, Home, and School* (Seattle: Pear Press, 2008), p. 84.

7. Medina, *Brain Rules*, pp. 84–88.

8. Sydney Finkelstein, *Why Smart Executives Fail: And What You Can Learn from their Mistakes* (New York: Penguin Portfolio Trade, 2003).

9. Ibid., p. 194.

10. Ibid., p. 196.

11. Claudia Wallis, "The Multitasking Generation," *Time*, March 19, 2006. http://www.time.com/time/magazine/article/0,9171,1174696-1,00.html (accessed August 14, 2009).

Chapter 20

ARE YOU TRAPPED IN A WORRY CIRCUIT?

WHAT'S THE STORY?

In *Never Good Enough*, therapist Monica Ramirez Basco describes a woman who exhausted herself trying to maintain a perfect home.[1] This perfectionist housewife eventually realized that her high standards were not reasonable. For example, her husband and kids didn't care if the sheets were ironed. In fact, down deep *she* didn't even care if the sheets were ironed. Yet she found it difficult to change her behaviors because the very thought of lowering her standards made her anxious.

Anxiety is a powerful motivator. To avoid anxiety, we will turn down a promotion that would require us to do some public speaking. We will fail to confront an employee about his tardiness because the thought of conflict makes our heart pound. Sometimes, we will walk up twenty flights of stairs because elevators make us nervous. If we discover that our anxiety can be relieved by organizing our cereal boxes alphabetically or by endlessly reworking a report, then we'll be inclined to carry out those actions. For many people, it feels nearly impossible to resist such impulses. This leaves them at the mercy of their own fears. The feeling of anxiety acts as a trigger that sets off a circuit of reactions, a "worry circuit," that some people can neither control nor resist.

It turns out that the idea of a worry circuit is more than a metaphor. Jeffrey Schwartz, a research professor of psychiatry at the University of

California, Los Angeles, School of Medicine, works with people diagnosed with *obsessive-compulsive disorder*, or OCD. People with OCD are plagued with obsessive, unwanted thoughts. They may continually fear that they left the door unlocked even after they have repeatedly checked. Or they feel compelled to repeat certain actions, such as washing their hands or counting the number of stoplights they pass on the way to work.

Brain scans of these patients reveal heightened activity in the *orbital frontal cortex*, a part of the brain that resides behind our eyes, folded under the front of our cortex. Research with rhesus monkeys shows that this part of the monkey brain reacts when something seems out of whack.[2] For example, one study showed that orbital frontal neurons fired rapidly when the researchers substituted salt water for the black currant juice that the monkeys had come to expect.[3] The orbital frontal cortex helps us recognize when something that is emotionally significant is not as it should be. This led Schwartz to believe that perhaps this part of the brain was malfunctioning in people with OCD, causing them to *wrongly* feel that things were out of kilter. As he puts it, "The result is like a computer's spell-check run amok, highlighting every word in a document."[4]

To test his hypothesis, Schwartz studied the brain scans of people with OCD; he observed activity in the orbital frontal cortex, but also in other areas. Consequently, he dubbed the set of brain networks that were active in OCD patients "the worry circuit." When patients with OCD were exposed to something that triggered their anxiety, such as a dirty towel being placed near them, their brain scans showed that the worry circuit was consistently activated. The bright colors of the brain scan signified brain activity associated with high anxiety. This anxiety drove rituals—excessive hand washing, counting stoplights, and so on—as patients attempted to calm themselves. For Schwartz, the burning question was whether it was possible to change this neural circuitry. Could we somehow derail the pattern in the brain that, like a broken record, repeats the same groove over and over again?

Schwartz took the unusual action of showing his patients their own brain scans so that they could see their worry circuits in action. He explained that their fears, such as the fear that the door might be unlocked, are feelings created by the brain that represent *inaccurate* error messages. He encouraged them to respond to the phony messages with "mindful awareness," assuming an inquisitive but accepting attitude toward what their brain was doing. They might tell themselves something like: "Oh, there goes my brain again, telling me to worry about whether or not I've locked the door. What is that message making me feel? Does the feeling make sense? Do I really think the door is unlocked?" Using mindfulness allowed people with OCD to relabel their experience: "What I'm experiencing is not a reasonable caution reminding me to check the door. What I'm experiencing is not even *me*. It's a brain glitch—a false message from my brain." Individuals suffering from OCD could then use these thoughts to trigger more adaptive thoughts and behaviors.

The therapy that Dr. Schwartz offered his patients is more complicated than this brief description conveys, and it is described in more detail in his books.[5] Schwartz's patients improved significantly. Moreover, brain scans before and after treatment showed that the OCD worry circuit itself had been altered. The worry circuit was still triggered by objects like a dirty rag, but as soon as patients reminded themselves that these anxious feelings were just a brain glitch, their thoughts activated a different set of neurons. The worry circuit was interrupted and a more adaptive cycle of responses was established —both neurologically and behaviorally. As Schwartz concludes, something "as insubstantial as a thought" can change the very circuitry of our own brains.[6]

INTERESTING, BUT SO WHAT?

HOW CAN I USE THIS INFORMATION AS A BUSINESS LEADER?

The stock market plummeted during the 2008 economic meltdown, triggering government bailouts of mortgage and automotive companies. Some investors became hypervigilant in response to their anxiety about these events. They tuned in to CNN with their first cup of coffee and compulsively checked market updates on the Internet throughout the day. From the perspective of how the brain works, these reactions only escalated their anxiety. These people were digging the groove of the worry circuit deeper with every minute that they stayed glued to the news' market reports. Even positive reports failed to relieve the chronic fear about what might happen next.

Leaders in industries affected by hard economic times cannot help but react with their own anxiety about the future. But they can borrow a neuroscience lesson from Dr. Schwartz's work to help them manage their own fears and guide others to do the same.

1. Leaders should notice what is triggering their anxiety. Is it a news report about the economy as a whole? A vague rumor about possible layoffs in the company? Or a clear directive to cut budgets? Leaders can notice if these events send their own thoughts spiraling from concern to anxiety, perhaps even to absolute panic. Does their stress trigger undesirable reactions, such as having an outburst in front of employees? Like Dr. Schwartz's patients, leaders who feel escalating anxiety can tell themselves, "This feeling is being created by my brain. It's not me. It doesn't necessarily represent the reality of the situation. It doesn't even necessarily reflect my own thoughts accurately, and it may be contrary to my intentions. Let me step back from this, take an interest in what my brain is telling me, and explore it further instead of letting this fear and anxiety dominate me unchallenged."

2. During that further exploration, leaders can ask themselves a variety of questions:

   • To what extent is my brain exaggerating the degree of fear that this situation warrants? How much of the fear is based more on the worst-case scenario for what the future might hold, rather than on what is really happening right now?
   • To the extent that my brain *is* sending me *accurate* messages about the present state of affairs, which of these fear alerts involve factors that I can control or influence? Which involve factors that I have no control over?

Based on their answers to these questions, leaders can reprogram their brains. For example, instead of excessively worrying over situations over which they have no control, a leader might think, "I have more important things to do than worry about what the European Union will do tomorrow. I can't do anything about that anyway. I'm going to turn my attention to something constructive. I am going to think about ways the company might delay some of its more expensive projects until we see how the dust settles."

A major benefit of this approach is that we can disrupt the worry circuit simply by stepping back to notice what our brain is telling us. When we ask ourselves questions about our experience, we interrupt the worry circuit. We don't deepen the groove by endlessly repeating a cycle of catastrophic thinking. Instead, we are doing what Schwartz's OCD patients did. We are using the worry itself as a trigger to shift to a different circuit—one that involves a more adaptive problem-solving cycle.

Leaders can also consider how to respond more constructively to the concerns of their employees. The worry circuit is not only an individual groove or a broken record in our own minds. It's contagious. Employees voice the same concerns over and over again at the coffee machine. This not only hurts productivity; it interferes with their work after they return to their desks. It is hard for people to give assignments their full attention when they are anxious.

Leaders can empathize with the fears that employees have. But at the same time, they can help employees notice that constant talk about worst-case scenarios only feeds those fears. As a first step, leaders need to reflect on their own fears and assess how valid they are. This will help them to identify which genuine fears they need to acknowledge. For example, leaders can tell employees that it is natural to be anxious when the future is uncertain. But once they have done that, leaders can emphasize more positive factors. For instance, they can let employees know what the company is doing to deal with the crisis. Leaders can also ask their team members to help keep panic at bay by not feeding into the cycle of cynical or hopeless thoughts. It may be a long time before people are able to view this tough time as an opportunity. But for the moment, leaders can shift the organizational worry circuit from worst-case scenarios to creative problem solving. They do this most effectively by identifying what employees can realistically do to address the situation, and then redirecting their attention to those tasks.

The insight that we can shift from deeply embedded circuits of fearful thoughts and compulsive behaviors to more adaptive cycles has an even broader application for business leaders. Neurally, activity patterns that are frequently repeated tend to occur faster and more easily. In well-practiced routines, information speeds faster through a neural network to trigger a behavioral response. This is what holds people with OCD so tightly in the grip of the well-worn worry circuit. It seems likely that this general principle applies not only to worry circuits but also to other habitual patterns like complaining.

Schwartz's experience with his patients shows that it is possible to use anxiety as a trigger to shift to a more adaptive and helpful circuit. Couldn't employees similarly use an event like "complaining" as a trigger to shift to a healthier circuit? And couldn't leaders find ways to intervene so that griping and blaming become the very cues that alert people that they need to do something different?

WHAT IF . . . ?

Most organizations have a number of broken records: the employee who repeatedly tells a tale of being victimized by others, the cynic whose rant becomes all too familiar, the blame game that one team predictably plays with another. It is not surprising that a leader's first instinct is to try to squelch this kind of negativity. Leaders manage to drive the annoying behavior underground. They no longer see it. But all too often, the complaining and cynicism continue when the leader is not present.

What if, instead, leaders use those negative behaviors as a signal to help people shift into a different circuit? Here are some typical broken records and ideas to shift the negative circuit to more constructive behaviors.

1. The Blame Game—"They"

"They are always messing up." "Why can't they communicate with us in a way that we can understand?" Phrases like these are often the opening volley in the blame game, in which it is "us versus them." Teams can learn to notice these phrases and say, "Okay, we're doing it again—we're playing the blame game." Then they can learn to use that realization to shift their thinking. For example, a team might find it helpful at that point to simply ask, "What can we do to make this better?"

2. THE VICTIM CYCLE—"YOU ALWAYS" AND "YOU NEVER"

"Always" and "never" are key words that often signal the victim cycle. When employees are in a victim cycle, they say things like "He never calls on me in a meeting" or "She always gets the best assignments." If individuals stuck in this cycle are motivated to change, they can learn to notice the "always" and "never," and react differently. For example, they might tell themselves, "There goes my brain again, seeing everything in black and white. Maybe there is more to it than that. Let me step back and think. I thought after we had lunch the other day my team leader would be sure to give me a good assignment at the next meeting, but she didn't. What do I need to do to have a better chance at those assignments?"

3. NOT TAKING RESPONSIBILITY— "IT'S POSSIBLE THAT MISTAKES WERE MADE."

One big red flag that people are failing to take responsibility is when they use the passive voice. That's why social psychologists Carol Tavris and Elliot Aronson named their book *Mistakes Were Made (But Not By Me)*.[7] The authors recount numerous evasions of responsibility. One of their examples is a statement that McDonald's issued as an apology to Hindus and other vegetarians for failing to let its customers know that McDonald's potatoes contained beef by-products. The statement said, "Mistakes were made in communicating to the public and customers about the ingredients in our French fries and hash browns."[8] Leaders can encourage people to notice when they are using the passive voice and challenge them to acknowledge their responsibility unequivocally.

4. INSTANT JUDGMENT—"WHAT AN IDIOT!" "HOW COULD THEY!"

When people are thinking (or saying) "What an idiot!" or "How stupid!" they can use these signs of frustration to go from furious to curious. In

Blind Spots: Why Smart People Do Dumb Things, psychologist Madeleine Van Hecke suggests that people try to notice when they are thinking that someone's actions are stupid or ridiculous.[9] Then they should try to go from furious to curious. What if people asked with genuine curiosity "Well, why would someone do that?" or "What might cause someone to believe that?" When people move away from labeling others as "stupid" or "idiotic," they are challenged to search for more insightful explanations.

Both leaders and their followers can get stuck in destructive ruts. People can repeatedly get caught up in fear, frustration, cynicism, and anger. By feeding into their fears and negative emotions, people reinforce their brain patterns and make it easier to become more fearful and angry in the future. The good news is that people can recognize the signs that negative circuits are being activated, and they can use those same signals as a reminder to choose a different, adaptive course.

NOTES

1. Monica Ramirez Basco, *Never Good Enough: How to Use Perfectionism to Your Advantage without Letting It Ruin Your Life* (New York: Touchstone, 2000).

2. E. T. Rolls, "The Orbitofrontal Cortex and Reward," *Cerebral Cortex* 10 (2000): 284–94.

3. S. J. Thorpe, E. T. Rolls, and S. Maddison, "The Orbitofrontal Cortex: Neuronal Activity in the Behaving Monkey," *Experimental Brain Research* 4 (1983): 93–115.

4. Jeffrey Schwartz and Sharon Begley, *The Mind and the Brain: Neuroplasticity and the Power of Mental Force* (New York: Harper Perennial, 2002), p. 65.

5. Ibid. See also, Jeffrey Schwartz and Beverly Beyette, *Brain Lock: Free Yourself from Obsessive-Compulsive Behavior* (New York: Harper Perennial, 1997).

6. Schwartz, *The Mind and Brain*, p. 90.

7. Carol Tavris and Elliot Aronson, *Mistakes Were Made (But Not by Me)* (New York: Harcourt, 2007).

8. Ibid., p. 1.

9. Madeleine Van Hecke, *Blind Spots: Why Smart People Do Dumb Things* (Amherst, NY: Prometheus Books, 2007).

Chapter 21

FIGHT, FLIGHT, OR FREEZE

WHAT'S THE STORY?

Twenty-five years ago Bernard Goetz, a thirty-seven-year-old, white, electrical engineer, was dubbed the New York City "subway vigilante" after he wounded four black teenagers who had accosted him on the train and demanded five dollars. His shots left one of the youths permanently paralyzed.

Goetz's actions were defended by some and denounced by others. At his trial, Goetz pled self-defense. In discussing this case, neurologist Richard Restak points out that the key legal question was whether Goetz's actions were those of "a reasonable person." The defense argued that they were, given Goetz's elevated level of fear. This fear was exacerbated by his experience of being mugged previously. The previous mugging was what led him to buy his .38-caliber Smith and Wesson in the first place.

The prosecution countered that while Goetz's initial shots may have been reasonable, his repeated firing after the danger had passed—even to the point of shooting two of his assailants in the back as they fled—was not an action reasonably called for in the situation.[1] According to this line of thinking, a reasonable person would have stopped shooting after the threat had subsided.

But would they? Richard Restak believes that "the reasonable person" test fails to take into account what we know today about the human brain. The part of the brain called the *limbic system* reacts when we are in peril. It includes a cluster of cells called the *amygdala*. The amygdala generates reactions of fear and rage. In normal circumstances it is regulated to some extent by the cortex—the more deliberative part of the brain. But in intense situations, the reactions of the amygdala can overwhelm the cortex and hijack our ability to act reasonably. "I'm convinced," Restak writes, "that no one acts reasonably when feeling threatened by death or severe bodily harm."[2]

Rather than acting reasonably, we react instinctively in one of three ways. Like Goetz, we may lash out and fight. At other times, we run for our lives to escape. These reactions constitute the famous "fight or flight" duo. But it turns out that the duo is really a trio, and sometimes—like a deer caught in the headlights—we freeze. In our initial reactions to a threat, we don't usually take the time to calculate which response would be to our best advantage; we react instinctively.

We act without thinking because of what happens in our brains when we notice danger. When light stimulates the cells in the retina of our eyes, it activates electrical impulses that travel through the optic nerve and on to the visual cortex of the brain. After the visual cortex registers those impulses, we can become consciously aware of what we see. But those impulses also take a second route that leads to the amygdala. This route, as Daniel Goleman notes, is "a smaller and shorter pathway—something like a neural back alley [that] allows the amygdala to receive some direct inputs from the senses and start a response before they are fully registered by the neocortex."[3] In other words, the amygdala can register danger and set off reactions to that danger before we are consciously aware of what we are doing. That's why we might immediately freeze at the sight of a snake, or something that looks a bit like a snake, before we fully realize what we have seen. In evolutionary terms, the ability of the amygdala to react faster than our conscious minds is a great advantage, but in daily life it can sometimes become a problem.

Once intense panic sets in, Restak maintains, it is unrealistic to expect that a person can calm down and behave rationally within a few minutes. In fact, "Once aroused, the limbic system can become a directive force for hours, sometimes days, and can rarely be shut off as if by flipping a switch. The heart keeps pounding; harsh and labored breathing burns in the throat; fear is replaced by anger and, finally, by murderous rage."[4] Given the physiology of fear, it may take a long time for reasonable people to regain rational control of their behavior. In this battle between rage and reason, the deliberation of the cerebral cortex can intervene, with effort, but sometimes rage wins.

However, what about less intense situations, ones that are emotional but not life threatening? What makes it possible for us to sometimes offset the natural reactions of the amygdala?

University of California, Los Angeles, neuropsychologist Matthew Lieberman thought that the key might be the ability to engage a different part of the brain. For example, surgeons don't have the reactions that most of us would have to the gory aspects of surgery, partly because their focus is on the demands of the job. They need to consider what they are seeing and make decisions. This kind of thinking engages the more rational part of the brain, the *prefrontal cortex*. Lieberman speculated that the reactions of the amygdala might be dampened if people had to do something that was cognitively demanding. Maybe something as simple as requiring them to make a judgment would increase activity in the prefrontal cortex and at the same time decrease activity in the amygdala.

To test this idea, Lieberman used a technique that other MRI studies have shown activates the amygdala. He showed research participants photos of people with different facial expressions, including fear and anger. As expected, the amygdala reacted when the person viewed the faces expressing emotion. But then Lieberman asked the participant to choose which of the two words below the photo—anger or fear, for example—best described the emotion being expressed. This cognitive task quieted the amygdala. In fact, the more active the prefrontal cortex

Figures 21.1 and 21.2. We react when we see facial expressions like these! But research using photographs of real people shows that we can dampen our emotional reactions.

was as participants made this judgment, the more the activity in the amygdala subsided.

No one is arguing here that it would have been easy for Bernard Goetz to gain control of his rage. But it might have helped if he had stopped to ask himself "What am I feeling?" when he had his gun aimed at the backs of his assailants. Certainly Lieberman's research suggests that when we are experiencing less intense emotions we might be able to quiet them by shifting to something as simple as giving that emotion a label. Like the patients with obsessive-compulsive disorder discussed in chapter 20, people were able to influence what was going on in their brain by directing their attention to something different.

One word of caution: research from neuroscientist Kevin Ochsner at Columbia University shows that activity in the prefrontal cortex can either subdue the amygdala—or galvanize it.[5] It depends on what we think about. For example, if we feel anxious about our upcoming sales presentation and we imagine terrible outcomes like "I'll probably lose my job if I flub this," the amygdala will react accordingly. But if we remind ourselves that we are taking many steps to ensure that our performance will be strong, the amygdala will quiet down.

INTERESTING, BUT SO WHAT?

HOW CAN I USE THIS INFORMATION AS A BUSINESS LEADER?

Unlike soldiers, firefighters, and paramedics who may have only moments to act, business leaders usually have more time to consider their decisions. In fact, leaders can often buy more time for themselves or their people because they are the ones who decide how urgent the situation is.

But despite the latitude that leaders have, they sometimes react as instinctively as Bernard Goetz and make poor decisions. It is likely that Andersen partner David Duncan's order to shred key Enron documents, a judgment that would ultimately bring the entire company down, was driven by panic. Intense fear can disrupt our ability to think rationally. The arousal of the amygdala can even disrupt memory, as anyone who has ever dialed 911 and then been unable to recall their own address can attest.

But even less intense emotions, like mild anxiety, frustration, and anger, can derail the prefrontal cortex. The prefrontal cortex is the executive part of the brain that normally does an excellent job analyzing information, deciding what to do, and creating workable plans—the very functions that leaders rely on to thrive. To keep the executive brain functioning optimally, leaders need to be able to manage their emotions. Indeed, emotional management is one of the key pillars of emotional intelligence that Goleman views as essential to effective leadership.[6] But how does one maintain "emotional management" during crisis situations?

The military designs training to help soldiers replace extreme emotions with calmer responses. Journalist Bob Drury describes an incident that occurred during his visit to Baghdad. After the telltale sound of a rocket launch propelled the soldiers into a bomb shelter, the men huddled there in the darkness. Drury shone a flashlight onto his own face and asked the men to describe what they saw. Drury's face was ghost white, exhibiting the instantaneous fear reaction that automatically occurs when we are under threat. Our bodies shuttle blood away from the face to other places where it might be more needed, such as to the muscles needed for fight or flight. But when Drury then pointed the flashlight toward one of the marines, the light revealed that the marine's face remained its normal color.

How is that possible? Part of the answer is in the body's adaptation to repeated exposures to threat. Training programs, such as those used for the navy's elite SEAL (Sea, Air, Land) corps, condition troops to overcome their natural fear of combat. As one SEAL explained, in practice exercises trainees "reach that level of fear where we think we're going to die, so when you do it for real, there's less fear. You go and do it just like you trained for it."[7]

Leaders don't want to train themselves to dampen the very survival mechanisms that might propel them out of the path of a moving car when they leave the office. But if marines and SEALs can stay cool in situations that pose a genuine threat to life and limb, shouldn't it be possible for business leaders to stay composed in situations that, though pressure-filled, are not nearly so dire? Research by both Lieberman and Ochsner suggests that leaders can train themselves to respond more calmly when they feel anxiety and anger. When a leader is angry with an employee who fails to complete a crucial assignment or anxious about meeting a key client, it might help to recognize the role of the brain in these reactions. Realizing that the amygdala is disrupting the executive functions of the prefrontal cortex, leaders can reclaim the authority of their thinking brain. By stepping back from their feelings and labeling them, or by reappraising the situation altogether, leaders can quiet the emotional response and move into a more rational mode.

Leaders can use a similar approach to enable their employees to regain emotional control as well. For example, let's say a team is panicking at an unanticipated glitch that appears to place the entire project at risk. What if the leader simply asks the team to start with a list of possible ways to address the problem? This step shifts the group from emotional reactions to engaging rational and thoughtful modes of their brains. Similarly, when a group is getting riled up over a disagreement, the leader could change the focus of the discussion. If the issue isn't pressing, the leader might say, "Let's put that in an idea bin for now" or "We can't really decide that today, so let's move forward and see what our common goal here is."

However, leaders need to be careful when they try to shift employees to a calmer state. Timing is important here, as anyone who has tried to calm an angry person knows. People need to feel that their concerns are being taken seriously. That sometimes means that they need time to vent instead of being prematurely urged to "calm down and talk about this rationally." If employees are frustrated, the leader's advice to calm down can make it seem as though their concerns are being trivialized. This is likely to *increase* their outrage. So leaders need to walk a fine line between redirecting emotional turmoil without appearing to make light of it.

WHAT IF . . . ?

1. WHAT IF LEADERS FOCUS ON BETTER MANAGING HOW THEY RESPOND TO THEIR EMPLOYEES?

Some leaders come across as being "outraged" at even the slightest error. Some actions *should* generate outrage—unethical behavior, lack of integrity, illegal behavior. Actions that lead to significant losses or hurt the business may also create outrage. But sometimes leaders invent or magnify the "hazard" and react disproportionately to its real damage.

For example, in one organization there was an extremely detail-oriented executive. He would comb through a twenty-five-page document and find every typo, inconsistent font, or inconsistent color. He did this even on rough drafts, before the content was final. Not only did he find the errors, but he made a big deal about them. People knew that a less-than-perfect presentation would generate outrage. They adapted their behavior. If they had an hour to work on a presentation, they would spend ten minutes on content and fifty minutes proofreading. The documents looked great, but most of them didn't say much.

Another intimidating behavior involves hoarding data. Sometimes leaders hold back information so that they can later use it as a weapon to argue against ideas they don't support. In other cases, leaders have disproportionate responses to honest mistakes or omissions. If missing a piece of data results in a reprimand, people will soon stop bringing ideas or recommendations to the table. Instead they'll regress to just providing simple facts and information. That's why it is so important for leaders to recognize how they respond to their employees by self-monitoring their brain activity and emotions.

2. WHAT IF LEADERS TRAIN THEMSELVES TO STAY CALMER?

What if leaders could identify the business situations that, for them, put the amygdala into high gear? Some of these would be common to many business leaders: dealing with a looming deadline, needing to fire an employee, writing a report for a particularly exacting board member, or giving a presentation to an audience with high expectations. Others might be more specific to particular individuals. But once they have identified their triggers, leaders can change their reactions to them.

Leaders can step back and label what they are experiencing, putting some distance between themselves and the intense emotions they are having. Alternatively, leaders can shift their attention to a task that engages the thinking mode of their brains, such as considering, "Should I deal with this now, or return to this problem later?"

Like the Navy SEALs, leaders may well need to *practice* shifting away from intense emotions and replacing them with a calmer response. One way that people do this is to use relaxation tapes or meditation to induce a tranquil state. Then they call to mind the situation that triggers anger or anxiety, so that they can practice remaining calm in the face of it. The idea is that eventually—like the Navy SEALs—they'll be able to experience the amygdala's signals of anxiety or anger unperturbed.

3. WHAT IF LEADERS HELP THEIR EMPLOYEES BETTER UNDERSTAND THE DIFFERENCE BETWEEN ACTUAL AND PERCEIVED HAZARDS?

Leaders who want their employees to remain composed can introduce training that helps employees manage their own emotions. Employees might imagine potential anxiety-inducing scenes, such as dealing with an irate client, and mentally rehearse staying calm and responding effectively. Although it seems simple, picturing the scene and practicing some possible opening replies can go a long way. These actions can enable employees to override their initial emotional reactions that disrupt thinking. Role-playing in a simulated experience is an even stronger means of accomplishing the same end. With enough practice, it's possible to maintain a calm response even while someone is screaming in your face. Like the SEALs, people can habituate to the threat and avoid shifting into high gear.

Leaders who are part of emotionally intense organizations, such as advertising agencies, may want to bring trainees into meetings that they wouldn't ordinarily attend. Normally leaders seek to include experienced people who can contribute to the outcome of a meeting. But in companies where people are often highly emotional, allowing trainees to get used to the fervor and outbursts can be very developmental. Like the SEALs trainees, the business or advertising trainees would experience live-fire environments so that they could get used to the emotional intensity in a low-risk situation.

4. WHAT IF LEADERS RECOGNIZE THAT THEY POSE A THREAT JUST BY THE NATURE OF THEIR STATUS?

The big job of the amygdala is to stay vigilant and detect threats in the environment. The threats that people in modern work environments face are subtler than being attacked by a cheetah on the savanna. For example, status is important to professionals. People want to be respected for their talents and intelligence, and they are therefore sensitive to their standing within the work group. It doesn't take much to inadvertently threaten someone's sense of status. David Rock, founder of the Neuroleadership Institute writes, "A status threat can occur through giving advice or instructions, or simply suggesting someone is slightly ineffective at a task. Many everyday conversations devolve into arguments driven by a status threat, a desire to not be perceived as less than another."[8] No wonder performance reviews are so threatening to many employees!

Just speaking to a person of higher status can trigger anxiety in employees. Simply because of their status, leaders can trigger anxiety even though they don't intend to do so. Sometimes all a leader needs to do is to innocently deviate from the norm. Maybe a leader merely sits in a different chair at a presentation because she is wearing a warm outfit and her normal chair is in the sun. But the presenter wonders, "Why is she doing that? She never sits there for other people's presentations." Or maybe a leader decides to shake things up a bit. At today's meeting, whenever someone makes a statement, he will challenge it by asking, "What is your basis for believing that?" His intention is to keep people on their toes, to get more energy flowing in the room—but the outcome might be that people freeze and become not only tongue-tied but also unable to think.

Such reactions remind leaders how easily anxiety can derail critical and creative thinking. The key is to be judicious in deciding when and where to trigger anxiety. As Rock notes, if a leader merely appears threatening (maybe simply because he or she is not smiling that day), "suddenly a whole meeting can appear threatening and the tendency can be to avoid taking risks."[9] Of course, the threat is much worse if the leader is verbally abusive or publicly critical.

Tiger Woods's dad would beat pots and pans while Tiger practiced shots so that he'd learn to ignore the distractions—including the distracting feelings of anger or frustration that might rise up inside himself. Like this world champion golfer, leaders who understand how our emotional brain can hijack our concentration and thinking will intentionally develop a set of skills to effectively manage their own emotions and those of their employees.

NOTES

1. Richard Restak, *The Brain Has a Mind of Its Own* (New York: Random House, 1991).

2. Ibid., p. 52.

3. Daniel Goleman, *Emotional Intelligence: Why It Can Matter More Than IQ*, (New York: Bantam Books, 2006), p. 18.

4. Restak, *The Brain Has a Mind of Its Own*, p. 56.

5. K. K. Ochsner and J. J. Gross, "The Cognitive Control of Emotion," *Trends in Cognitive Sciences* 9 (2005): 242–49.

6. Goleman, *Emotional Intelligence*.

7. Bob Drury, "Bravery and How to Master It," *Men's Health*, April 2008, p. 162.

8. David Rock, "SCARF: A Brain-Based Model for Collaborating with and Influencing Others," *Neuroleadership Journal* 1 (2008): 46–47.

9. Rock, "SCARF: A Brain-Based Model," p. 46.

Chapter 22

MEMORIES

The Way We Never Were?

WHAT'S THE STORY?

"When twenty-seven-year-old Henry M. entered the hospital in 1953 for radical brain surgery that was supposed to cure his epilepsy, he was hopeful that the procedure would change his life for the better. Instead, it trapped him in a mental time warp where TV is always a new invention and Truman is forever president."[1] This is how Yale University graduate student Joanna Schaffhausen describes the plight of Henry Molaison. Molaison, the most studied individual in brain research, was written up anonymously in countless case studies as "H. M." On December 2, 2008, Henry Molaison died at the age of eighty-two and his identity was finally revealed.

At the time of Molaison's surgery as a young man, he was experiencing ten or more *grand mal* epileptic seizures a week. His surgeon hoped that he could put an end to Henry's seizures by removing the sections of the brain that were the seizures' focal starting points. The segments removed included the front portion of both *temporal lobes*. The temporal lobes lie on the sides of the brain, roughly near each ear. Within this portion of the temporal lobe there is a structure that is now known to be crucial for memory—the *hippocampus*.

When Molaison came out of the surgery, most of his memories formed prior to the operation were intact. He did not have the kind of amnesia popular on soap operas, forgetting his name and his whole life up to that point. But Molaison's ability to learn new information changed drastically. Moments after a new doctor left the room, for example, he would forget that they had ever met. Molaison lived in a void. As he told his biographer, Philip Hilts, "You see, at this moment everything looks clear to me, but what happened just before? That's what worries me. It's like waking from a dream. I just don't remember."[2]

The repercussions of Molaison's memory loss were devastating. He couldn't work, form new friendships, or adapt to any change in his life. If his family were to move, for example, he would never be able to find his way home again because he would seek them at the old address. Years after his mother's death, Molaison would experience the same shock and grief when hearing that she was no longer alive as he had when first informed of her death.

Research with Henry Molaison and other neurological patients has taught us a great deal. Fortunately, current neurosurgical procedures include safeguards against disabling both temporal lobes and producing an amnesia like Molaison's. For example, surgeons now only remove tissue on one side and verify the health of tissue on the other side. Also, when performing surgery on patients with epilepsy, neurosurgeons routinely thread tiny electrodes into the region of the hippocampus or into any brain area they believe to be a focal point of the person's seizures. This enables the surgeon to verify exactly where epileptic brain activity first arises. They can then restrict the tissue removal to the smallest possible portion that will lead to a successful outcome.

In some cases, the electrodes are left in place for several days after surgery. This allows researchers to learn more about the brain. With the cooperation of patients at the University of California, Los Angeles, Israeli and American researchers took advantage of this opportunity to investigate how we form new memories.[3] On the basis of prior studies of patients with amnesia, and from animal studies, we know that hippocampal neurons play a key role in the initial storage of a memory. They also play a major role when the memory is recalled a short time later. The researchers observed this neuronal activity in recordings made from electrodes implanted in the hippocampus and nearby *entorhinal* cortex. Patients first viewed brief video clips, such as scenes from *Seinfeld* and *The Simpsons*. Over half of the neurons responded principally to one or more of the clips. The researchers discovered that those same cells were active again when the patients recalled the correlating clips. In fact, the connection was so specific that when a particular cell became active just before the person spoke, the researchers could predict, "Oh, now he's going to remember something about the *Seinfeld* video."

As Molaison's case and subsequent studies have shown, the hippocampus and adjacent cortical structures are critical for the formation of new memories. For these memories to endure, however, additional memory processing is required.[4] We store a vast repertoire of knowledge in multiple regions of the cortex, distant from the hippocampus itself. When we recall events, we're gathering memory impressions from these different regions—including some of the same areas that originally processed what we experienced. For example, when we go on a vacation, the layout of the hotel initially registers in parts of the brain that process spatial relationships. The face of the bartender who annoyed us registers in visual cells especially devoted to processing facial information. The beautiful song we heard may be stored in the auditory cortex. Our long-lasting memories of the hotel, the bartender, and the song will eventually be consolidated in a network of cortical neurons. A complicated process involving the hippocampus is required before our brains consolidate the memories, however. For example, there is a period of time when the hippocampus has to activate the various brain areas that hold these different memories—of the hotel, the bartender, and the song—so that we can remember the vacation as a whole rather than activating only disjointed fragments.

Remembering is not like viewing a film that we have stored in the brain. Instead, when we remember we are patching stored impressions together to form a cohesive recollection. We are, essentially, *reconstructing* what happened. This is important because it explains why our memories can sometimes prove so faulty.[5] We have all experienced the fallibility of memory. We might recall a hilarious family scene at Aunt Joan's house in which our goofy brother-in-law Scott decided to throw some popcorn kernels into the blazing fireplace. Everyone laughs at the memory, but then someone says, "That couldn't have been at Joan's. Joan's house didn't have a fireplace." And we all pause as we realize that somehow things have gotten distorted.

What has happened? Neuroscientists believe that our memories can go awry not only because we forget but also because our recollections are reworked each time we bring them to mind. If we tell a story about what happened at a McDonald's to a bunch of friends while we are sitting in a Burger King, there is a chance that the next time we tell that story, we may think it happened at the Burger King.

One of the biggest lessons of this research is that our memories of events are more fallible than we might realize. Indeed, merely *imagining* something can lead us to believe that it actually occurred. One method for generating false memories of this sort was used by neuroscientists Brian Gonsalves and Ken Paller.[6] In their experiment, people imagined various objects in their minds—a cauliflower or a briefcase, for example—visualizing numerous objects upon reading the corresponding object names. Now and then, they also saw actual photographs of some of the objects.[7] Later, participants listened to a list of words in a memory test, including the names of objects they had only visualized. For each object, they were asked whether they had seen a photograph of that object. Thirty percent of the time, they claimed to have seen it, when in reality they had only imagined it. Analyses of brain activity pointed to the source of these errors. Based on electroencephalographic, or EEG, recordings, the initial visualization was particularly vivid for objects that people later misremembered as having been seen and not just imagined.[8] Given this information about the brain and memory formation, we should be slower to assert that we *know* something happened because we remember it.

INTERESTING, BUT SO WHAT?

HOW CAN I USE THIS INFORMATION AS A BUSINESS LEADER?

Many people don't realize how pliable our memories are. In business, false memories can cause conflict. Imagine that a leader is at a bar having a drink with his team after concluding some tense negotiations. During the discussion, the team members realize that there was a point that they failed to mention during the negotiations. Everyone now recognizes that the team should have pushed for some action on this item. After discussing this a bit, the leader decides that the best the team can do is make sure to bring it up the following year. But by that time, the group remembers things differently. Members of the team recall that big sticking point—but they don't remember that the conversation about it occurred in a bar *after* the negotiations were over. Instead, they remember bringing it up *during* the discussions. Now they are mad that, for the past year, no one has done anything about the concern. They enter the new negotiations with ruffled feathers.

On a more individual level, leaders and subordinates sometimes disagree on the nature of assignments that were given. A leader gives an assignment and has a picture in his mind of the output that he hopes to receive. Maybe he imagines a particular type of report in a certain style with specific kinds of information—the kind of report that the leader would produce if he were doing it himself. The leader doesn't give detailed instructions about what he wants. But having earlier *imagined* exactly what he wanted, that leader may later feel sure that he conveyed

Figure 22.1. Did the boss really discuss the big promotion she sees in her mind? Maybe not. Research shows why we sometimes have false memories.

that information to the employee who received the assignment. Like the research participants who felt certain that they had actually seen a brief-case when in fact they had only imagined one, the leader will feel sure that he told the employee exactly what he wanted. The employee may remember the incident very differently.

Because memories are constructed, our brains can create false memories. There is also an upside to the fact that memories are constructed. Leaders can intentionally influence the collective memories of the organization in a positive way. As a simple example, many facilitators use flip charts to "construct the group memory." They often do this consciously. By structuring the charts to note "our ideas" rather than identifying the ideas of specific individuals, the facilitator reinforces the sense of a team working together. Later, as memories blend, members will say, "I can't remember exactly who said this but we came up this great idea . . ."

Memories, accurate or false, can impact the group and its culture. In fact, group memories take on a life of their own. They may begin with the recollections of old-timers in the organization. But as new hires hear these stories, they come to share memories of events that they never experienced firsthand. Sometimes, for example, a rather recent hire will comment that the culture of the company is not the way it used to be. Senior executives will nod in wise agreement. But the recent hire really has no knowledge of how things used to be—he was never there!

As the stories of the organization are told again and again, what starts out as a vague memory of an individual or small group becomes a hardened reality. An organization can also be misled by memories that are distorted or false. For example, a CEO institutes changes designed to get a company to return to its roots. She thinks the company has drifted from its initial vision and culture. She believes that if she can get people to recall "the real company" or "the way we used to be," it will "put heart back" into the organization. But what she remembers as "the real company" exists mainly in her constructed and elaborated memories. If those aren't accurate to begin with, the changes she makes won't put heart into the organization. She may well be remembering "the way we never were."

Finally, leaders can use stories to help guide employees. Books on how to improve memory often propose using stories as a mnemonic device.[9] This approach is based on the assumption that people remember stories more easily than they remember isolated facts. Annette Simmons, author of *The Story Factor*, believes that employees bring stories to mind when they are trying to decide what to do. She writes, "Most of the time, you won't be present when the people you want to influence make the decision, choose the behaviors you were hoping to influence, or both. . . . You cannot easily predict the specifics of the situation in which they might find themselves, so how do you get them to do what you want? Story is like the mental software that you supply so your listener can run it again later using new input specific to the situation."[10]

WHAT IF . . . ?

1. "JUST FOR THE RECORD"

Given the fallibility of our memories, leaders should make sure that someone takes a few minutes at the end of meetings to document what occurred. What major decisions were made? Who agreed to take responsibility for what, and by when? Who else should hear about that meeting and its outcomes? By reviewing these notes before the meeting ends leaders can ensure that consensus exists. Documentation also prevents later confusion and can help resolve differences.

Sometimes leaders make decisions during informal discussions. When these decisions are significant, leaders should keep track of them. For example, a decision is made in a leadership meeting. The next day, having coffee with a vice president, the leader adds something to that decision. Those memories blend. So later the leader erroneously believes that he made this addition during the leadership meeting itself. Later, he can't understand why the team claims to know nothing about it and hasn't acted upon it.

Keeping track of decisions can also help leaders identify success factors for the next project. A leader who negotiates a successful merger, for example, could create a file called "Next time I negotiate a merger . . ." In the same way, managers who are responsible for planning annual meetings will save a lot of time in subsequent years if there are organized notes on what worked well and what was problematic. It's easy to forget the details involved in events that only happen once a year. Documentation of success factors can really help in these situations.

Leaders sometimes hear information long before the time comes to inform employees of the news. For example, leaders may repeatedly hear about a proposed change during various executive meetings. Over time, the information becomes familiar to them. The leader might have the passing thought, "Oh, I'd better tell my team about this." If he pictured himself informing the team, he might later have a false memory that he actually did inform them. As a result, when he finally does tell the team about the change, he may be surprised at people's reaction. "What's the big deal?" he asks. "Why are you so upset about this? We've been talking about it for months." But in reality, the team is hearing about it for the first time. The leader has had months to get used to the idea, while the team feels blindsided.

2. WHAT IF LEADERS INTENTIONALLY USE STORYTELLING TO COMMUNICATE WITH EMPLOYEES?

For the sake of efficiency, leaders summarize and condense information. But it is hard to convey information meaningfully when it is reduced to a bullet point. A leader may believe that, "I told them to make customer service a priority!" because it was the lead bullet point in her PowerPoint presentation. But without stories to translate those bullet points into memorable images, employees may fail to remember them and apply them.

What if leaders look at their bulleted lists and ask themselves, "What story could I tell that would really make this point in a vivid way?" In his book, *What's Your Story?* Craig Wortmann describes many examples of leaders doing just that.[11] One leader was addressing three hundred employees, fifty of whom were part of a newly acquired organization. He wanted to make the point that the parent company encouraged collabo-ration. As Wortmann notes, that leader could have put a phrase like "We value working collaboratively" on a slide.[12] Instead, he told the story of a previous merger situation. The company had sacrificed this previous merger, even though it would have been financially lucrative, because the target organization did not value collaboration. This made the point more powerfully than a bullet point ever could.

Wortmann, former CEO of Wisdom Tools, a company that develops story-based training for corporations, believes that people need stories to hold information together. In fact, he argues, they need stories to hold the organization itself together. Wortmann sees stories as one of the natural resources of an organization. Leaders can use stories to ignite performance, communicate values, and connect more authentically to employees. In *What's Your Story?*, Wortmann offers a matrix system for recalling and organizing stories. In this system, leaders categorize stories according to type of story, such as success and failure stories. These are listed on one axis of the matrix, while the other axis lists different areas, such as teamwork. For example, imagine that the leader has a powerful story about a time when a client became an investor in the company. This is a success story; if that success occurred because of teamwork, the leader would summarize the story in the segment of the matrix where success and teamwork cross. Leaders can use this system to recall the right story for different circumstances.

3. COULD IMAGINING WHAT IS POSSIBLE HELP PEOPLE SEE THAT THEY ARE ALREADY ACHIEVING IT?

Most leaders are familiar with the idea that the first step to achieving a vision is to begin by imagining it. As people picture the kind of product they want to invent or the kind of organization they want to become, they begin to move toward that image. The memory research described earlier shows that we can believe that we have already experienced something that we have only imagined. This raises an interesting possibility. Maybe leaders who communicate a vivid picture of what they are striving for might create a memory of already being well on the way.

The point is not for leaders to try to create false memories of accomplishments that have not occurred. The point is that leaders who paint a vibrant picture of the vision can then point to the small ways in which it is already here. This helps people see that the vision isn't a pipe dream. In this way, leaders can use constructed memories to show that the vision is an achievable dream. The organization is already on its way.

Once business leaders recognize the importance of memories—how they're made, how they can change, and how they can influence an organization—leaders can communicate more effectively and craft first-rate change management plans, and thereby create a more effective means of operation.

NOTES

1. Joanna Schaffhausen, "The Day His World Stood Still," *Brain Connection*, http://www.brainconnection.com/topics/?main=fa/hm-memory (accessed January 3, 2009).

2. Philip Hilts, *Memory's Ghost: The Strange Tale of Mr. M. and the Nature of Memory* (New York: Touchstone, 1996).

3. Hagar Gelbard-Sagiv et al., "Internally Generated Reactivation of Single Neurons in Human Hippocampus during Free Recall," *Science* 3 (2008): 96–101.

4. K. A. Paller, "Memory Consolidation: Systems," in *Encyclopedia of Neuroscience*, ed. L.R. Squire (Oxford: Academic Press, 2009), pp. 741–49.

5. D. L. Schacter, K. A. Norman, and W. Koutstaal, "The Cognitive Neuroscience of Constructive Memory," *Annual Review of Psychology* 49 (1998): 289–318.

6. Brian Gonsalves and Ken A. Paller, "Mistaken Memories: Remembering Events That Never Happened," *Neuroscientist* 8 (2002): 391–395.

7. You can get a sense of what these participants experienced by taking a similar memory test yourself at Ken Paller's Web site, http:/www.northwestern.edu/people/kap (accessed March 27, 2009).

8. Brian Gonsalves and Ken A. Paller, "Neural Events That Underlie Remembering Something That Never Happened," *Nature Neuroscience* 3 (2000): 1316–21.

9. Kenneth Higbee, *Your Memory: How It Works and How to Improve It* (New York: DaCapo Press, 2001).

10. Annette Simmons, *The Story Factor* (New York: Basic Books, 2006), p. 41.

11. Craig Wortmann, *What's Your Story? Using Stories to Ignite Performance and Be More Successful* (New York: Kaplan Publishing, 2006).

12. Ibid.

Chapter 23

WHAT DOESN'T KILL YOU WILL MAKE YOU STRONGER?

WHAT'S THE STORY?

Between 1980 and 1988, twenty-eight thousand workers in a Boston shipyard were exposed to low levels of radiation as they handled toxic materials. Other workers in the same shipyard—some thirty-two thousand of them—never touched the toxic materials. The potential harm to the exposed workers was disturbing. But the situation also created a perfect opportunity to assess the long-term effects of low-dose radiation on workers' health. The US Department of Energy carried out this study by comparing the health histories of the two groups.

Did the Department of Energy find differences between the two sets of workers? You bet they did. But amazingly, what they discovered was that the *exposed* workers were healthier, enjoying a 24 percent lower mortality rate than the nonexposed workers. Harvard Medical School psychiatrist John Ratey, who describes this research in his book *Spark*, writes, "Somehow the toxins that everyone feared were ruining the workers' health were doing just the opposite."[1] In high levels, radiation damages healthy cells and stimulates the growth of cancerous cells. But in low doses, these toxins apparently strengthened the workers.

How is this possible? The answer lies in the notion that the cells in our bodies can become more robust when they are mildly stressed. This "stress inoculation" idea underlies the theory called *hormesis*. Biologist

Mark Mattson describes hormesis as a process where "organisms exposed to low levels of stress or toxins become more resistant to tougher challenges."[2] Mattson, who is also a professor of neuroscience at Johns Hopkins University, points out that some chemicals that are carcinogenic in high doses can impede the growth of cancer cells when taken in low doses.

In the brain, there are also substances that are toxic in high doses but helpful in low doses. *Glutamate*, a chemical that is understood to aid in the learning process, is one of these. Glutamate mediates communication between neurons. It also plays a role in promoting neuronal growth. At high levels, glutamate is extremely toxic—it destroys brain cells. But the small amounts of glutamate released when we learn something are beneficial. Why? Because the small amounts trigger cells to repair themselves. It is important to note, however, that this beneficial effect occurs only when the brain cells have time to recover from the small doses.

So what about stress? Could stress be either helpful or toxic depending on the "dose"? The answer is yes. Short-term stress can sometimes be adaptive. It gives us the kind of adrenaline surge that once helped our ancestors escape from a lion pounding across the savanna. That's the message of Stanford University neuroscientist Robert Sapolsky's witty book *Why Zebras Don't Get Ulcers*.[3] But as Sapolsky also points out, few stressors in today's world last only minutes. The stress reaction that once helped save our lives can shorten them when it occurs continuously. That is why so many authors who write about stress emphasize the term "chronic." If stress hormones are released repeatedly over a long period of time, our bodies and minds become damaged.

You may have heard of the stress hormone called *cortisol*. In addition to contributing to poor overall health, cortisol can harm thinking and learning. "If you put a neuron in a Petri dish and flood it with cortisol," John Ratey of Harvard Medical School tells us, "its vital connections to other cells retract. Fewer synapses develop and the dendrites wither."[4] John Medina, author of *Brain Rules*, agrees that stress hormones disconnect the neural networks most involved in learning and memory. Indeed, "they can stop the hippocampus from giving birth to brand-new baby neurons. Under extreme conditions, they can even kill hippocampal cells. Quite literally, severe stress can cause brain damage in the very tissues most likely to help your children pass their SATs."[5] So, stress doesn't reduce productivity just because it distracts us (as conventional wisdom says). It literally destroys connections in the brain.

Even when stress doesn't have such extreme effects, it impairs cognitive abilities. Medina summarizes research showing that when we are under stress, we don't solve math problems well or process language efficiently. Stress also interferes with learning. In one study, adults who experienced chronically high levels of stress performed substantially more poorly on cognitive tests when compared with adults who had low stress levels.[6]

There is a two-pronged neuroscience lesson in these findings. The first is the familiar lesson above that unremitting stress is undoubtedly damaging. But as biologist Mark Mattson writes, "There has perhaps been too much emphasis on the unhealthy aspects of stress, on the assumption that all types of stress are bad."[7] The second lesson is the more positive message that, "depending upon its quantity and duration, stress can improve the length and quality of life."[8] Mattson believes that we can enhance our brain functioning by engaging in activities that demand thinking and new learning. This works well, as long as we leave time for "recovery" from the glutamate that learning activates. "Intellectually challenging occupations," Mattson asserts, "reduce your risk of developing neurodegenerative diseases [such as Alzheimer's] because of the beneficial stress imposed on active neurons."[9] Whether neurodegenerative diseases can actually be avoided in this manner is unclear. But as Mattson points out, intellectual challenges increase the number of connections among brain cells and enhance their information-processing capacity.

INTERESTING, BUT SO WHAT?

HOW CAN I USE THIS INFORMATION AS A BUSINESS LEADER?

As numerous business articles have recounted, the price tag of chronic stress is high. It includes healthcare costs associated with stress-related disorders and the costs of hiring and retraining that result from the firing or resigning of unproductive employees.

It is harder to measure the negative impact that stress has on learning, memory, and problem solving in the business setting. But it is likely that businesses pay a toll for these consequences as well. It is also likely that the fast pace of today's business world exacerbates the stress that leaders and employees face each day.

Decades ago, psychologists Thomas Holmes and Richard Rahe developed a stress scale that assigned a number of "stress points" to different life events.[10] More stressful events received more points. A divorce, for example, scored seventy-three points, while getting a traffic ticket received only eleven. People could review the list, check off the events that had happened to them in the past year, and add up the resulting points. Holmes's initial research showed that this measure of stress predicted the likelihood that a person would get a stress-related illness in the future.

What surprised some people was that the list included not only negative events, such as getting fired (forty-seven points) but positive events, such as getting married (fifty points). Why? Holmes argued that all change, whether positive or negative, involves adaptation, and adapting can be stressful. If you have to adjust too quickly to changes, such as increased responsibilities associated with a promotion, stress will escalate even if you have been coveting that spot for years. Similarly, when an entire organization has to adapt to change, stress will be one of the by-products, even if the changes themselves are positive and successfully implemented.

It is particularly stressful to be in circumstances where we have little or no control over the situation that is stressing us. This can lead to a feeling of *learned helplessness*. In early studies of learned helplessness, dogs would hear a buzzer that meant an electric shock would come through the grid they were standing on. They were unable to escape the shocks. Later in the experiment, the barrier in the cage was lowered so that the dogs could easily escape the shock by jumping out when they heard the buzzer. But they didn't move. Having learned that there was nothing they could do, they continued to act as if they were helpless. Animal studies like this one are no longer conducted because current ethical standards prohibit such cruelty. But this research spurred psychological studies of learned helplessness in people—research that revealed that people, too, can become helpless when they are unable to control negative events in their lives.[11] If employees are put into situations over which they have little control, yet are held accountable for the consequences nonetheless, these employees might experience learned helplessness. Seeing themselves as helpless victims, these employees may be unable to help themselves even in controllable situations.

Given the relationship between lack of control and stress, business guru W. Edwards Deming's classic observations about how employees feel caught in the middle are important.[12] One of Deming's most significant contributions was to point out how often employees are blamed for problems that are really caused by a system glitch. A simple example is a situation in which line supervisors were blamed whenever a product failed to meet inspection standards. This problem occurred only when certain vendors were used to supply the raw materials. Yet those same supervisors were required by the chief financial officer to contract with the cheapest vendors, which resulted in poor-quality raw materials.[13] When managers feel caught in the middle of situations in which they are held responsible but cannot control the factors that determine success, their stress will escalate.

On the other hand, leaders can create "beneficial" stress experiences by managing the pace of change and new learning. Every time leaders decide to stretch themselves by taking on new challenges or encourage their followers to do the same, they are promoting new learning. Brain cells can benefit from that new learning as long as they have sufficient "recovery time." Leaders can successfully factor in recovery time when they control the pace of employee training experiences. When employees are immersed in learning-intensive situations that leave little downtime, they may find themselves "in over their heads." There is simply too much that is new, too little time to absorb it, and too little time to recuperate from the stress involved. In that case, the challenge undermines people's resiliency rather than strengthening it. Leaders who are aware of how stress can impact their employees, both positively and negatively, are in a better position to manage the degree of stress that employees experience. In this way, they can reduce the odds that stress will impair performance and productivity.

WHAT IF . . . ?

1. WHAT IF LEADERS MANAGE THE DEGREE OR "DOSE" OF STRESS THAT EMPLOYEES EXPERIENCE?

What if leaders proactively manage stress in the same way that they allocate money or time in their departments? This would mean taking people's level of stress into account when assigning tasks. For example, leaders might go easy on people who are just coming off highly stressful assignments. Keeping tabs on stress levels can be as simple as asking "How is your workload right now?" or "Is there anything work-related that's keeping you up at night?"

The goal is to become more sensitive to individual employee's stress points. The same assignment that puts one person over the top could be a welcome challenge to another. Psychiatrist Edward Hallowell in his article on "overloaded circuits" advises leaders to monitor the degree to which they challenge employees to move out of their comfort zones.[14] When people take on tasks that don't lie within their areas of strength or their natural talents, they will be stressed. They'll have the anxiety of doing an unfamiliar task. They will also have the cognitive load of learning something new. People do best with low doses of challenge, repeated periodically, and with sufficient bounce-back time in between.

2. WHAT IF LEADERS IDENTIFY AND ELIMINATE THE CHRONIC SOURCES OF STRESS CAUSED BY LACK OF CONTROL?

As the following examples illustrate, it is very stressful to be responsible for an outcome in situations where we can't control the results. This means that increasing our control or aligning responsibility with the elements that we *can* control will reduce stress. Leaders can often influence these factors.

- "My big mistake," one professional said, "was taking a job where I had to report to two different people, both of whom had an equal say in what I was supposed to be doing. What a nightmare! When they didn't agree, I was caught in the middle and there was no way to satisfy both of them. Eventually, I just quit."

- "What's driving me crazy is that I am responsible for containing costs. But two of the people who purchase supplies have seniority over me, and I can't control what they do. So I am consistently over budget, blamed for something I can't do anything about!"

Leaders can identify which people or departments experience chronic stress. Then they can examine whether lack of control is contributing to that stress. Maybe members of one department feel in danger of failing to meet deadlines because they have to rely on information or resources from a different department. Maybe one executive feels stymied because her proposals are applauded by the board but then underfunded.

Here are some key questions leaders can ask their team members to assess the extent to which they feel responsible for factors beyond their control.

- How many different masters do you have to please in carrying out this assignment?

  With the advent of matrix organizations, many people are in situations where they have more than one "boss." Maybe a number of people have to sign off on a proposal or design. Maybe several people are depending on the success of a presentation or project. If the expectations of some of these individuals clash with the desires of others, the employee is placed in a difficult position.

- How much does the success of your work depend on the quality of what others do?

  Often the success of a project depends on at least two different people or teams. Maybe one team provides an initial cost estimate, while another comes up with the project design. Leaders can look at the handoffs between teams to see if one team feels its work is hampered by the performance of other teams.

- To what extent are you trying to do your job in the dark?

  In some organizations in which people work independently, an atmosphere of distrust can evolve, which leads them to be not only isolated but also secretive and suspicious. Little information is exchanged. Sometimes leaders will similarly withhold information from employees. They may do this to avoid triggering stress. Yet the more information that leaders provide, the more employees will feel in control of what is happening—this decreases their stress. This is an area where what leaders do can have an immediate and significant impact on the stress that people experience.

- What are the odds that you will be held responsible for a slipup that is caused by factors outside your control?

  Leaders are in a position to recognize when factors are truly out of the control of an individual or department. They need to ensure that people will not be held responsible for those elements. Even more important, leaders who recognize that there is a failure in the system can work toward changing that system. This will benefit the organization as a whole as well as relieve frustration and stress.

  Sometimes the work environment is inherently unpredictable. Hospital emergency rooms are a prime example of an intrinsically unpredictable environment. An ER can change from nearly empty to overflowing in a matter of minutes. Leaders who realize that their employees experience diminished control because of unpredictable factors can decrease stress by openly acknowledging that the employees are doing the best they can. In this way, employees won't feel unjustly blamed.

3. WHAT IF LEADERS ALIGN PEOPLE'S ACCOUNTABILITY, CONTROL, AND AUTHORITY?

In one company, salespeople's goals included product quality. Yet the salespeople had no control over any aspect of the production process. To reduce their perceived risk, the salespeople attempted to assert some control. They began micromanaging those who did have control over product quality—the production managers. This prevented the production managers from fully focusing on their jobs. Sometimes the salespeople would go around the production managers and talk directly to the production managers' supervisors and employees. By giving the salespeople a goal over which they had no control, the organization increased their stress and perception of risk. The result was dysfunctional behavior and performance.

What should leaders do? It is clear that leaders should align people's accountability, control, and authority. But this is easier said than done. In too many cases, there is shared accountability. The problem is that the lines of responsibility within that shared area are not clear. Leaders should not hold people accountable for what is produced by resources that are outside of their control. At times, some simple clarification of the lines of responsibility or reassignment of tasks can solve this problem.

4. WHAT IF LEADERS MONITOR THEIR EXPECTATIONS?

Leaders can also manage stress by placing reasonable expectations on their people. As Deming pointed out, leaders should anticipate a certain amount of natural variation in results. Not every new addition to a product line will be a hit. The training program won't reach every employee to the same degree or at the same speed. The ad that results in top sales in October might have a much lower impact in June. Leaders should remember that some of this variability is statistically predictable and unavoidable.

This doesn't mean that leaders can't push for improvement. Developing scorecards and challenging people to improve on their monthly metrics is one way to do this. But what leaders won't do, if they understand statistical variability, is choose the top performer—the hit product, the group that mastered the training the fastest, or the highest sales month—and ask, "Why can't you do that all the time?" This demand is not only unrealistic, it is statistically unachievable. It once again places managers in a situation where they are responsible for producing results that are not under their control—a sure recipe for stress.

NOTES

1. John J. Ratey and Eric Hagerman, *Spark: The Revolutionary New Science of Exercise and the Brain* (Boston: Little, Brown, and Company, 2008), p. 61.

2. Mark Mattson and Edward Calabrese, "Best in Small Doses," *New Scientist* 199, no. 2668 (2008): 36–39.

3. Robert Sapolsky, *Why Zebras Don't Get Ulcers* (New York: W. H. Freeman/Owl Books, 2004), p. 262.

4. Ratey, *Spark*, p. 125.

5. John Medina, *Brain Rules: 12 Principles for Surviving and Thriving at Work, Home, and School* (Seattle: Pear Press, 2008), p. 179.

6. Diane Coutu, "The Science of Thinking Smarter: A Conversation with Brain Expert John Medina," *Harvard Business Review* (May 2008): 1–4.

7. Mattson and Calabrese, "Best in Small Doses," p. 39.

8. Ibid.

9. Ibid.

10. Thomas Holmes and Richard Rahe, "Holmes-Rahe Life Changes Scale," *Journal of Psychosomatic Research* 11 (1967): 213–18.

11. Christopher Peterson, Steven F. Maier, and Martin E. P. Seligman, *Learned Helplessness: A Theory for the Age of Personal Control* (New York: Oxford University Press, 1995).

12. W. Edwards Deming, *Out of the Crisis* (Cambridge, MA: Massachusetts Institute of Technology, 1986).

13. Joseph R. Jablonski, *Implementing TQM*, 2nd ed. (Hoboken, NJ: Pfeiffer Wiley, 1993).

14. Edward Hallowell, "Overloaded Circuits: Why Smart People Underperform," *Harvard Business Review* (January 2005): 1–9.

Chapter 24

CAN WORKING LESS GENERATE MORE?

WHAT'S THE STORY?

Why did students in the elite Chicago suburb of Naperville have heart rate monitors before they had the Internet?

In 1990, physical education instructor Phil Lawler was sipping coffee and reading a newspaper article about the declining health of kids in the United States. Children in public schools in Illinois have physical education class daily. So Lawler's reaction to the article was, as he put it, "We have these kids everyday; shouldn't we be able to affect their health? If this is our business, I thought, we're going bankrupt."

The story of what happened next in Naperville School District 203 is the opening vignette in John Ratey's book *Spark: The Revolutionary New Science of Exercise and the Brain.*[1] Ratey, an associate clinical professor of psychiatry at Harvard Medical School, describes how Lawler tested, "a new-fangled heart monitor." Lawler tried the monitor out on a thin, nonathletic, sixth-grade girl who seemed to be dragging as she slogged around the field. Ordinarily Lawler might have pushed her to speed up. But when he checked her heart monitor at the end of her run, he was shocked to see that her average rate was 187—and 209 is the theoretical maximum heart rate for an eleven-year-old! Lawler recognized that this apparently sluggish child was working harder than his top athletes.

Lawler's realization led to many changes in the District 203 physical education program. In the new program, every student engaged in aerobic exercise. But students would no longer be graded on their speed or skill. Now, their grade would depend on their ability to keep their heart rates within their target zones. Today, at a time when 30 percent of students in the United States are overweight, only 3 percent are overweight in District 203. Of course, there are other factors that contribute to weight issues. But surely the exercise program in District 203 has helped the thousands of students who have participated over the years to stay more fit.

As it also turned out, the students' exercise helped their brains as well as their bodies. The aerobic exercise classes were introduced gradually into the school system. This gave researchers an opportunity to compare students who were involved in the aerobic program with those in regular physical education classes. In one revealing study, researchers scrutinized poor readers in the district who were enrolled in a special class to give them additional literacy help. The students who engaged in aerobic exercise just before their literacy class improved 17 percent in their reading and comprehension that term. In contrast, the kids who took regular physical education that term only improved 10.7 percent in the literacy class—a statistically significant difference.

Why would student learning improve after a demanding physical education class? Ratey explains that exercise can enhance learning because what happens in the brain during exercise has long-term benefits. Exercise stimulates brain activity. During exercise, more oxygen is carried to the brain. This helps the brain transform glucose into additional energy. But energy transformation has a downside. It results in potentially toxic waste by-products. The brain counters this by generating protective enzymes to destroy the by-products. These protective enzymes repair and strengthen nerve cells. Not only that, but exercise stimulates the development of new neurons in the hippocampus, a brain structure that is heavily involved in learning. No wonder one physical education coordinator wryly remarked, "In our department, we create the brain cells. It's up to the other teachers to fill them."[2]

There are also other ways that the brain benefits from exercise. One is that vigorous exercise results in more positive moods. Students might be more ready to learn when they are in a good mood. Another advantage of exercising during the day is that we then tend to sleep better at night, which also improves brain function.

Indeed, all the ways in which we care for, or neglect, our bodies can impact the brain. One way we impair brain function, all too often, is through sleep deprivation. As biologist John Medina concludes in *Brain Rules*, "The bottom line is that sleep loss means mind loss."[3] Medina summarizes research indicating that sleep loss "hurts attention, executive function, immediate memory, working memory, mood, quantitative skills, logical reasoning ability, [and] general math knowledge."[4]

In addition to hindering our thinking, sleep deprivation also interferes with our ability to learn. Of course, simply being sleepy can interfere with learning. But more than that, learning that begins when we are awake may also continue when we are asleep. Researchers studied rats as they learned how to navigate mazes. During this learning period, certain neural circuits were active. These same circuits were active again when they slept. The rats were, in effect, using sleep time to consolidate the learning that occurred earlier in the day.[5]

It turns out that humans, too, replay their learning experiences during sleep. In one study, people had to watch a set of lights. There was a button below each light. Their job was to press that button every time the light above it flashed. The lights flashed in a particular pattern, and

Figure 24.1. Our brain continues to work, even in our sleep.

over time, the participants learned the pattern. People accomplish a similar sort of learning when they play the interactive video game Guitar Hero. PET scans of the participants showed that, during the night after training, the same brain regions that were active while they were learning this task were again active during sleep.[6]

It's also clear that this practice during sleep can actually help us improve our performance on whatever task we've been rehearsing. Indeed, different types of memory may be improved by different types of brain processing during sleep. Harvard Medical School professor Robert Stickgold at the Center for Sleep and Cognition points out numerous studies using a variety of tasks to demonstrate this. A volunteer learns something new. Afterward, the volunteer is tested and his or her score is recorded. When tested again the next day, after a night's sleep, the volunteer's score often improves. But scores *don't* improve if the same amount of time passes during the day, without sleep.[7]

Confirming these results, memory processing has also been directly manipulated during sleep. Jan Born and his colleagues had research participants play a computer game similar to the card game called Memory or Concentration. In this game, you see a set of facedown cards and then turn cards over two at a time in order to discover where matching pairs are located. You have to remember where the pairs are in order to match the same cards later, so the game challenges your memory. What is intriguing about this research is that participants experienced whiffs of rose-scented air while they played the game and learned the card locations. That night, they were exposed to rose-scented air again—this time during deep sleep. The researchers reasoned that the scent might trigger a replaying of the game during sleep and so improve their memories of where the pairs were located. And that, apparently, is just what occurred. When participants were retested the following day, the participants who were exposed to the scent during sleep remembered more locations than those who were not.[8]

This kind of research, in addition to his own studies, led Stickgold to conclude that "converging evidence . . . leaves little doubt that offline memory reprocessing during sleep is an important component of how our memories are formed and ultimately shaped."[9] *Offline memory reprocessing* refers to the brain networks' practicing of what has been learned as we sleep. If you learned how to create slides for a Powerpoint presentation, for example, that night your brain might replay specific elements, such as how to move a text box on a slide. Northwestern University memory researcher Ken Paller agrees, and goes even further. Paller speculates that memory reprocessing during sleep not only reinforces individual pieces of our daily experiences but can consolidate them as a higher-order unit. This memory consolidation allows us to later reconstruct a cohesive memory of the event.[10] For example, the episode of attending training about Powerpoint might include specific knowledge about moving text boxes, along with who was with us in the room and new ideas for a great presentation we imagined.

In addition, which memories are reprocessed during sleep may be influenced by whatever is important to us. Sometimes we may recruit experiences to reprocess because those experiences are subtly connected to our current concerns and goals. For example, research showed that recently divorced people often had dreams in which they were working out strategies for coping with the new challenges in their lives.[11] One of the most intriguing possibilities coming out of this research is that we may not need to remember our dreams in order to benefit from them. We may reap the benefits of dreaming on our waking behavior and decision making even if we don't recall our dreams. We may just need to "sleep on it."

INTERESTING, BUT SO WHAT?

HOW CAN I USE THIS INFORMATION AS A BUSINESS LEADER?

Leaders want their employees to perform at their best, including their intellectual best. Exercise could help. Neuroscience research shows that it is not only children whose cognitive abilities are boosted by exercise. There are substantial benefits for adults as well, even for people in their seventies.[12] Brain expert John Medina writes, "Exercisers outperform couch potatoes in tests that measure long-term memory, reasoning, attention, [and] problem solving."[13] They also perform better on tasks that assess fluid intelligence, a measure of creativity.

In addition to staying sharper, employees who keep fit benefit their companies in others ways. They take fewer sick days and make fewer medical claims. Employees who participated in the corporate exercise program at Northern Gas Company took 80 percent fewer sick days than those who did not. At General Electric, the employees in the company's aircraft division who were members of its fitness center lowered the number of medical claims they filed by 27 percent, while nonmembers in the same period *increased* in their claims by 17 percent.[14]

Such studies are always open to the alternative explanation that healthier people are more likely to participate in these programs in the first place. Ideally, results from people who were told whether or not to exercise would provide the strongest evidence. Yet, other research does support a link between exercise and employee productivity. One of these studies was conducted at a company in Leeds, England.[15] In this study, employees ended each workday by filling out a questionnaire that measured factors related to productivity. For example, they rated themselves on how effectively they felt they had managed their time, related to their colleagues, handled their workloads, and met their deadlines. They also indicated whether they had used the company gym that day.

Workers who used the gym were more productive than those who did not. In addition, the researchers compared how the people who worked out answered questions on their gym days versus their off days. They found significant differences. On days they had exercised, people did better on several of the productivity measures. Moreover, they felt less stressed, less fatigued in the afternoon, and more positive about their jobs. These kinds of results, along with the possibility that exercise will reduce medical claims and absenteeism due to illness, have encouraged companies to build on-site gyms or to subsidize employee memberships at health clubs.

The research related to the importance of sleep and the debilitating effects of sleep deprivation also holds important lessons for business leaders. The detrimental effects of sleep loss for society are extensive, including decreased productivity and safety.[16] For instance, driver fatigue due to sleep loss is a serious safety hazard in the transportation industry. Similarly, shift-work employees are at risk for making poor decisions because shift work disrupts the sleep cycle that is natural to human beings—a cycle in which we typically sleep roughly 8 hours out of 24, during darkness. When this cycle is disrupted, as it is for shift-work employees, people may experience symptoms similar to jet lag, which include fatigue and disorientation.[17] Shift work often also involves sleep deprivation. For example, medical residents may fail to get enough sleep for long stretches of time because of the shifts involved. Leaders may not be able to eliminate shift work, but they can think about how best to counteract its possible negative consequences.

One obvious implication is that whenever possible leaders should ensure that employees are not working extensive overtime for prolonged periods. In *Brain Rules*, Medina points out that Boeing executives, concerned about the potential negative effects of inadequate sleep, no longer have teams work late into the night. Another company that has recognized the cognitive costs of overwork is the largest privately held software company in the world, SAS Institute. SAS believes that being overtired just increases the risk of errors. In fact, the company proverb is "After eight hours, you're probably just adding bugs."[18]

Given the links between sleep, learning, and memory consolidation, it is not surprising that adequate rest appears to be necessary to develop high levels of expertise. In their discussion of "expert performers," Ericsson and his associates point out that expert performers require more sleep, often in the form of naps. This is especially true when they are engaged in periods of intensive training or performing.[19] Concentration takes energy. We need sleep to renew that energy. Once we have had the opportunity to renew our energy, we can concentrate more and perform expertly.

Business leaders know that inadequate sleep and exercise, like poor nutrition, have a detrimental effect on the body. What the neuroscience research reminds us is that they also impact people's thinking and performance—much more than we realized.

WHAT IF . . . ?

Many leaders today are mindful of the importance of work-life balance for their employees. But they may not be as mindful about the specific elements of exercise and sleep. What would leaders do differently if they took these factors into account?

1. WHAT IF LEADERS ENCOURAGE A "FITNESS" MENTALITY BY INCORPORATING MORE PHYSICAL MOVEMENT INTO EVERYDAY WORK ACTIVITIES?

Most people naturally follow the least physically demanding routine. We search for the parking place that is closest to the building and take the elevator rather than the stairs. Leaders can encourage a different mentality—one that incorporates activity into otherwise sedentary activities. On the disc that accompanies *Brain Rules*, Medina shows an executive reading e-mail on his laptop while walking on a treadmill. This feat is made possible by the Steelcase product Walkstation.[20] But exercise is also available more cheaply. Medina suggests climbing stairs while talking on cell phones, and having "walking meetings."

Many organizations can't afford on-site gyms for their employees. Still, there are inexpensive ways to encourage physical activity. Climbing staircases rather than taking the elevator is a no-cost means of adding regular exercise. Leaders can also think about how to use discretionary time in more active ways. Though people tend to groan when you insist they get up, stretch, and walk about the room for a few minutes, consistently encouraging physical movement might get employees to re-think their attitude toward exercise.

These small steps aren't going to stimulate the growth of new neurons. But they might encourage a "fitness mentality." Leaders themselves can adopt the practice of "management by walking around." Roderick W. Gilkey, executive director of the Center for Healthcare Leadership and a professor at the Emory University School of Medicine, suggests that stopping by the production floor, loading docks, or employee cafeteria can broaden the perspective of leaders as well as helping them keep more fit.[21]

It would be even better if leaders could support a fitness mentality with policies that make it easier for employees to visit a gym. Sometimes simply having the option of an extended lunch hour or a somewhat later starting time will enable employees to engage in a regular exercise program. As John Ratey says, "The most important thing is to do *something*."[22] Exercise boosts learning, memory, and creativity, as well as bolstering our overall physical health.

2. WHAT IF LEADERS FACTOR SLEEP INTO THE PRODUCTIVITY EQUATION?

Leaders who take the research about sleep deprivation seriously will consider whether the *cognitive* costs of working late are worth the progress made. It is tempting to pile on the hours when important projects are running behind schedule, but the gains may not be as great as the leader hoped for, especially if fatigued employees are not only less efficient but more prone to errors. Moreover, fatigue signals all sorts of other detrimental neurological processes that have serious long-term effects. Burning the candle at both ends doesn't just reduce productivity during those pressured hours. It impairs the quality of thinking, and it may interfere with learning if it reduces the sleep needed to consolidate new learning. Most leaders don't intentionally work people this hard. But layoffs are common during depressed economic times. And layoffs often mean that fewer people are trying to do the same amount of work.

These lessons apply as much to leaders themselves as they do to employees. Many leaders push themselves to the limit, setting family, friends, and other interests aside as they pursue success. Advocates of work-life balance sometimes act as if the main reason for encouraging balance is to make employees happier and more fully engaged when they return to their work. But for leaders themselves as well as for employees, work-life balance is crucial for other reasons as well. Even people who are more than willing to work extra hours are adversely affected. They may work long hours because the work is intrinsically satisfying to them or because the financial rewards keep them motivated. But they will ultimately pay a cognitive price for such relentless exertion. Ironically, working at this pace may weaken these leaders' chances of achieving the very victory for which they were willing to sacrifice those hours of sleep.

NOTES

1. John J. Ratey and Eric Hagerman, *Spark: The Revolutionary New Science of Exercise and the Brain* (Boston: Little, Brown, and Company, 2008).
2. Ibid., p. 18.
3. John Medina, *Brain Rules: 12 Principles for Surviving and Thriving at Work, Home, and School* (Seattle: Pear Press, 2008), p. 163.

4. Ibid.

5. W. E. Skaggs and B. L. McNaughton, "Replay of Neuronal Firing Sequences in Rat Hippocampus during Sleep following Spatial Experience," *Science* 271 (1996): 1870–73.

6. P. Maquet et al., "Experience-Dependent Changes in Cerebral Activation during Human REM Sleep," *Nature Neuroscience* 3 (2000): 831–36.

7. R. Stickgold, "Sleep-Dependent Memory Consolidation," *Nature* 427 (2005): 1272–78.

8. Björn Rasch et al., "Odor Cues during Slow-Wave Sleep Prompt Declarative Memory Consolidation," *Science* 315 (2007): 1426–29.

9. Stickgold, "Sleep-Dependent Memory Consolidation."

10. Ken A. Paller and Joel L. Voss, "Memory Reactivation and Consolidation during Sleep," *Learning and Memory* 11 (2004): 664–70.

11. R. Cartwright et al., "Relation of Dreams to Waking Concerns," *Psychiatry Research* 141, no. 3 (2006): 261–70.

12. E. Naylor et al., "Daily Social and Physical Activity Increases Slow-Wave Sleep and Daytime Neuropsychological Performance in the Elderly," *Sleep* 23, no. 1 (2000): 87–95.

13. Medina, *Brain Rules*, p. 14.

14. Ratey and Hagerman, *Spark*, p. 83–84.

15. Ibid., p. 83.

16. National Sleep Foundation, "Shift Work and Sleep," http://www.sleepfoundation.org/site/c.huIXKjM0IxF/b.4813151/k.5CF2/Shift_Work_and_Sleep.htm (accessed March 27, 2009).

17. WebMD, "Sleep and Circadian Rhythm Disorders," http://www.Webmd.com/sleep-disorders/guide/circadian-rhythm-disorders-cause (accessed August 13, 2009).

18. Richard Florida and Jim Goodnight, "Managing for Creativity," *Harvard Business Review* (July/August 2005): 5.

19. K. Anders Ericsson, "The Acquisition of Expert Performance: An Introduction to Some of the Issues," in *The Road to Excellence: The Acquisition of Expert Performance in the Arts and Sciences, Sports and Games*, ed. K. Anders Ericsson (Mahwah, NJ: Lawrence Erlbaum Associates, 1996), p. 24.

20. For product information, visit http://www.steelcase.com (accessed March 27, 2009).

21. Roderick Gilkey and Clint Kilts, "Cognitive Fitness," *Harvard Business Review* (November 2007): 1–10.

22. Ratey and Hagerman, *Spark*, p. 250.

HOW WILL TODAY'S BRAIN RESEARCH SHAPE THE FUTURE?

How will the new brain research discussed in *The Brain Advantage* change society? It is impossible to tell for sure. But we can glimpse some "possible futures" based on what is happening now. Here are some examples.

1. "LET'S GET A BASELINE ON YOUR BONE DENSITY . . . OH, AND ON YOUR COGNITIVE FUNCTIONING TOO."

It is now common practice for women who are at high risk for osteoporosis to have a bone scan around age fifty. This gives their doctors a baseline. If later scans show that the woman has lost bone mass, she can be treated to prevent the disease or reverse its adverse effects.

The day may come when doctors similarly recommend cognitive testing for adults around fifty years old. These tests would measure basic brain functions, such as working memory and attention. In later years, if a patient wonders "Is my memory deteriorating?" physicians would have a way to answer that question. Patients could retake the tests and see how their scores compared with their baseline.

Local hospitals already provide tests that could yield helpful baseline cognitive scores. These are based on individual testing, typically conducted by a clinical neuropsychologist. But in the future, primary care physicians might have patients take a Web-based test right in the doctor's own office. Brain Resource Corporation is an example of one company that already provides Web-based tests that could be used in this way. Brain Resource has compiled preexisting tests that assess functions such as attention, new learning, memory, and language fluency into a battery of tests it calls "IntegNeuro."[1] A large database of norms is available to help people interpret scores from these tests. Though more research is needed to see how well these test scores predict people's functioning in everyday life, one early study of its validity is promising.[2]

Such computerized tests can make assessments more widely available than the paper or face-to-face methods used in the past. Of course, there also might be something lost in computerized testing because a good neuropsychologist has special expertise in administering tests, navigating a patient's difficulties and quirks, and interpreting the entire clinical picture.

2. "HEY, COACH, I THOUGHT THE TEAM WAS PRACTICING TODAY— WHY ARE THEY ALL SITTING AT COMPUTERS?"

To reach their peak performance, basketball players have to keep track of everyone's location on the court. They also have to predict what is going to happen next, make fast decisions, and shift their attention quickly. All of these capabilities have more to do with players' minds than with their bodies. According to cognitive psychologist Daniel Gopher, software programs designed to train these capabilities can improve players' performance.[3] One such program, Basketball IntelliGym was introduced in 2006 and it is used today by NBA players and college teams. The producer of this training program, ACE (Applied Cognitive Engineering), is now working on a similar training tool for hockey players. Hockey IntelliGym should be available in 2010.

Daniel Gopher is a professor of cognitive psychology and human factors engineering at the Technion, Israel's Institute of Science. As Gopher points out, most people think that the best training simulates the actual situation as closely as possible. For example, flight and driving simulation courses try to replicate the physical experiences of flying and driving. But Gopher argues that this kind of "physical fidelity" is not nearly as important as "cognitive fidelity." *Cognitive fidelity* means that the training replicates the same cognitive skills that the task itself involves. In Gopher's words, training "should faithfully represent the mental demands that happen in the real world."[4] Gopher's own research in the 1990s established this principle. He showed that flight cadets who spent only ten hours playing the computer game Space Fortress improved their actual flying performance by 30 percent.[5] Another study showed that cadets who completed a computer simulation of flying a Blackhawk helicopter that was very realistic, but did not include critical cognitive skills, did not improve in their performance nearly as much as others who played Space Fortress.[6]

3. "Hey, Grandma, your place is cool. It has a pool, a gym, and a cognitive fitness center."

Today people investigating retirement communities and assisted-living facilities look into amenities. Is there a swimming pool? A golf course? A fitness center filled with cardio machines and weights? In the future, potential residents at these facilities may also look for *cognitive* fitness centers filled with computers and video games. Alvaro Fernandez, CEO of Sharp Brains, estimates that four hundred US continuing-care facilities already boast programs designed to improve a variety of cognitive functions that tend to decline as we age.[7]

Can these programs help older people stay sharp? Although many brain fitness programs remain untested, research shows that some programs can have a positive effect. For example, University of Illinois neuroscientist Arthur Kramer and his colleagues used a video game to improve the thinking of older adults.[8] All the participants in this study were over age sixty—the average age was sixty-nine. The participants spent a total of twenty-three hours playing a computer role-playing game called Rise of Nations. In contrast to a comparison group, posttests showed that the players had improved in three areas. First, they were better at switching between tasks. This is a useful skill; it enables us to do a better job at shifting our attention so we don't lose precious minutes wondering "Now where was I?" Second, the participants were better at holding more information in "working memory." This ability is used when we remember a telephone number long enough to dial it, but it also comes into play to help us follow a conversation or keep in mind the factors we need to consider in making a decision. Finally, after playing Rise of Nations, the participants were better at tests of reasoning.

Does this mean that playing such games might delay the onset of Alzheimer's disease, or slow down its effects after onset? We don't yet have the answer to that question. But researchers have found that cognitive training can have positive long-term effects. In research dubbed the ACTIVE study, older adults spent two hours a week for five weeks going through mental training exercises. They also received booster training at the end of one year and again after three years. As predicted, the training improved their thinking at the end of the first five weeks. But even more impressive, they continued to show gains when tested five years later.[9] As ACTIVE researcher Jerri Edwards at the University of South Florida's School of Aging Studies said, "The payoff from cognitive training, or what we can call "mental exercise," seemed far greater than we are accustomed to getting from physical exercise. Just imagine if you could say that ten hours of workouts at the gym every day this month was enough to help keep you fit five years from now."[10]

These positive results are promising but consumers need to be cautious. At this point, very few brain fitness products have demonstrated effectiveness despite the claims that some companies make. Before adopting any cognitive training program, such as those pitched to older people, it is important to have solid evidence showing that they actually help. Consumers should look to see if independent researchers have evaluated the product. One positive example of this kind of research is a study showing that Cogmed's program for enhancing working memory helped children and adolescents who had attention deficits.[11]

4. "YOUR HONOR, THIS WITNESS IS LYING! JUST LOOK AT HER MRI."

Two US companies offer brain scan technology for the purpose of detecting lies. They are California-based No Lie MRI and Cephos of Tyngsboro, Massachusetts. Cephos presented at a September 2008 conference on neuroscience and the law. The company announced that it had achieved an unprecedented 97 percent accuracy with its lie detection system. Yet, as of this book's printing, no US court has admitted brain scans for the purpose of determining the truth or falsity of witnesses' statements.

The ability to "peek" inside your head may cause profound changes in the way we do things in the future.

Why not? Studies show that certain parts of the brain are more active when people lie, presumably because lying takes more effort.[12] It is this increased activity that is interpreted as evidence of deceit. But so far, there are no thorough studies showing similar results with people accused of real-world crimes. No one has demonstrated that real criminals, who have more at stake, or who may be adept at lying, would have the same brain scan results as volunteers in research studies. Equally important, field studies of falsely accused people are needed to show how often these methods incorrectly indicate that truthful people are lying.

Will brain-based lie detection be admitted as evidence in court someday? In some parts of India, it already has been. In June 2008, a twenty-four-year-old Indian woman was convicted of murdering her former fiancé by poisoning him. The basis for her conviction was, in part, her results on a brain-based lie detector test (the BEOS, Brain Electrical Oscillations Signature).[13] During the BEOS, Aditi Sharma—with electrodes taped to her head—listened as an investigator read a series of statements. Some of these referred to the crime, such as, "I bought arsenic." Others were neutral statements, like "The sky is blue." Though she was silent as she listened to these statements, prosecutors argued that her brain betrayed her by reacting in ways that indicated that she had "experiential knowledge" of the crime.

THE BRAINY CONSUMER

Aditi Sharma's conviction dramatically illustrates why we have to be careful about using "brain-based" services and products. The neuro-science field is exploding with new findings and new products. For example, companies now offer services to help market researchers choose the most effective advertising and packaging for their products. One such company, NeuroFocus, uses neural recordings to investigate a host of factors of interest to market researchers.[14] Such factors include identi-fying which aspects of an advertisement attract consumers' attention and engage them emotionally, as well as which price seems reasonable to them. No doubt new products and services will be developed in the years to come.

But how can we be sure that they really work?

Leaders can take three steps to become more intelligent consumers of brain-based programs. First, they can keep up to date about these products. Second, they can test products out themselves. Third, they can take brain research with a grain of salt. Here's how.

1. KEEP UP TO DATE.

The single best resource we have found to date to help leaders keep abreast of brain fitness products is the Sharp Brains Web site.[15] The free monthly newsletter for this site reviews a wide range of brain fitness research, programs, and products. It also alerts readers to breaking neu-roscience news and features thoughtful interviews with researchers. Fer-nandez, CEO of Sharp Brains, is careful to vet the information that appears on the site. For example, reported research must be from science journals that use a peer-review process. Fernandez also issues supplementary reports, including market research reports. The market research reports describe the state of the brain fitness industry, market data and trends, emerging leaders, and best practices. They also discuss the degree to which research validates a product's effectiveness.[16]

Many private and government-sponsored Web sites also summarize a host of relevant research. The National Institutes of Health provide information at two Internet sites.[17]

In addition to keeping up with the brain fitness industry, leaders can keep tabs on attempts to apply brain research to leadership issues. Executive coach David Rock, author of *Your Brain at Work*, has spearheaded Neuroleadership Summits in Italy, Australia, and the United States.[18] These summits bring top neuroscientists together with business leaders to explore ways in which brain research can be applied to leadership practices. Rock also coedits the *Neuroleadership Journal*, which includes articles by both researchers and practitioners in the field.[19]

Leaders need to be somewhat cautious when they hear claims about what brain research has demonstrated. First, of course, they need to keep in mind that they can't believe everything they read on the Internet. Second, they need to remember that neuroscientists are now using brain-imaging methods that have not been around very long. Even newer and more accurate technologies will be used in the coming years. When more research is done, neuroscientists may well reach a consensus about theories that are hotly debated today. But until that consensus occurs, leaders need to be careful not to place too much faith in any single study. There is still much work to be done.

2. Do Your Own Testing.

When a brain-based program offers potential benefits to an industry, leaders can pilot test its effectiveness. For example, Posit Science Corporation has a program called InSight, which is purported to improve visual processing.[20] Because visual processing affects driving, Allstate Insurance is currently offering InSight free to its Pennsylvania policyholders aged fifty to seventy-five. Policyholders who volunteer for the training program devote at least ten hours to cognitive training exercises. When the study is completed in 2009, Allstate will see whether using the program has resulted in fewer accidents.[21] If so, then Allstate might offer the program to older policyholders across the nation.

There are currently brain fitness programs available that promise to improve specific cognitive functions such as working memory. Leaders can experiment with these programs to gauge their effectiveness. Let's say, for example, that an organization wants to help its leaders improve their brains' "executive functions." These functions involve planning goals, resolving conflicts, keeping track of progress, and making decisions and changes as needed. Imagine that the CEO selects a program that promises to improve these functions, such as a training program offered by Posit Science or CogMed. Leaders could use Brain Resource's Web-based assessments of executive functions to see whether the training has improved pretraining test scores. Leaders could also draw on Brain Resource's large database to see how scores on tests relate to other factors, such as productivity, and to compare competing training programs.[22]

Beyond improving test scores, leaders will want to know if the training actually changes what people do on the job. People's scores on an assessment might improve after training. But have people become more effective at doing their actual work? This, of course, is a more difficult question to answer. For some work processes, there are clear measures that can be adapted for this purpose. For example, companies who apply Six Sigma methods will often have extensive measures to analyze the effectiveness of their processes. Measures used for productivity, customer satisfaction, defect rates, and so on can be used in "before and after" studies to measure brain fitness programs as well.

Obviously, this kind of research does not have the controls that more scientific research requires. For example, employees who have invested time in a training program might improve in their productivity simply because they feel more is now expected of them. Without the controls that could eliminate these kinds of alternative explanations, leaders can't be sure that it is the training itself that led to the improvement. Despite these limitations, the kind of exploratory research that leaders can do is a step in the right direction. Most training programs now use "smile sheets" where participants evaluate the training *experience* but not the long-term *impact* of the training. Using real business measures can help assess that impact.

In chapter 19 on multitasking, we discussed the productivity lost through distractions. What if leaders ran a test where they measured productivity during equal time periods both with and without typical distractions? Measures could include lines of code written, number of errors or defects in work produced, number of accounting transactions processed, and so on. Not only are these studies fairly simple to run, but they also could provide valuable data to motivate people to change their behavior. It is one thing to tell employees that they are unproductive when they work, text, and listen to music at the same time. It is another to show them that their own errors increase by a significant margin or that their productivity drops dramatically when they multitask.

Leaders who would like to conduct more controlled research but lack the resources should consider contacting local colleges and universities for help. Students are often looking for opportunities to conduct research for their honors projects or master's theses, and would welcome "real-life" opportunities to do so. And many PhD students in experimental psychology are trained in exactly these sorts of assessments.

3. DON'T OUTSOURCE YOUR OWN BRAIN! TAKE BRAIN RESEARCH WITH A GRAIN OF SALT.

In his *Science* article "Don't Be Seduced by the Brain," Greg Miller warns that people may be overly influenced by claims based on brain research.[23] Miller reports that undergraduates were more likely to accept far-fetched conclusions when the fake reports they were reading included MRI brain images. For example, one fake report claimed that the areas of the brain that are active when we do math are also active when we watch television. Then it drew the false conclusion that watching TV improves math skills. Readers were more likely to accept this conclusion as true when a photo of the brain accompanied the article.

Leaders who are aware of the dangers and who have a basic understanding of how the brain functions will be less likely to fall into such traps. For example, some products claim to take ten years off your "brain age." But as Sharp Brains CEO Fernandez points out, "brain age" is a muddy concept. We can't measure brain functioning as a whole and assign it an "age." We can only measure specific cognitive skills that reflect distinct brain functions. Some skills are related to perception, memory, and language. Others are related to our ability to think abstractly, focus our attention, or make plans. As Fernandez writes, "All science-based brain fitness products in the market today target specific cognitive skills. The research that has been published shows how specific brain functions can be improved. But there is no general "brain age" that can be measured or trained in a meaningful way."[24]

In fact, the claim of being able to take ten years off your brain age is probably based on the study in which older adults whose average age was about seventy participated in an intensive auditory training program. This improved their auditory cognitive skills, including auditory-related attention and memory skills that were not directly trained. In fact, after training they did as well on these tests as people who were sixty years old.[25] But does this mean that their brain is now, overall, comparable to a sixty-year-old brain? "Just think about this," Fernandez says. "If, by attending an intensive tennis camp, you were able to serve at a level comparable to people ten years younger than your age . . . would you say that your body is now ten years younger? Probably not. You'd say that now you play tennis better."[26]

Talking about how a program improves a specific function, like reaction time or working memory, isn't as flashy as claiming that it makes your brain younger. But training in reaction time or working memory *can* improve people's performance. Remember the research showing that cognitive fidelity is more important than physical fidelity? When people strengthen areas like working memory, their performance may improve in a number of areas. This is no small advantage. For example, research shows that people who practice memorizing lists of words get better and better at just that—memorizing words. But they show no improvement in memorizing numbers.[27] In contrast, people who receive training designed to improve memory skills more generally might improve their memory across all sorts of situations.

Leaders don't want to jump on a bandwagon and embrace every practice that claims to be backed by brain research. But leaders can sustain their "Brain Advantage" by keeping up with recent neuroscientific discoveries and continuing to explore possibilities in their own practices.

Significant scientific advances often come when new technology enables scientists to observe what was always there, but was invisible to the human eye. The invention of the telescope allowed Galileo to see the moons of Jupiter, changing astronomy—and our understanding of the earth's place in the universe—forever. The microscope enabled Louis Pasteur to see that microbes were the cause of disease. Current neuroscientific technologies allow us to see more clearly what is going on in the human brain. These tools open our eyes to a world that, for the most part, has been hidden.

It's always a challenge for us to accept the existence of hidden worlds and adapt to their implications. Galileo was vilified. Louis Pasteur was ridiculed. The newspaper *La Press* scorned in 1860: "I am afraid that the experiments you quote, M. Pasteur, will turn against you. The world into which you wish to take us is really too fantastic."[28]

The brain research of the past two decades does, indeed, lead us into a fantastic world, the hidden world inside the brain that influences us so dramatically, often without our awareness. As with other discoveries, knowing about what was previously hidden is a tremendous advantage. With *The Brain Advantage* in hand, leaders can align what they do to the natural workings of our greatest resource: the human brain.

NOTES

1. Brain Resource, "Enabling Optimal Solutions for Brain Health," http://www.brainresource.com (accessed March 2, 2009).

2. R. H. Paul et al., "The Validity of 'IntegNeuro': A New Computerized and Standardized Battery of Neurocognitive Tests," *International Journal of Neuroscience* 115 (2005): 1549–67.

3. Alvaro Fernandez, "Cognitive Training for Basketball Game Intelligence: Interview with Professor Daniel Gopher," *Sharp Brains*, November 2, 2006, http://www.sharpbrains.com/blog/2006/11/02/cognitive-simulations-for-basketball-game-intelligence-interview-with-prof-daniel-gopher/ (accessed January 7, 2009).

4. Ibid.

5. D. Gopher, M. Weil, and T. Baraket, "Transfer of Skill from a Computer Game Trainer to Flight," *Human Factors* 36 (1994): 1–19.

6. S. G. Hart and V. Battiste, "Flight Test of a Video Game Trainer," *Proceedings of the Human Factors Society 26th Meeting* (1992): 1291–95. For updated information, see also W. L. Shebilske et al., "Revised Space Fortress: A Validation Study," *Behavior Research Methods* 37 (2005): 591–601.

7. Alvaro Fernandez, "The State of the Brain Fitness Software Market, 2008." *SharpBrains*, March, 2008, http://www.sharpbrains.com (accessed March 28, 2009).

8. C. Basak et al., "Can Training in a Real-Time Strategy Video Game Attenuate Cognitive Decline in Older Adults?" *Psychology and Aging* 23, no. 4 (2008): 765–77.

9. Sherry L. Willis et al., "Long-Term Effects of Cognitive Training on Everyday Functional Outcomes in Older Adults," *Journal of the American Medical Association* 296 (2006): 2805–14.

10. Fernandez, "The State of the Brain Fitness Software Market, 2008," p. 38.

11. T. Klingberg et al., "Computerized Training of Working Memory in Children with ADHD—A Randomized, Controlled Trial," *Journal of the American Academy of Child and Adolescent Psychiatry* 44 (2005): 177–86.

12. Frank A. Kozel et al., "A Replication Study of the Neural Correlates of Deception," *Behavioral Neuroscience* 118, no. 4 (2004): 852–56.

13. Anand Giridharadas, "India's Novel Use of Brain Scans in Courts Is Debated," *Asia Pacific Edition, New York Times* (Mumbai) September 14, 2008, http://www.nytimes.com/2008/09/15/world/asia/15brainscan.html?_r=1 (accessed March 28, 2009).

14. NeuroFocus, http://neurofocus.com (accessed April 1, 2009).

15. SharpBrains, "The Brain Fitness Authority," http://sharpbrains.com (accessed March 28, 2009).

16. Fernandez, "The State of the Brain Fitness Software Market, 2008."

17. National Institutes of Health Web sites include News in Health, http://newsinhealth.nih.gov (accessed March 21, 2009) and US Department of Health and Human Services, National Institutes of Health: The Nation's Medical Research Agency, http://health.nih.gov (accessed March 21, 2009).

18. David Rock, *Your Brain at Work: Strategies for Overcoming Distraction, Regaining Focus, and Working Smarter All Day Long* (New York: HarperBusiness, 2009).

19. NeuroLeadership Institute, "Breaking New Ground in Our Ability to Transform Human and Workplace Performance," http://www.neuroleadership.org (accessed March 28, 2009).

20. PositScience, "Our Products: Brain Fitness Programs That Work," http://www.positscience.com/products (accessed January 5, 2009).

21. "Protecting Pennsylvania Drivers, One Brain at a Time," *PR Newswire*, October 1, 2008, http://www.prnewswire.com/cgi-bin/stories.pl?ACCT=104 &STORY=/www/story/10-01-2008/0004895850&EDATE= (accessed March 28, 2009).

22. For a detailed discussion of how researchers can use Brain Resource and its database, see Evian Gordon, "Neuroleadership and Integrative Neuroscience: It's about VALIDATION, Stupid!" *Neuroleadership Journal* 1, (2008): 71–80.

23. Greg Miller, "Neuroimaging: Don't Be Seduced by the Brain," *Science* 320, no. 5882 (2008): 1413.

24. Alvaro Fernandez, "Posit Science, Nintendo Brain Age, and Brain Training Topics," *SharpBrains*, June 24, 2008, http://www.sharpbrains.com/blog/2008/06/24/brain-age-posit-science-and-brain-training-topics/ (accessed January 7, 2008).

25. G. E. Smith et al., "A Cognitive Training Program Based on Principles of Brain Plasticity: Results from the Improvement in Memory with Plasticity-based Adaptive Cognitive Training (IMPACT) Study." *Journal of the American Geriatrics Society* 4 (2009): 594-603.

26. Fernandez, "Posit Science, Nintendo Brain Age, and Brain Training Topics."

27. K. A. Ericsson and P. F. Delaney, "Working Memory and Expert Performance," in *Working Memory and Thinking*, ed. R. H. Logie and K. J. Gilhooly (Hillsdale, NJ: Erlbaum, 1998), pp. 93–114.

28. Chris Trueman, "Louis Pasteur," History Learning Site, http://www.historylearningsite.co.uk/louis_pasteur.htm (accessed August 17, 2009).

Afterword

THE ADVANTAGES OF BRAIN RESEARCH

C ontemporary brain research might seem like a funny place for people to look for ideas about how to improve their leadership skills. After all, neuroscience is about understanding the brain, not helping leaders run their organizations.

Leadership was not on the curriculum when I was a graduate student in neuroscience, but it did come up once. I recall reading a local newspaper article about some new findings from the laboratory of Steve Hillyard, one of my mentors at the University of California, San Diego. The article described investigations of brain potentials in people who visited the lab to volunteer for the recordings—so far, so good. But the journalist's overstatement was that modern brainwave technology could provide scientific predictions about a person's future success through a brain measure called the "leadership potential." This brings to mind bizarre visions of a corporate culture in which each employee is regularly hooked up to a machine to look inside the brain, and then the machine decides who gets a promotion and who gets sacked. In actuality, the journalist must have been making a pun, conflating leadership capacity with electricity in the form of brain potentials.

Indeed, neuroscientists have discovered many interesting brain potentials—including face-processing potentials, memory-formation potentials, decision-making potentials, error-monitoring potentials, and so on—but as far as I know, no one has yet discovered one that deserves to be called the leadership potential. Still, journalistic word play aside, there may be some truth to the idea that brain science can help build better leadership qualities.

Leaders want to understand human thought and behavior in order to be more effective. As this book shows, understanding scientific research on the human brain is essential to that endeavor.

After all, the reasons why we behave as we do, and explanations for human cognition more generally, derive from the way the human brain works. Even the way we comprehend reality is, in no small part, a function of human perceptual capabilities. Human beings do not know the world in an absolute sense. What we know is conditioned by the types of environmental signals that can be registered by our sense organs. We see only certain wavelengths of electromagnetic radiation (light). We hear only certain frequencies of pressure waves travelling through the air (sound). We recognize only certain chemicals that make their way to the right place on our bodies (taste and smell). And the story doesn't stop there because our take on these sensory signals is a function of our ability to analyze and extract meaning from them. It is our brainpower that determines how we make sense of the world. In a very real sense, our world is not really a separate external place. What we know is a function of the outside world and of the inside—a result of neural processing.

In many more concrete (and less esoteric) ways, neuroscience research seeks greater understanding of perception, memory, decision making, and all other aspects of human behavior.[1] As this understanding continues to develop, we become better able to explain mental abilities in adults, how these abilities develop in children, and how they change as people's brains get older. These scientific approaches often connect directly to disorders of brain function, informing the diagnosis and treatment of various diseases. As we understand more about how learning takes place, we strive for ways to improve educational methods. And as our understanding of emotion deepens, we seek better methods for dealing with our emotions and emotional malfunctions. Acquiring knowledge about the basic principles of brain function can lead us in surprising new directions with unforeseen benefits; we don't always know in advance where the next miracle cure, novel insight, or boon for society might materialize. The scope of the potential implications of neuroscience research is remarkably wide ranging.

Although the chief aim of this book is to provide useful leadership advice, it also includes a glimpse into how neuroscience contributes to understanding the mind. Of course, evaluating specific neuroscientific findings is very different from evaluating the practical advice this book provides. In this vein, I'd like to take a moment to examine how advances in neuroscience arise.

The scientific challenge includes various steps required to understand basic brain mechanisms. Consider the possibility that some scientific claims about the brain may ultimately turn out to be incorrect. Would this impugn the leadership ideas prompted by the science and offered in this book?

Certainly many of the scientific findings that Madeleine, Lisa, and Brad selected to include in the leadership context could, in another context, be analyzed, probed, and questioned in great detail. Neuroscientists love to do that. These are the steps that are regularly taken in the course of research. There may be alternative or more complex interpretations of the results, shortcomings in experimental designs, and countless factors that limit the confidence one might have in the evidence acquired or the conclusions drawn.

Usually we begin by asking questions of nature. Then we strive to obtain sensible answers based on observations that are interesting and convincing, answers that make the most sense when considering all the alternatives. Some of these answers will stand the test of time—the test of future experiments that could either produce converging findings or findings that cast doubt on the original results. Many experts in the field will judge and weigh all the evidence. The most convincing scientific propositions will be those supported not by just a single experiment but by the weight of evidence from many research studies.

To make the best use of neuroscience research in a leadership context, then, should we wait for the final word, the conclusion verified by the most weighty and convincing evidence? As it happens, there is no such thing as the final word. All scientific hypotheses are provisional—every single one. Scientists must always be open to the prospect of changing their minds in the face of new evidence that demands a new understanding. At least, that's the ideal. We may not always be completely open to change. People like to grasp on to hypotheses that they have long held close. Neuroscientists are people too, subject to these same tendencies. But at least in principle, our scientific understanding of the human brain is fluid, always on the move—sometimes unpredictably so.

In many places in this book, presumed functions of particular brain areas are brought up to help make a leadership point. However, the human cerebral cortex is a vast and mysterious collage of brain networks and our current knowledge of how to map specific functions to each patch of cortex is a work in progress. When I see a statement like "activation was found in brain area X, which is thought to be essential for cognitive function Y," I often wonder—thought by whom? Perhaps by one set of investigators who are in battle with a different set of investigators who think that brain area X does something entirely different. These controversies abound, but for the purposes of this book, putting them aside is best.

Besides, in time these controversies tend to resolve into a consensus and an enriched understanding. And yet, we can't always foresee who will win the argument and what our future understanding might hold. In some cases the role attributed to a brain region in cognition fits with evidence from many neuroscience methods. We might then relax our concerns about the shortcomings of any single research method. The hypothesis can then be considered relatively firm. Other times, speculations have a weaker basis.

The challenge of developing hunches and speculations into solid scientific advances is extended yet further when we attempt to translate neuroscientific knowledge so that it can be applied outside the laboratory. Whereas all our hypotheses are subject to change, in subtle ways or with an all-out refutation, this state of affairs does not necessarily take away from the potential usefulness of the leadership implications drawn out in this book. The question is whether these ideas are useful. If they help a leader to be more effective, then they should be taken seriously.

I'd also like to highlight how engaging a challenge it can be to attempt to solve a mystery, in this case the mystery of how each little patch of the human cerebral cortex contributes to mental functions. In light of the way one cortical network can routinely interact with other networks located in distant regions of the brain, cognition is seemingly a product of the whole. Nearly the whole brain might become involved in some complex computation. Nonetheless, discrete networks in the brain do carry out unique sorts of computations. We are reminded of this by the dramatically specific problems people sometimes experience after damage to the brain.[2] There are many examples in which brain injury produces one cognitive disability alongside otherwise preserved abilities:

- preservation of elementary visual abilities with impaired access to the meaning of objects (*visual agnosia*),
- preservation of some object perception with impaired face perception (*prosopagnosia*),
- preservation of some visual abilities with impaired conscious vision (*blindsight*), and
- preservation of many abilities to learn from experience with impaired storage of memories for autobiographical episodes and complex facts (*amnesia*).

Among other more outlandish examples, a patient with *Capgras syndrome* may recognize his wife's face but suffer from the delusion that she is an imposter, not really his wife. Other examples are described in the "What's the Story?" sections of this book.

We can learn about the human mind not only from these selective cognitive impairments in patients but also from technologies that provide complementary evidence and that make it possible to examine the brain in exquisite detail and to monitor it in action. Many brain scanning and brainwave recording methods can be applied in healthy individuals with minimal risks to the volunteers.

While this research advances our scientific understanding step by step, we also acknowledge the enormity of this challenge. Neuroscientists often focus on a specific cognitive function or brain region and attempt to gain some understanding. A standard tactic is to isolate one phenomenon for study by holding other phenomena constant or putting everything else aside. How is this done? Ideally, we try to carve nature at her joints, meaning that we strive to isolate the topic of study in a way that makes good sense. Perhaps in some instances we have mistakenly subdivided phenomena, cutting in the wrong place, failing to carve up nature properly. This certainly happens.

But even when we succeed in finding the appropriate divisions so as to carve nature exactly at each joint, we may still do violence by this carving.[3] In other words, the very divisions and categorization schemes that we use to identify and study distinct phenomena can introduce some distortion. It seems that we must zero in and identify the parts to achieve any understanding, but in doing so we may neglect aspects of the whole that are out of focus when only analyzing the parts. Neurocognitive phenomena need to be understood both in relative isolation and in context. The context may involve the individual's other cognitive functions, hormones, diet, social milieu, broader culture, and all the influences that have accrued through that individual's lifelong development and shape the kinds of thoughts he or she experiences.

After taking the pieces apart in our analyses, we can attempt to remedy this situation by putting the pieces back together (in theory) in a way that calls attention to the interdependence among them. We still have much to learn about how the presumed function of each patch of cortex operates in a greater context, such as in the midst of large-scale cortical networks[4] and in the face of an array of environmental and cultural influences.[5] These complexities are no cause for disillusionment for neuroscientists. Rather, it remains an exciting time to be in the business of deciphering the mysteries of human neurocognitive functions.

As a final thought about the relevance of neuroscience for leadership, I'd like to put some stress on integrity. This book is full of useful ideas that emerge from neuroscientific considerations. However, ethics may not always come along for the ride when we learn about all the ways in which we might use our brains better and improve our talents.[6] In the workplace, as anywhere, allowing our actions to be guided by ethical principles is of primary importance. Integrity and compassion for others should be Job Number One. Hopefully a neuroscientific understanding of the human mind will ultimately shed further light on why these principles are so important.

Ken A. Paller, PhD
Professor of Psychology, Northwestern University
Evanston, Illinois

Notes

1. M. S. Gazzaniga, R. B. Ivry, and G. R. Mangun, *Cognitive Neuroscience: The Biology of the Mind*, 3rd ed. (New York: Norton, 2008); A. Zeman, *Consciousness: A User's Guide* (New Haven, CT: Yale University Press, 2002); M.-M. Mesulam, ed., *Principles of Behavioral and Cognitive Neurology* (Oxford: Oxford University Press, 2000).

2. Ibid.

3. K. A. Paller, J. L. Voss, and C. E. Westerberg, "Investigating the Awareness of Remembering," *Perspectives on Psychological Science* 4 (2009): 185–99.

4. M.-M. Mesulam, "Large-Scale Neurocognitive Networks and Distributed Processing for Attention, Language, and Memory," *Annals of Neurology* 28 (1990): 597–613.

5. J. Y. Chiao and N. Ambady, "Cultural Neuroscience: Parsing Universality and Diversity across Levels of Analysis," in *Handbook of Cultural Psychology*, ed. S. Kitayama and D. Cohen (New York: Guilford Press, 2007), pp. 237–54.

6. M. J. Farah, "Emerging Ethical Issues in Neuroscience," *Nature Neuroscience* 5 (2002): 1123–29; M. S. Gazzaniga, *The Ethical Brain: The Science of Our Moral Dilemmas* (New York: HarperCollins, 2005).

BIBLIOGRAPHY

Allstate Insurance Company. "Protecting Pennsylvania Drivers, One Brain at a Time." *PR Newswire*, October 1, 2008. http://www.prnewswire.com/cgi -bin/stories.pl?ACCT=104&STORY=/www/story/10-01-2008/00048958 50&EDATE= (accessed March 28, 2009).

Amabile, Teresa. "How to Kill Creativity." *Harvard Business Review* (May 2007): 1–13.

Amabile, Teresa, and Mukti Khaire. "Creativity and the Role of the Leader." *Harvard Business Review: Leading Creative People* (October 2008): 2–13.

Barr, Alistair, and Ronald D. Orol. "Madoff Arrested in Alleged Ponzi Scheme: Ex-Nasdaq Chairman, Investor Charged with Securities Fraud, FBI Says." *MarketWatch*, December 11, 2008. http://www.marketwatch.com/news/ story/madoff-arrested-charged-may-facing/story.aspx?guid=%7BB7353 DBD-688D-47D4-B7F8-D257A018405F%7D&dist=msr_14 (accessed January 12, 2009).

Barsade, Sigal G. "The Ripple Effect: Emotional Contagion in Groups." *Yale School of Management Working Paper Series, OB-01* (August 2001). http:// papers.ssrn.com/abstract=250894 (accessed November 7, 2008).

Bart, William M., and Michael Atherton. "The Neuroscientific Basis of Chess Playing: Applications to the Development of Talent and Education." Paper presented at the American Educational Research Association Meeting, Chicago, IL, April 2003.

Bartel, Caroline A., and Richard Saavedra. "The Collective Construction of Work Group Moods." *Administrative Science Quarterly* 45, no. 2 (2000): 197–231.

Basak, C., W. R. Boot, M. W. Voss, and A. F. Kramer. "Can Training in a Real-Time Strategy Video Game Attenuate Cognitive Decline in Older Adults?" *Psychology and Aging* 23, no. 4 (2008): 765–77.

Basco, Monica Ramirez. *Never Good Enough: How to Use Perfectionism to Your Advantage without Letting It Ruin Your Life*. New York: Touchstone, 2000.

Baumgartner, T., M. Heinrichs, A. Vonlanthen, U. Fischbacher, and E. Fehr. "Oxytocin Shapes the Neural Circuitry of Trust and Trust Adaptation in Humans." *Neuron* 58 (2008): 639–50.

Bechara, A., H. Damasio, D. Tranel, and A. R. Damasio. "Deciding Advantageously before Knowing the Advantageous Strategy." *Science* 275 (1997): 1293–95.

Begley, Sharon. *Train Your Mind, Change Your Brain*. New York: Ballantine Books, 2008.

Beilock, S. L., S. L. Carr, and T. H. Carr. "On the Fragility of Skilled Performance: What Governs Choking under Pressure?" *Journal of Experimental Psychology General* 130 (2001): 701–25.

Beilock, S. L., and S. Gonso. "Putting in the Mind versus Putting on the Green: Expertise, Performance Time, and the Linking of Imagery and Action." *Quarterly Journal of Experimental Psychology* 61 (2008): 920–32.

Bergeron, Louis. "Suppression as Coping Mechanism Increases Stress." *Stanford News Service*, March 24, 2008. http://storybank.stanford.edu/stories/suppression-coping-mechanism-increases-stress (accessed June 7, 2008).

Berns, Gregory. *Iconoclast*. Boston: Harvard University Press, 2008.

BlessingWhite. "Employee Engagement Report 2008—North American Overview." *BlessingWhite Intelligence* (April/May 2008). http://www.blessingwhite.com/EEE__report.asp (accessed March 20, 2009).

Brain Resource. "Enabling Optimal Solutions for Brain Health." http://www.brainresource.com (accessed March 2, 2009).

Brett, Jeanne. *Negotiating Globally: How to Negotiate Deals, Resolve Disputes, and Make Decisions Across Cultural Boundaries*. San Francisco: Jossey-Bass, 2007.

Brett, Jeanne, Kristin Behfar, and Mary C. Kern. "Managing Multicultural Teams." *Harvard Business Review* (November 2006): 1–11.

Brockner, Joel. "Why It's So Hard to Be Fair." *Harvard Business Review* (March 2006): 1–10.

Bryner, Jeanna. "Monkeys Fuss over Inequality." *Live Science* (November 12, 2007). http://www.livescience.com/animals/071112-monkey-treats.html (accessed September 22, 2008).

Burton, Robert. *On Being Certain: Believing You Are Right Even When You're Not*. New York: St. Martin's Press, 2008.

Butler, E. A., B. Egloff, F. W. Wilhelm, N. Smith, E. A. Erickson, and J. J. Gross. "The Social Consequences of Expressive Suppression." *Emotion* 3 (2003): 48–67.

Cameron, Lisa A. "Raising the Stakes in the Ultimatum Game: Experimental Evidence from Indonesia." *Economic Inquiry* 37 (1999): 47–59.

Carey, Benedict. "A Shocker: Partisan Thought Is Unconscious." *New York Times*, January 24, 2006. http://www.nytimes.com/2006/01/24/science/24find.html?ex=1190260800&en=345d50dbc467f552&ei=5070 (accessed July 8, 2008).

Cartwright, R., M. Y. Agargun, J. Kirkby, and J. K. Friedman. "Relation of Dreams to Waking Concerns." *Psychiatry Research* 141, no. 3 (2006): 261–70.

Case, John. "Panel on the Neuroscience of Leadership," Comments made as part of the 2008 annual NeuroLeadership summit, New York, October 30, 2008.

Catmull, Ed. "How Pixar Fosters Collective Creativity." *Harvard Business Review* (September 2008): 1–12.

Chen, Ming-Jer. *Inside Chinese Business: A Guide for Managers Worldwide.* Boston: Harvard Business School Press, 2001.

Chiao, J. Y., and N. Ambady. "Cultural Neuroscience: Parsing Universality and Diversity across Levels of Analysis." In *Handbook of Cultural Psychology,* edited by S. Kitayama and D. Cohen, 237–54. New York: Guilford Press, 2007.

Chiao, Joan Y., Tokiko Harada, Hidetsugu Komeda, Zhang Li, Yoko Mano, Daisuke Saito, Todd B. Parrish, Norihiro Sadato, and Tetsuya Iidaka. "Neural Basis of Individualistic and Collectivistic Views of Self." *Human Brain Mapping* (forthcoming). http://www.interscience.wiley.com/.

Choi, Charles Q. "The Bright Side of Spite Revealed." *Live Science,* July 16, 2007. http://www.livescience.com/animals/070716_spite_chimps.html (accessed September 22, 2008).

Collins, Jim. *Good to Great: Why Some Companies Make the Leap—and Others Don't.* New York: HarperCollins, 2001.

Collinson, David. "Managing Humour." *Journal of Management Studies* 39 (2002): 269–88.

Comeau, Allan J. "Why Rejection Really Hurts." http://www.drcomeau.com/Why-rejection-really-hurts.htm (accessed January 15, 2009).

Consalvo, C. M. "Humor in Management, No Laughing Matter." *Humor: International Journal of Humor Research* 2 (1989): 285–97.

Cooper, Joel, Frank Drews, and David Strayer. "What Do Drivers Fail to See When Conversing on a Cell Phone?" *Proceedings of the 48th Human Factors and Ergonomics Society Annual Meeting.* New Orleans (September 20–24, 2004): 2213–17.

Coutu, Diane. "The Science of Thinking Smarter: A Conversation with Brain Expert John Medina." *Harvard Business Review* (May 2008): 1–4.

Csikszentmihalyi, Mihaly. *Flow: The Psychology of Optimal Experience.* New York: Harper Perennial Modern Classics, 2008.

Damasio, Antonio R. *Descartes' Error: Emotion, Reason, and the Human Brain.* New York: Penguin Putman, 1994.

De Bono, Edward. *Six Thinking Hats.* Boston: Back Bay Books, 1999.

Deming, W. Edwards. *Out of the Crisis.* Cambridge, MA: Massachusetts Institute of Technology, 1986.

DeQuervain, Dominique, Urs Fischbacher, Valerie Treyer, Melanie Schellhammer, Ulrich Schnyder, Alfred Buck, and Ernst Fehr. "The Neural Basis of Altruistic Punishment." *Science* 305, no. 5688 (2004): 1254–58.

Dirks, Tim. "The History of Film: Film History of the 1980s." *AMC Filmsite*. http://www.filmsite.org/80sintro.html (accessed August 6, 2009).

Doidge, Norman. *The Brain That Changes Itself.* New York: Penguin, 2007.

Donaldson, Margaret. *Human Minds.* New York: Penguin, 1993.

Drury, Bob. "Bravery and How to Master It." *Men's Health* (April 2008): 158–62.

Eagly, A. H., R. D. Ashmore, M. G. Makhijani, and L. C. Longo. "What Is Beautiful Is Good, but . . . : A Meta-analytic Review of Research on the Physical Attractiveness Stereotype. *Psychological Bulletin* 110 (1991): 109–28.

Eisenberger, Naomi I., Matthew D. Lieberman, and Kipling D. Williams. "Does Rejection Hurt? An fMRI Study of Social Exclusion." *Science* 302 (2003): 290–92.

Elbert, T., C. Pantev, C. Wienbruch, B. Rockstroh, and E. Taub. "Increased Cortical Representation of the Fingers of the Left Hand in String Players." *Science* 270 (1995): 305–307.

Ericsson, K. A., and P. F. Delaney. "Working Memory and Expert Performance." In *Working Memory and Thinking*, edited by R. H. Logie and K. J. Gilhooly, 93–114. Hillsdale, NJ: Erlbaum, 1998.

Ericsson, K. Anders. "The Acquisition of Expert Performance: An Introduction to Some of the Issues." In Ericsson, *The Road to Excellence*, 1–50.

———, ed. *The Road to Excellence: The Acquisition of Expert Performance in the Arts and Sciences, Sports and Games.* Mahwah, NJ: Lawrence Erlbaum Associates, 1996.

Faber, Judy. "CBS Fires Don Imus over Racial Slur." *CBS News*, April 12, 2007. http://www.cbsnews.com/stories/2007/04/12/national/main2675273_page 2.shtml (accessed February 1, 2009).

Farah, M. J. "Emerging Ethical Issues in Neuroscience." *Nature Neuroscience* 5 (2002): 1123–29.

Fehr, Ernst, and Bettina Rockenbach. "Human Altruism: Economic, Neural, and Evolutionary Perspectives." *Current Opinion in Neurobiology* 14 (2004): 784–90.

Fernandez, Alvaro. "Cognitive Training for Basketball Training Intelligence: Interview with Professor Daniel Gopher." *SharpBrains* (November 2, 2006). http://www.sharpbrains.com/blog/2006/11/02/cognitive-simulations-for-basketball-game-intelligence-interview-with-prof-daniel-gopher/ (accessed January 7, 2009).

———. "Posit Science, Nintendo Brain Age, and Brain Training Topics." *SharpBrains* (June 24, 2008). http://www.sharpbrains.com/blog/2008/06/

24/ brain-age-posit-science-and-brain-training-topics/ (accessed January 7, 2008).

———. "The State of the Brain Fitness Software Market, 2008." A publication of *SharpBrains* (March 2008). http://www.sharpbrains.com/ (accessed March 28, 2009).

Finkelstein, Sydney. *Why Smart Executives Fail: And What You Can Learn from Their Mistakes.* New York: Penguin Portfolio Trade, 2004.

Fisher, Roger, William L. Ury, and Bruce Patton. *Getting to Yes: Negotiating Agreement without Giving In.* New York: Penguin, 1991.

Florida, Richard, and Jim Goodnight. "Managing for Creativity." *Harvard Business Review* (July/August 2005): 1–10.

Freiberg, Kevin, and Jackie Freiberg. *Nuts! Southwest Airlines' Crazy Recipe for Business and Personal Success.* New York: Random House Broadway Books, 1998.

Friesen, W. V. "Cultural Differences in Facial Expressions in Asocial Situations: An Experimental Test of the Concept of Display Rules." Unpublished PhD diss., University of California, San Francisco, 1972.

Frith, Chris. *Making Up the Mind: How the Brain Creates Our Mental World.* Malden, MA: Blackwell, 2008.

Gardner, Howard. *Leading Minds: An Anatomy of Leadership.* New York: Basic Books, 1995.

Gawande, Atul. "The Checklist." *New Yorker*, December 10, 2007. http://www.newyorker.com/reporting/2007/12/10/071210fa_fact_gawande?currentPage=1 (accessed December 17, 2008).

Gazzaniga, M. S. *The Ethical Brain: The Science of Our Moral Dilemmas.* New York: HarperCollins, 2005.

Gazzaniga, M. S., R. B. Ivry, and G. R. Mangun. *Cognitive Neuroscience: The Biology of the Mind.* New York: Norton, 2008.

Gelbard-Sagiv, Hagar, Roy Mukamel, Michal Harel, Rafael Malach, and Itzhak Fried. "Internally Generated Reactivation of Single Neurons in Human Hippocampus during Free Recall." *Science* 3 (2008): 96–101.

George, J. M., and A. P. Brief. "Feeling Good—Doing Good: A Conceptual Analysis of the Mood at Work—Organizational Spontaneity Relationship." *Psychological Bulletin* 112, no. 2 (1992): 310–29.

Gigerenzer, Gerd. *Gut Feelings: The Intelligence of the Unconscious.* New York: Viking, 2007.

Gilkey, Roderick, and Clint Kilts. "Cognitive Fitness." *Harvard Business Review* (November 2007): 1–10.

Gilliland, Steve. "Steve Gilliland: Entertaining. Inspiring. Real." http://www.stevegilliland.com (accessed October 4, 2008).

Giridharadas, Anand. "India's Novel Use of Brain Scans in Courts Is Debated."

Asia Pacific Edition, New York Times, Mumbai, September 14, 2008. http://www.nytimes.com/2008/09/15/world/asia/15brainscan.html?_r=1 (accessed March 28, 2009).

Gladwell, Malcolm. *Blink: The Power of Thinking without Thinking.* Boston: Little, Brown, and Company, 2005.

Goffee, Rob, and Gareth Jones. "Managing Authenticity: The Paradox of Great Leadership." *Harvard Business Review* (December 2008): 86–95.

Goldin, Claudia, and Celia Rouse. "Orchestrating Impartiality: The Impact of Blind Auditions on Female Musicians." *American Economic Review* 90 (2007): 715–41.

Goldin, Philippe R., Kateri McRae, Wiveka Ramel, and James J. Gross. "The Neural Basis of Emotion Regulation: Reappraisal and Suppression of Negative Emotion." *Biological Psychiatry* 6 (2008): 577–86.

Goldstein, Bruce. *Cognitive Psychology: Mind, Research, and Everyday Experience.* Belmont, CA: Wadsworth, 2008.

Goleman, Daniel. *Emotional Intelligence: Why It Can Matter More Than IQ.* New York: Bantam Books, 2006.

Goleman, Daniel, Richard Boyatzis, and Annie McKee. "Primal Leadership: The Hidden Driver of Great Performance." *Harvard Business Review* (December 2001): 46–56.

———. *Primal Leadership: Learning to Lead with Emotional Intelligence.* Cambridge, MA: Harvard Business School Press, 2004.

Gonsalves, Brian, and Ken A. Paller. "Mistaken Memories: Remembering Events That Never Happened." *Neuroscientist* 8 (2002): 391–95.

———. "Neural Events that Underlie Remembering Something That Never Happened." *Nature Neuroscience* 3 (2000): 1316–21.

Gonzales, Laurence. *Everyday Survival: Why Smart People Do Stupid Things.* New York: Norton, 2008.

Goodfield, June. *Quest for the Killers.* Boston: Birkhauser, 1985.

Gopher, D., M. Weil, and T. Baraket. "Transfer of Skill from a Computer Game Trainer to Flight." *Human Factors* 36 (1994): 1–19.

Gordon, Evian. "Neuroleadership and Integrative Neuroscience: It's about VALIDATION, Stupid!" *Neuroleadership Journal* 1 (2008): 71–80.

Gostick, Adrian, and Scott Christopher. *The Levity Effect.* Hoboken, NJ: Wiley, 2008.

Groopman, Jerome. *How Doctors Think.* New York: Mariner, 2007.

Gross, James J. "Emotional Regulation." In *Handbook of Emotions*, edited by Michael Lewis, Jeannette Haviland-Jones, and Lisa Feldman Barrett, 497–512. New York: Guildford, 2008.

Gross, J. J., and O. P. John. "Mapping the Domain of Expressivity: Multimethod

Evidence for a Hierarchical Model." *Journal of Personality and Social Psychology* 74 (1998): 170–91.

Grossman, Dave, and Loren W. Christensen. *On Combat: The Psychology and Physiology of Deadly Conflict in War and Peace*. Milstadt, IL: Warrior Science Publications, 2008.

Haeckel, Stephan. *Adaptive Enterprise: Creating and Leading Sense-and-Respond Organizations*. Boston: Harvard Business School Press, 1999.

Hallowell, Edward. "Overloaded Circuits: Why Smart People Underperform." *Harvard Business Review* (January 2005): 1–9.

Hammermesh, D., and J. E. Biddle. "Beauty and the Labor Market." *American Economic Review* 84 (1994): 1174–94.

Hart, S. G., and V. Battiste. "Flight Test of a Video Game Trainer." *Proceedings of the Human Factors Society 26th Meeting* (1992): 1291–95.

Hatfield, Elaine, John T. Cacioppo, and Richard L. Rapson. *Emotional Contagion*. Cambridge, MA: Cambridge University Press, 1993.

Heath, Dan, and Chip Heath. "Heroic Checklists: Why You Should Learn to Love Checking Boxes." *Fast Company*, February 14, 2008. http://www.fast company.com/magazine/123/heroic-checklist.html (accessed October 27, 2008).

Hedden, Trey, Sarah Ketay, Arthur Aron, Hazel Rose Markus, and John D.E. Gabrieli. "Cultural Influences on Neural Substrates of Attentional Control." *Psychological Science* 19, no. 1 (2008): 12–17.

Higbee, Kenneth. *Your Memory: How It Works and How to Improve It*. New York: DaCapo, 2001.

Hilts, Philip. *Memory's Ghost: The Strange Tale of Mr. M. and the Nature of Memory*. New York: Touchstone, 1996.

Hoffman, Martin L. "Developmental Synthesis of Affect and Cognition and Its Implications for Altruistic Motivation." *Social and Personality Development: Essays on the Growth of the Child*, edited by William Damon, 258–77. New York: Norton, 1983.

Hofstede, Geert. *Culture's Consequences: Comparing Values, Behaviors, Institutions, and Organizations across Nations*. Thousand Oaks, CA: Sage, 2001.

Holmes, Thomas, and Richard Rahe. "Holmes-Rahe Life Changes Scale." *Journal of Psychosomatic Research* 11 (1967): 213–18.

Hurley, Robert. "The Decision to Trust." *Harvard Business Review* (September 2006): 7.

Iacoboni, Marco. *Mirroring People: The New Science of How We Connect with Others*. New York: Farrar, Straus, and Giroux, 2008.

Isen, A. M., K. A. Daubman, and G. P. Nowicki. "Positive Affect Facilitates Creative Problem Solving." *Journal of Personality and Social Psychology* 52 (1987): 1122–31.

Jablonski, Joseph R. *Implementing TQM*. 2nd ed. Hoboken, NJ: Pfeiffer Wiley, 1993.

Johnson, George. "Sleights of Mind." *New York Times*, August 21, 2007. http://www.nytimes.com/2007/08/21/science/21magic.html?_r=1 (accessed October 16, 2008).

Jung-Beeman, Mark, Edward M. Bowden, Jason Haberman, Jennifer L. Frymiare, Stella Arambel-Liu, Richard Greenblatt, Paul J. Reber, and John Kounios. "Neural Activity When People Solve Problems with Insight." *Public Library of Science Biology* (April 2004). http://biology.plosjournals.org/perlserv/?request=get-document&doi=10.1371/journal.pbio.0020097&ct=1 (accessed July 5, 2008).

Kabat-Zinn, Jon. *Wherever You Go, There You Are*. New York: Hyperion, 1994.

Keim, Brandon. "Magic Tricks Reveal Inner Workings of the Brain." *Wired Science*, http://www.wired.com/wiredscience/2008/07/the-science-of/ (accessed September 12, 2008).

Klein, Gary. *The Power of Intuition*. New York: Doubleday, 2003.

Kleiner, Art. *The Age of Heretics A History of the Radical Thinkers Who Reinvented Corporate Management*. San Francisco: Jossey-Bass, 2008.

Klingberg, T., E. Fernell, P. J. Olesen, M. Johnson, P. Gustafsson, K. Dahlstrom, C. G. Gillberg, H. Forssberg, and H. Westerberg. "Computerized Training of Working Memory in Children with ADHD—A Randomized, Controlled Trial." *Journal of the American Academy of Child and Adolescent Psychiatry* 44 (2005): 177–86.

Knoch, Daria, Alvaro Pascual-Leone, Kaspar Meyer, Valerie Treyer, and Ernst Fehr. "Diminishing Reciprocal Fairness by Disrupting the Right Prefrontal Cortex." *Science* 314, no. 5800 (2006): 829–32.

Kolar, Brad. "When SMART Goals Are Dumb." *Brad Kolar Associates* (2007). http://www.kolarassociates.com/articles/When%20SMART%20goals%20are%20dumb.pdf (accessed February 1, 2009).

Kosfeld, M., M. Heinrichs, P. J. Zak, U. Fischbacher, and E. Fehr. "Oxytocin Increases Trust in Humans." *Nature* 435 (2005): 673–76.

Kozel, Frank A., Ralph H. Johnson, Tamara M. Padgett, Mark S. George, and Ralph H. Johnson. "A Replication Study of the Neural Correlates of Deception." *Behavioral Neuroscience* 118, no. 4 (2004): 852–56.

Krueger, Frank, Kevin McCabe, Jorge Moll, Nikolaus Kriegeskorte, Roland Zahn, Maren Strenziok, Armin Heinecke, and Jordan Grafman. "Neural Correlates of Trust." *Proceedings of the National Academy of Sciences* 104, no. 50 (2007): 20084–89.

Lehrer, Jonah. "The Eureka Hunt." *New Yorker*, July 28, 2008, pp. 40–48.

———. *How We Decide*. New York: Houghton Mifflin Harcourt, 2009.

Libet, Benjamin. *Mind Time: The Temporal Factor in Consciousness*. Cambridge, MA: Harvard University Press, 2004.

Limb, Charles J., and Allen R. Braun. "Neural Substrates of Spontaneous Musical Performance: An fMRI Study of Jazz Improvisation." *PLoS ONE* 3, no. 2 (February 2008). http://www.plosone.org/article/info%3Adoi %2F10.1371%2Fjournal.pone.0001679 (accessed March 14, 2008).

MacDonald, Geoff, and Mark R. Leary. "Why Does Social Exclusion Hurt? The Relationship between Social and Physical Pain." *Psychological Bulletin* 131, no. 2 (2005): 202–23.

Mack, D., and D. Rainey. "Female Applicants' Grooming and Personnel Selection." *Journal of Social Behavior and Personality* 5 (1990): 399–407.

Maquet, P., S. Laureys, P. Peigneux, S. Fuchs, C. Petiau, C. Phillips, J. Aerts, C. Smith, and A. Cleeremans. "Experience-Dependent Changes in Cerebral Activation during Human REM Sleep." *Nature Neuroscience* 3 (2000): 831–36.

Masuda, T., and R. E. Nisbett. "Attending Holistically versus Analytically: Comparing the Context Sensitivity of Japanese and Americans." *Journal of Personality and Social Psychology* 82 (2001): 922–34.

Mattson, Mark, and Edward Calabrese. "Best in Small Doses." *New Scientist* 199, no. 2668 (2008): 36–39.

Mayer, Roger C., James H. Davis, and F. David Schoorman. "An Integrative Model of Organizational Trust." *Academy of Management Review* 20, no. 3 (1995): 709–34.

Medina, John. *Brain Rules: 12 Principles for Surviving and Thriving at Work, Home, and School*. Seattle: Pear, 2008.

Mesulam, M.-M. "Large-Scale Neurocognitive Networks and Distributed Processing for Attention, Language, and Memory." *Annals of Neurology* 28 (1990): 597–613.

———, ed. *Principles of Behavioral and Cognitive Neurology*. Oxford: Oxford University Press, 2000.

Miller, Greg. "Neuroimaging: Don't Be Seduced by the Brain." *Science* 320, no. 5882 (2008): 1413.

Miller, Steve. "Interview with Phil Rosenzweig, Author of *The Halo Effect*." *BeyeNETWORK*, July 31, 2007. http://www.b-eye-network.com/view/5649 (accessed January 5, 2009).

Milton, J. G., A. Solodkin, P. Hlustik, D. Crews, and S. S. Small. "Expert Motor Performance: Limbic Activation Is Inversely Related to Skill Level." *Neurology* 60 (2003): A345.

Morgan, Nick. "How to Become an Authentic Speaker." *Harvard Business Review* (November 2008): 115–19.

Morling, B., S. Kitayama, and Y. Miyamoto. "Cultural Practices Emphasize Influence in the United States and Adjustment in Japan." *Personality and Social Psychology Bulletin* 28 (2002): 311–23.

Mulrine, Anna. "To Battle Groupthink, the Army Trains a Skeptics Corps." *U.S. News & World Report*, May 15, 2008. http://www.usnews.com/articles/news/world/2008/05/15/the-army-trains-a-skeptics-corps-to-battle-groupthink.html (accessed March 31, 2008).

National Institutes of Health. *News in Health.* http:/newsinhealth.nih.gov (accessed March 21, 2009).

———. US Department of Health and Human Services: The Nation's Medical Research Agency. http://health.nih.gov (accessed March 21, 2009).

National Sleep Foundation. "Shift Work and Sleep." *National Sleep Foundation.* http://www.sleepfoundation.org/site/c.huIXKjM0IxF/b.4813151/k.5CF2/Shift_Work_and_Sleep.htm (accessed March 27, 2009).

Naylor, E., P. D. Penev, L. Orbeta, I. Janssen, R. Ortiz, E. F. Colecchia, M. Keng, S. Finkel, and P. C. Zee. "Daily Social and Physical Activity Increases Slow-Wave Sleep and Daytime Neuropsychological Performance in the Elderly." *Sleep* 23, no. 1 (2000): 87–95.

NeuroFocus, Inc. http://neurofocus.com/ (accessed April 1, 2009).

NeuroLeadership Institute. "Breaking Ground in Our Ability to Transform Human and Workplace Performance." http://www.neuroleadership.org (accessed March 28, 2009).

Newman, G. E., H. Choi, K. Wynn, and B. J. Scholl. "The Origins of Causal Perception: Evidence from Postdictive Processing in Infancy." *Cognitive Psychology* 57, no. 3 (2008): 262–91.

Nisbett, Richard. *The Geography of Thought: How Asians and Westerners Think Differently.* New York: Free Press, 2003.

Ochsner, K. K., and J. J. Gross. "The Cognitive Control of Emotion." *Trends in Cognitive Sciences* 9 (2005): 242–49.

Orwell, George. *1984.* New York: Signet Classics, 1950.

Oyserman, D., H. M. Coon, and M. Kemmelmeier. "Rethinking Individualism and Collectivism: Evaluation of Theoretical Assumptions and Meta-Analyses." *Psychological Bulletin* 128, no. 1 (2002): 3–72.

Paller, K. A. "Memory Consolidation: Systems." In *Encyclopedia of Neuroscience,* edited by L.R. Squire, 741–49. Oxford: Academic Press, 2009.

Paller, K. A., J. L. Voss, and C. E. Westerberg. "Investigating the Awareness of Remembering." *Perspectives on Psychological Science* 4 (2009): 185–99.

Paller, Ken A., and Joel L. Voss. "Memory Reactivation and Consolidation during Sleep." *Learning and Memory* 11 (2004): 664–70.

Paul, R. H., J. Lawrence, L. M. Williams, R. C. Clark, N. Cooper, and E.

Gordon. "The Validity of 'IntegNeuro': A New Computerized and Standardized Battery of Neurocognitive Tests." *International Journal of Neuroscience* 115 (2005): 1549–67.

Pescosolido, Anthony. "Emotional Intensity in Groups." Unpublished PhD diss., Department of Organizational Behavior, Case Western University, 2000.

Peterson, Christopher, Steven F. Maier, and Martin E. P. Seligman. *Learned Helplessness: A Theory for the Age of Personal Control.* New York: Oxford University Press, 1995.

Pink, Daniel. *A Whole New Mind.* New York: Penguin, 2006.

Pogrebin, Robin. "In Madoff Scandal, Jews Feel an Acute Betrayal." *New York Times,* December 23, 2008. http://www.nytimes.com/2008/12/24/us/24jews.html (accessed January 12, 2009).

PositScience. "Our Products: Think Faster, Focus Better, Remember More." http://www.positscience.com/products (accessed January 5, 2009).

Project Implicit. "Implicit Associations Test (IAT)." https://implicit.harvard.edu/implicit/ (accessed March 9, 2009).

Ramachandran, V. S., and Sandra Blakeslee. *Phantoms in the Brain.* New York: Harper Perennial, 1998.

Rasch, Björn, Christian Büchel, Steffen Gais, and Jan Born. "Odor Cues during Slow-Wave Sleep Prompt Declarative Memory Consolidation." *Science* 315 (2007): 1426–29.

Ratey, John J., and Eric Hagerman. *Spark: The Revolutionary New Science of Exercise and the Brain.* Boston: Little, Brown, and Company, 2008.

Restak, Richard. *The Brain Has a Mind of Its Own.* New York: Crown Trade Paperbacks, 1991.

———. *The Naked Brain: How the Emerging Neurosociety Is Changing How We Live, Work, and Love.* New York: Three Rivers, 2007.

Richards, Jane M., and James J. Gross, "Personality and Emotional Memory: How Regulating Emotion Impairs Memory for Emotional Events." *Journal of Research in Personality* 40, no. 5 (October 2006): 631–51. http://www.sciencedirect.com/science?_ob=ArticleURL&_udi=B6WM0-4H0YYSW-1&_user=7438643&_rdoc=1&_fmt=&_orig=search&_sort=d&view=c&_acct=C000050221&_version=1&_urlVersion=0&_userid=7438643&md5=765992aa971a92711382b75b2c8b27d2 (accessed November 15, 2008).

Richeson, Jennifer A., Abigail A. Baird, Heather L. Gordon, Todd F. Heatherton, Carrie L. Wyland, Sophie Trawalter, and J. Nicole Shelton. "An fMRI Investigation of the Impact of Interracial Contact on Executive Function." *Nature Neuroscience* 6 (2003): 1323–28.

Rizzolatti, G., R. Camarda, L. Fogassi, M. Gentilucci, G. Luppino, and M. Matelli. "Functional Organization of Inferior Area 6 in the Macaque

Monkey. II. Area F5 and the Control of Distal Movements." *Experimental Brain Research* 71 (1988): 491–507.

Rock, David. "SCARF: A Brain-Based Model for Collaborating with and Influencing Others." *Neuroleadership Journal* 1 (2008): 44–52.

———. *Your Brain at Work: Strategies for Overcoming Distraction, Regaining Focus, and Working Smarter all Day Longer.* New York: HarperBusiness, 2009.

Rock, David, and Jeffrey Schwartz. "The Neuroscience of Leadership," *Strategy + Business*, February 6, 2007. http://www.strategy-business.com/press/freearticle/06207 (accessed March 22, 2009).

Rogers, Carl. *On Becoming a Person.* London: Constable, 1961.

Rolls, E. T., "The Orbitofrontal Cortex and Reward." *Cerebral Cortex* 10 (2000): 284–94.

Root-Bernstein, Robert, and Michele Root-Bernstein. *Sparks of Genius.* New York: Houghton, Mifflin, and Company, 1999.

Rosenzweig, Phil. *The Halo Effect: How Managers Let Themselves Be Deceived.* New York: Free Press, 2009.

———. "From Halo to Hell." *Chief Executive*, June 4, 2007. http://www.chief executive.net/ME2/dirmod.asp?sid=&nm=&type=Publishing&mod =Publications%3A%3AArticle&mid=8F3A7027421841978F18BE895F87F 791&id=88A15F4EFD1C40279AC05827677F79EF&tier=4 (accessed March 27, 2009).

Sala, Fabio. "Laughing All the Way to the Bank." *Harvard Business Review* (September 2003). http://hbr.harvardbusiness.org/2003/09/laughing-all-the -way-to-the-bank/ar/1 (accessed October 8, 2008).

Sapolsky, Robert. *Why Zebras Don't Get Ulcers.* New York: Freeman/Owl Books, 2004.

Schacter, D. L., K. A. Norman, and W. Koutstaal. "The Cognitive Neuroscience of Constructive Memory." *Annual Review of Psychology* 49 (1998): 289–318.

Schaffhausen, Joanna. "The Day His World Stood Still." *Brain Connection.* http://www.brainconnection.com/topics/?main=fa/hm-memory (accessed January 3, 2009).

Schooler, J. W., S. Ohlsson, and K. Brooks. "Thoughts beyond Words: When Language Overshadows Insight." *Journal of Experimental Psychology: General* 122 (1993): 166–83.

Schoorman, F. David, Roger C. Mayer, and James H. Davis. "An Integrative Model of Organizational Trust: Past, Present, and Future." *Academy of Management Review* 32, no. 2 (2007): 344–54.

Schrage, Michael. "Daniel Kahneman: The Thought Leader Interview." *Strategy + Business*, January 7, 2009. http://www.dailygood.org/more.php ?n=3556 (accessed January 9, 2009).

Schwartz, Jeffrey, and Sharon Begley. *The Mind and the Brain: Neuroplasticity and the Power of Mental Force*. New York: Harper Perennial, 2002.

Schwartz, Jeffrey, and Beverly Beyette. *Brain Lock: Free Yourself from Obsessive-Compulsive Behavior*. New York: Harper Perennial, 1997.

Senge, Peter. *The Fifth Discipline: The Art and Practice of the Learning Organization*. New York: Doubleday Business, 2006.

Shapiro, Stephen. "Unleash Your Inner Motivator." *Stephen Shapiro's 24/7 Innovation*. http://www.steveshapiro.com/unleash-your-inner-innovator (accessed March 3, 2009).

Shebilske, W. L., R. A. Volz, K. M. Gildea, J. W. Workman, M. Nanjanath, S. Cao, and J. Whetzel. "Revised Space Fortress: A Validation Study." *Behavior Research Methods* 37 (2005): 591–601.

Simmons, Annette. *The Story Factor*. New York: Basic Books, 2006.

Simons, Daniel J., and Daniel T. Levin. "Failure to Detect Changes to People during a Real-World Interaction." *Psychonomic Bulletin and Review* 5 (1998): 644–49.

Singer, Tania, and Ernst Fehr. "The Neuroeconomics of Mind Reading and Empathy." *American Economic Review* 95, no. 2 (2005): 340–45.

Singer, Tania, Ben Seymour, John P. O'Doherty, Holger Kaube, Ray J. Dolan, and Christopher D. Frith. "Empathy for Pain Involves the Affective but Not Sensory Components of Pain." *Science* 303, no. 5661 (2004): 1157–62.

Skaggs, W. E., and B. L. McNaughton. "Replay of Neuronal Firing Sequences in Rat Hippocampus during Sleep following Spatial Experience." *Science* 271 (1996): 1870–73.

Smith, G. E., P. Housen, K. Yaffe, R. Ruff, R. F. Kennison, H. W. Mahncke, and E. M. Zelinski. "A Cognitive Training Program Based on Principles of Brain Plasticity: Results from the Improvement in Memory with Plasticity-Based Adaptive Cognitive Training (IMPACT) Study." *Journal of the American Geriatrics Society* 4 (2009): 594–603.

Soldati, Patricia. "Employee Engagement: What Exactly Is It?" *Management-Issues*, March 8, 2007. http://www.management-issues.com/2007/3/8/opinion/employee-engagement-what-exactly-is-it.asp (accessed March 11, 2009).

Spreier, Scott W., Mary H. Fontaine, and Ruth L. Malloy. "Leadership Run Amok: The Destructive Potential of Overachievers." *Harvard Business Review*, (June 2006). http://harvardbusiness.org/product/leadership-run-amok-the-destructive-potential-of-o/an/R0606D-PDF-ENG (accessed August 6, 2009).

Stauffer, David. "Yo, Listen Up: A Brief Hearing on the Most Neglected Communication Skill." *Harvard Management Update* (July 1998): 1–3.

Stickgold, R. "Sleep-Dependent Memory Consolidation." *Nature* 427 (2005): 1272–78.

Sullins, Ellen. "Emotional Contagion Revisited: Effects of Social Comparison and Expressive Style on Mood Convergence." *Personality and Social Psychology Bulletin* 17, no. 2 (1991): 166–74.

Surowiecki, James. *The Wisdom of Crowds*. New York: Doubleday, 2004.

Taber, Charles S., Damon Cann, and Simona Kucsova. "The Motivated Processing of Political Judgments." *Social Science Research Network* (September 25, 2008). http://papers.ssrn.com/sol3/papers.cfm?abstract_id=1274028 (accessed August 7, 2009).

Talbot, Margaret. "Duped." *New Yorker*, July 2, 2007. http://www.new yorker.com/reporting/2007/07/02/070702fa_fact_talbot (accessed December 7, 2008).

Taleb, Nassim Nicholas. *The Black Swan: The Impact of the Highly Improbable*. New York: Random House, 2007.

Tavris, Carol, and Elliot Aronson. *Mistakes Were Made (but Not by Me)*. New York: Harcourt, 2007.

Thorndike, E. L. "A Constant Error on Psychological Rating." *Journal of Applied Psychology* 82 (1920): 665–74.

Thorpe, S. J., E. T. Rolls, and S. Maddison. "The Orbitofrontal Cortex: Neuronal Activity in the Behaving Monkey." *Experimental Brain Research* 4 (1983): 93–115.

Trueman, Chris. "Louis Pasteur." History Learning Site. http://www.history learningsite.co.uk/louis_pasteur.htm (accessed August 17, 2009).

Van Hecke, Madeleine. *Blind Spots: Why Smart People Do Dumb Things*. Amherst, NY: Prometheus Books, 2007.

Vital Smarts Industrial Watch. "Silence Kills." *Vital Smarts* (2005). http://www.silencekills.com/Download.aspx (accessed December 21, 2008).

Wagner, Richard K. "Smart People Doing Dumb Things: The Case of Managerial Incompetence." In *Why Smart People Can Be So Stupid*, edited by Robert J. Sternberg, 42–63. New Haven, CT: Yale University Press, 2003.

Wallis, Claudia. "The Multitasking Generation." *Time*, March 19, 2006. http://www.time.com/time/magazine/article/0,9171,1174696-1,00.html (accessed August 14, 2009).

Ward, Jamie. *The Frog Who Croaked Blue: Synesthesia and the Mixing of the Senses*. New York: Routledge, 2008.

WebMD. "Sleep and Circadian Rhythm Disorders." *WebMD: Sleep Disorders Guide*. http://www.Webmd.com/sleep-disorders/guide/circadian-rhythm-disorders-cause (accessed August 13, 2009).

Weinstein, Matt. *Managing to Have Fun: How Fun at Work Can Motivate Your*

Employees, Inspire Your Coworkers, and Boost Your Bottom Line. New York: Fireside, 1997.

Westen, Drew, Pavel S. Blagov, Keith Harenski, Clint Kilts, and Stephan Hamann. "Neural Bases of Motivated Reasoning: An fMRI Study of Emotional Constraints on Partisan Political Judgment in the 2004 US Presidential Election." *Journal of Cognitive Neuroscience* 18 (2006): 1947–58.

Wilber, Del Quentin. "A Crash's Improbable Impact: '82 Air Florida Tragedy Led to Broad Safety Reforms." *Washington Post,* January 12, 2007.

Williams, K. D. "Social Ostracism." In *Aversive Interpersonal Behaviors,* edited by R. Kowalski, 133–70. New York: Plenum, 1997.

Williams, K. D., and B. Jarvis. "Cyberball: A Program for Use in Research on Ostracism and Interpersonal Acceptance." *Behavior Research Methods, Instruments, and Computers* 38 (2006): 174–80.

Willis, Paul, Louise Heywood, and Leonie Hansell. "Pain of Rejection." *ABC News Story Archive,* September 9, 2004. http://www.abc.net.au/catalyst/stories/s1195656.htm (accessed October 4, 2008).

Willis, Sherry L., Sharon Tennstedt, Michael Marsiske, Karlene Ball, Jeffrey Elias, Kathy Mann Koepke, John Morris, George Rebok, Frederick Unverzagt, Anne Stoddard, and Elizabeth Wright. "Long-Term Effects of Cognitive Training on Everyday Functional Outcomes in Older Adults." *Journal of the American Medical Association* 296 (2006): 2805–14.

Wilson, Timothy. *Strangers to Ourselves: Discovering the Adaptive Unconscious.* Cambridge, MA: Belknap Press of Harvard University Press, 2002.

Wolfe, M. "Stand Up to Desk Rage—and Rude People at Work." *AOL Find a Job,* August 5, 2008. http://jobs.aol.com/article/_a/stand-up-to-desk-rage-and-rude-people-at/20080723151509990001 (accessed September 4, 2008).

Wortmann, Craig. *What's Your Story? Using Stories to Ignite Performance and Be More Successful.* New York: Kaplan, 2006.

INDEX